STANLEY BALDWIN

Oil painting by Sir Oswald Birley
1938

STANLEY BALDWIN

G. M. YOUNG

RUPERT HART-DAVIS
SOHO SQUARE LONDON
1952

First published 1952
Second impression 1952

Made and printed in Great Britain by
William Clowes and Sons, Limited, London and Beccles

νῦν τις ἐνηείης Πατροκλῆος δειλοῖο
μνησάσθω· πᾶσιν γὰρ ἐπίστατο μείλιχος εἶναι

CONTENTS

CONTENTS

LIST OF ILLUSTRATIONS

PREFACE

WHEN Lord Baldwin asked me, somewhat languidly I thought, whether I would care to write his life I said yes, but I said it with misgiving, thinking of the mass of documents which must have accumulated about him in his years of office and in Opposition. Actually, my difficulties were of another kind. The papers bequeathed to Cambridge and by the kindness of the University authorities placed at my disposal were certainly abundant—for example, one file, innocently labelled "Notes for Drury Lane Speech," contained departmental briefs running to 150 pages, while the birth of the *Listener* was the occasion of as many more. For the most part, however, the papers were of general rather than of personal interest, and I had undertaken to write a life, not a history of the Conservative party, its legislation, its administration, its successes and its failures. But Baldwin kept no diary: circulated no memoranda to his colleagues: rarely wrote a political letter: "I hate writing about these things, come and see me": and still more rarely made a copy of anything he did write. Later I learned that a large collection of papers had been destroyed shortly after his death, and by a further mischance another collection reached me only when my book was drafted and much of it in type. For some passages in Baldwin's career I was able to use records made at the time by others. But on a general review of the material I felt that the fully documented life, which the public might expect and historians value, could not yet be written and that either I must lay the book aside or write it in a different form and with a different intention.

The rough popular judgment of Baldwin is that he deceived the people in the matter of national defence in order to maintain himself in office and his party in power. So he stands branded in a book for which, if for any book

of our time, immortality may safely be predicted, Churchill's
Gathering Storm;

> Baldwin, Stanley, confesses putting party before country.

Thus in the index, and, in the text:

> That a Prime Minister should avow that he had not done his
> duty in regard to national safety because he was afraid of
> losing the election was an incident without parallel in our
> Parliamentary history.

No one who remembers the early months of the Second
War can deny that Churchill is here giving voice to the judgment, or the sentiment, of multitudes. Nor can anyone
deny that for what befell us in 1939 and all that has befallen
us since, Baldwin must take his share of blame. Only—
history may add that, but for Baldwin, what befell us might
have been far worse. We are proud, and rightly proud, of our
unity in 1939 and in the terrible years that followed. Are we
so sure that without Baldwin that unity could have been
achieved, and maintained? I have given, as faithfully as I
can, the evidence on which the answer must be grounded.

G. M. Y.

1952

ACKNOWLEDGMENTS

I am particularly grateful for the assistance afforded me by the author of the obituary notice in *The Times*; by Mr. Austin Hopkinson; the Rt. Hon. Lord Citrine; Sir Horace Wilson; The Hon. Mrs. Geoffrey Dawson; Sir Geoffrey Fry, Bart.; and others who will perhaps accept this general expression of thanks for letters and memories with which they have furnished me.

His late Majesty King George VI graciously allowed me access to the royal archives at Windsor.

For permission to print unpublished letters I have to thank Mrs. George Bambridge, Lord Birdwood, the Earl of Birkenhead, Sir Maurice Bonham-Carter, Mrs. Neville Chamberlain, the Rt. Hon. Winston S. Churchill, O.M., C.H., M.P., the Marchioness Curzon of Kedleston, the Hon. Mrs. Geoffrey Dawson, Mr. Geoffrey Keynes, the literary executors of the late Mr. Mackenzie King, the Rt. Hon. Lord Kirkwood, Mrs. Harold Laski, the Marquis of Londonderry, the Rt. Hon. Malcolm MacDonald, Baroness Ravensdale, and Susan Lady Tweedsmuir.

Leave to reprint published material has kindly been given by the editor of *The Times*, the Controller of Her Majesty's Stationery Office, Messrs Cassell & Co. Ltd, and Messrs Hodder & Stoughton Ltd.

I trust that other benefactors and copyright-owners whom I have failed to trace or thank will accept my gratitude and forgive my shortcomings.

G. M. Y.

STANLEY BALDWIN

CHAPTER I

EARLY YEARS

STANLEY BALDWIN was born on August 3rd 1867 at Bewdley in Worcestershire, and brought up at Wilden; the only Prime Minister, he would say, whose first years were passed within hearing of machinery. The Baldwins were by origin small gentry in Shropshire, of the rank that sent younger sons into the town, to be apprenticed, and earn their livings, as tradesmen and manufacturers. In the eighteenth century, when coal and iron were beginning to assert their ascendancy in the national economy, two pioneering brothers migrated, one into Staffordshire, the other south to Wilden, where the new canal entered the Severn. There, in 1788, he set up his foundry. A son, George Pearce Baldwin, by skilful amalgamations and the purchase of collieries in South Wales, raised the family to affluence, which in the hands of his son Alfred became wealth.

Alfred Baldwin married (1866) Louisa Macdonald. Her family had left the Highlands after the Forty-five and settled awhile in Fermanagh. James Macdonald (1761-1833) was bidden by John Wesley himself to come to England as a Methodist preacher.

> He was a man who could never have had more than a couple of pounds a week, but he was a natural scholar. He taught himself many languages and educated his son to take a scholarship at Cambridge.

Of this son, George Brown Macdonald, who married a Welsh girl, Hannah Jones, from the Vale of Clwyd, we have a contemporary portrait by Crabb Robinson, who met him in a coach between Preston and Ambleside:

> He was a handsome man of 36 with a very fine voice and his style of conversation good—no cant, but altogether marked by religious expressions indicating discrimination so that I said "you are in the Ministry." He gave a very flattering

account of Wesleyanism. Macdonald has been a preacher 13 years. He began at 20—he has much to do but finds time to read 5 or 6 hours a day—Shakespeare never off his table— he had a good classical education.

"And so," Baldwin once remarked, after reciting the strains of Welsh and Highland in his ancestry, "I am almost a foreigner."

To this Macdonald and his Welsh wife were born two sons and five daughters. One of the sons, by all accounts a man of some erratic genius, went to America; the other, who followed the Wesleyan tradition of his family, was President of Conference in 1899. Of the daughters four made famous marriages, Georgiana Burne-Jones; Agnes Poynter; Alice Kipling; and Louisa Baldwin, Alfred's wife. Mrs. Alfred Baldwin, indeed, enjoyed some modest celebrity in her own right as the author of sundry tales of rural life and a book of ghost stories.

Alfred Baldwin—in face and figure, it was said, something between a Spanish grandee and a Hebrew prophet—was an eminently successful man: strict, dominant and prosperous in all his undertakings.

He was a man of business [his father-in-law wrote] and if I said he was the finest specimen of his order I ever knew, I should not be saying too much. Few men carried heavier burdens of responsibility and duty, yet I do not know that I ever saw him irritable, or greatly depressed, or so engrossed as to close his mind to religion, or books, or the happy interests of his home, or the troubles of other people. By conviction an Anglican, he represented to me the Church of England layman, in a form that had my admiration.

Stanley, named after another Wesleyan minister, his great-grandfather Jacob Stanley, was an only child; and though his mother lived to see him twice Prime Minister, she was always frail, much given to resting in hushed rooms with all the curtains drawn. Her one unmarried sister was the little boy's companion: with her, and to her, he read Scott and Bunyan, Marryat, Dickens and the *Morte d'Arthur*: and he has left on record his earliest venture in literary criticism, a firm refusal to find poetry in the words:

The street that from Oxford hath borrowed its name.

Part of each year, he once told an audience of artists, he spent in London "in a little house in a remote part called Wood Green," at one time occupied by Walter Crane, and then by Sir Edward Poynter: an old-fashioned house in a garden—afterwards occupied by a power station—and, across the way, open fields and the lane to Wormwood Scrubbs. He remembered squeezing flake white on to his uncle's palette, and with a large brush he was allowed to make his contribution to *Atalanta's Race*.

With no brothers or sisters and few playfellows to treasure, or invent, stories of his early days, Baldwin's childhood goes almost unrecorded. In holiday time, Rudyard Kipling was his chief friend, with Ambrose Poynter as a third in the party. But one incident, preserved in the memory of an older cousin, seemed to his friends in later life to be truly significant.

> You and Ambrose Poynter, both aged seven, were playing in the verandah. Suddenly, I found a great commotion going on: Ambrose at dancing point, more and more shrill; you still quietly answering. At last he fairly shrieked, while your voice grew lower and lower, "Why do you speak like that? Why don't you speak louder, Stan?" And you answered, down in the depths, "Because if I spoke any louder, I should hit you."

His letters from his preparatory school, Hawtrey's, are true to the form of most schoolboys—" a postal order for 5*s.*, or 10*s.*, please, as I have only 1*s.* and I want to put something in the collection; thirty or forty stamps, please, as I write a great many letters." Indeed, between childhood and old age few men can ever have written more. "I try not to nibble my nails and I wash better than I ever did: the loopha is lovely." He is notably observant and lively in his description of plays or fireworks or the feats of conjurors; and a visit to Madeira produced a well-written diary—sustained for two days. A Highland story in the manner of Scott held out rather longer. Photographs of later boyhood show a dull face inclining to the saturnine—his "inexpressive features," and the knobby nose which teased the cartoonists, were a matter of placid mirth to the end.

At Eton his scholarship might have ripened, but his father was advised to send him to Harrow. There he displays only the faintest interest in passing events, and his one essay in classical

criticism is brief and final: "We are doing the hardest
speech in Thucydides. Dreadful rubbish." Baldwin accepted
the belief of his generation that, after all, the preparatory
school, the public school and the university were the natural
training for boys of what was still the governing class. And that
training made unexpected appearances. Once we were sitting
in the library at Astley—it was a few months before his death
—when he suddenly said, out of a long silence, "ἔν τινι
φρουρᾷ, that's from the *Phaedo*, isn't it?" "I think so," I
replied, "but I will make sure." I took from the shelf his
Plato, Baiter-Orelli in one volume, a Harrow prize, and
found the place. "And how would you translate it? On
guard, on outpost duty?" "Yes, something like that." "I
thought so. I may not have built much on my foundations,
but those were sound." And silence settled down again. I
told him of an American officer who had said to me: "Of
all the things I learnt at school, the one that has been of
most use to me in the Army is Latin Prose." He glowed
with delight, and again when I complained that the new
pronunciation had made Latin a foreign language. "The
very thing I am always telling them." Malicious tongues
sometimes suggested that, like Bagehot's Oxford man,
Baldwin's learning, Greek or Latin, did not go much further
than a firm conviction that there are such languages, but
it went far enough to give him an insight into the simplicity,
the subtlety and directness of antique speech: an insight
which served him well when his own turn came. If I had to
say what utterance in our time came nearest to the ancient
ideal, most exactly conformed to what the ancients meant
by true rhetoric, I should hesitate between his favourite, the
speech on the Political Levy, 1925, and my own, the speech
on the Abdication, 1936.

But one incident in his later time at Harrow seemed to
some who were nearest to him to have left a deeper trace
than anything he learnt. Some boyish prank got him into
trouble with the Headmaster, Montagu Butler, who would
not make him a prefect. It was not so much the injustice
to himself, as the sense of power misused that stuck in his
mind and memory. The immediate consequences were unlucky. Butler became Master of Trinity when Baldwin went

Aged seven					At Harrow

Aged twenty-four

up. He dropped his classics, put his name down for History, idled over some of his books and never opened the others. The standard of History in those days, whether at Cambridge or Oxford, was not high; even so, his Third would seem to be a correct evaluation of his academic attainments. In old age he would often regret those wasted years. But his devotion to Cambridge, of which he became Chancellor in 1930, was unclouded and munificent. In 1921 he gave his cousin, Philip Burne-Jones, a thousand guineas for his father's designs for the Kelmscott Chaucer, so that they might be preserved in the Fitzwilliam.

"But don't get a Third in life," his father said; and after a journey to America, Stanley settled down to life by entering the family business and keeping the cash books at a salary of £2 a week. He had a passing fancy for Holy Orders, and he was for a short time a subaltern in the Artillery Volunteers at Shoeburyness. The American trip left very pleasant memories. At Worcester (Mass.) he found his old nurse, married to a Stourport weaver, now a manufacturer of carpets. He had an introduction from Burne-Jones to a famous collector in Boston who came back from a country holiday on purpose to show the visitors his pictures, an unexpected attention to an unknown youth which Baldwin always gratefully remembered. At Chicago he and his companion debated—San Francisco or New Orleans? Baldwin preferred Old France to Modern America and to New Orleans they went.

The American visit happened to be so timed as to make a lasting impression on the young business man. McKinley was running on the high Protection ticket. In 1892 the new tariff came into operation and in two years Baldwins had lost their best market. First the cheap stuff went, tinplate that anyone could make; then the quality goods, specialities of the old English firm. They found new markets, but America was closed; and Baldwin threw over, once and for all, the orthodox economics of his father's generation. To the electors of Kidderminster in 1906 he said: "You and I will live to know what competition from Eastern labour means. Cotton has felt it. Iron and steel will feel it. And Protection will come—from the Labour Party."

CHAPTER II

IN PARLIAMENT

By now the Baldwin family might count itself among the wealthy. But the old English hierarchy had not been overthrown, and a large fortune, Harrow and Cambridge, did not carry a man across the line, still visible, between the upper middle classes and the aristocracy. Nor did families like the Baldwins much desire to cross it. In their own neighbourhood they could usually have a seat in Parliament for the asking. They could sway the new County Councils. They desired to be known as model employers, in the country as model landlords. In firms like Alfred Baldwin's, generations of work-people were still familiarly known to generations of employers: the nexus was personal, a kind of industrial feudalism which had never had to take much account of banks or trade unions, of mechanization or scientific research. In that long summer afternoon of aristocracy and industry Stanley Baldwin grew up. It was a good world for the rich; and no bad world for the labourer in a trade where there were no strikes, no unemployment, a sound friendly society and a fair-to-generous master. Whether Baldwin ever really understood the structure of modern industry was sometimes doubted: if he had, it was once said, he would have been a Socialist. What he did understand was the relationships in the old industry—that curious blend of discipline and good nature, fairmindedness and competition, sound workmanship and indifference to science, which floats hazily over the great creations of Victorian industry, as indeed the historian sometimes feels it floating over Baldwin's party and Baldwin's Cabinets.

Girls who knew about him as the best match in the West Midlands found him shy, silent and unsure of himself. In old age he once wrote:

I thought I was making a modest success on my own, but I have *never* made any real impression on a woman. I may have had a modest success for an evening if the party was particularly dull, but to be remembered next day, much less next week, NEVER.

Lucy Ridsdale, whom he married in 1892, was by name a daughter of the North, by temperament of the South, of Sussex, where they met and played cricket together. There was not much passion in their mating, but a deep and lasting affection: and she made it her pride to see that whatever part he was called to undertake he should play it correctly. For intellectual sympathy he had to look elsewhere. But if she was not sensitive, she had understanding; she was never indiscreet; and she furnished something astringent and positive which was lacking in his temperament. Six children were born to them, two sons and four daughters. But his interests seemed to flow over the inner ring of the family and expand themselves more freely among the cousinhood—of Kiplings, Poynters and Mackails. A certain discomfort in nearer relationships showed itself in the statesman too. Young followers were sometimes puzzled, sometimes hurt, by his constraint; he could write things that he could not bring himself to say. He was happier in the House than in Cabinet, and happiest of all in great meetings, giving and taking affection without personal intimacy or individual concern.

In the Conservative rout of 1906 Alfred Baldwin held the seat, West Worcestershire or Bewdley, which he had first won in 1892. Stanley, who stood for Kidderminster,* was beaten. The constituency had the reputation of being as corrupt as any in the kingdom: the common answer to the canvasser was "Call at a quarter to eight," when the electors were guided or carried to the polling station, not clearly knowing what to do when they got there. So at least it was said, and Baldwin was fond of relating a story to illustrate the danger from an indiscreet supporter. A Conservative speaker averred that the Liberal candidate had

---

* The letter to the electors began: "I have acceded to a request that I would come forward as the Conservative candidate." The candidate makes a pencil emendation "should." He offered himself for Worcester but the Local Executive preferred an Irishman.

been warned off the race-course at Nice for pulling his horse. "And why shouldn't he?" a Liberal voice demanded. "It was his own horse, wasn't it?"—thus anticipating the sentiment of Baldwin and four-fifths of his countrymen when in 1936 Hitler occupied the Rhineland. "And why shouldn't he? It's his own country, isn't it?" Baldwin did not like the business of electioneering and meetings at night in the thick air of the Kidderminster public-houses. Years later he told the Classical Association how he used to return to his hotel and cleanse his mind with Homer or Horace. In somewhat similar circumstances Asquith, forgetting that he had a meeting to address, was found reading Wordsworth's *Prelude*; and, modestly disclaiming the title for himself, Baldwin liked to think that he too was sustaining the tradition of scholar-statesmen.

But at the moment what he needed was not books but a long country walk.

So I took an early train to Kingham and took to my legs. I saw wagons in a fold yard with the romantic name of Mervyn Wingfield and somehow found myself in Burford. At an inn with the innocent sign of the *Lamb* I ate cold meats, washed down with ale. Next I got to Minster Lovel, and dug out old Crom Price (the Head of *Stalky and Co*) and sponged on him for high tea. I walked in the twilight to Witney where I had a long conversation in the bar with a traveller in boots. Next morning I tramped in the rain to Oxford where I ran into the Mackails and made my way home by rail, arriving a new man and purged of my humours. That was my first and last visit to Burford. But it remains in my memory in a golden mist.

The sudden death of Alfred Baldwin in 1908 put the Bewdley division—almost a family borough—into Stanley's hands. It was part of his good fortune, at least of his fortune, that he was never called upon to fight hard for a seat. He had sat—without distinction—for some years in the Worcestershire County Council, and he entered Parliament at forty-one with no great expectation of achieving greater distinction there. Nor did he achieve it. In six years he spoke five times—once "as an employer who had never had a strike or a lock-out." He was well liked but little known:

"One of the nicest fellows in the House," was Asquith's judgment; "No use to God or man," his own. After seven or eight years he thought of quitting Parliament altogether, but he and his wife decided to give it a ten years' trial and then, if nothing had happened, go back to the County Council and the family business, now greatly flourishing on wartime contracts; to books, to travel, perhaps to the management of a landed estate. I say perhaps, because Baldwin's deep love for the soil did not include any corresponding interest in the working of the soil. The poetry, the charm, the beauty of rural England: the names, the family records, the speech, the proverbs, of our villages: the angle of a gable, the build of a cart: of all that makes appeal to eye or ear; of Abberley and Woodbury, of the Teme and the Shropshire border, and the Cathedral church of Worcester, he was enamoured. But that Baldwin on the land was no better than a permanent week-ender, if said with more acerbity than understanding, was not said without some truth, as his rustic neighbours knew. "Live in the country and grow pigs? Ay, that'll be one of Master Stanley's jokes."

Alfred Baldwin greatly esteemed Bonar Law, and in return Bonar Law, now Chancellor of the Exchequer, made Stanley his Parliamentary Private Secretary and, in June 1917, Financial Secretary to the Treasury, an office which is as important as the occupant chooses to make it: to an ambitious man it is only one step below the Cabinet. Baldwin's qualifications were that he was honest, amenable and acceptable to the House. "But," said Chalmers, the Head of the Treasury, "never sit on the front bench unless you have business there. If you are absent the House says 'Where is the Financial Secretary?' But if you are present they say, 'What does the Financial Secretary think?'" Of Baldwin's tenure, one story survives in the mythology of Whitehall—the story of a minute-paper bearing only the words:

Chancellor of Exchequer: I agree. S. B.
Financial Secretary: I see you do. But why? A. C.

Once I remarked, "You were Financial Secretary under Austen, I think?" "Under," he replied, "is a well chosen word. I was to wind up for the Government in an Irish debate. Austen sent for me. 'Remember,' he said, 'this is not an occasion for levity.'" Austen was easily shocked. In 1926 the Conservative Central Office proposed to film Ministers at Work, with officials in their shirtsleeves bearing files and boxes. "Bovril may do this," Austen wrote, "but should Baldwins?"

On June 24th 1919 a letter appeared in *The Times* over the signature F. S. T.

Sir, [it ran] It is now a truism to say that in August 1914 the nation was face to face with the greatest crisis in her history. She was saved by the free-will offerings of her people. The best of her men rushed to the Colours; the best of her women left their homes to spend and be spent; the best of her older men worked as they had never worked before, to a common end, and with a sense of unity and fellowship as new as it was exhilarating. It may be that in four and a half years the ideals of many became dim, but the spiritual impetus of those early days carried the country through to the end.

To-day, on the eve of peace, we are faced with another crisis, less obvious, but none the less searching. The whole country is exhausted. By a natural reaction, not unlike that which led to the excesses of the Restoration after the reign of the Puritans, all classes are in danger of being submerged by a wave of extravagance and materialism. It is so easy to live on borrowed money; so difficult to realize that you are doing so.

It is so easy to play; so hard to learn that you cannot play for long without work. A fool's paradise is only the ante-room to a fool's hell.

How can the nation be made to understand the gravity of the financial situation; that love of country is better than love of money?

This can only be done by example, and the wealthy classes have to-day an opportunity of service which can never recur.

They know the danger of the present debt; they know the weight of it in the years to come. They know the practical difficulties of a universal statutory capital levy. Let them impose upon themselves, each as he is able, a voluntary levy. It should be possible to pay to the Exchequer within 12 months such a sum as would save the taxpayer 50 millions a year.

I have been considering this matter for nearly two years, but my mind moves slowly; I dislike publicity, and I hoped that someone else might lead the way. I have made as accurate an estimate as I am able of the value of my own estate and have arrived at a total of about £580,000. I have decided to realise 20 per cent of that amount or, say, £120,000, which will purchase £150,000 of the new War Loan, and present it to the Government for cancellation.

I give this portion of my estate as a thank-offering in the firm conviction that never again shall we have such a chance of giving our country that form of help which is so vital at the present time.

The example was not followed. In place of the expected £50,000,000 the taxpayer was relieved by some half-million. Baldwin had learned one of the most useful lessons of public life, but a lesson which had to be repeated before he could master it—and in the end perhaps it mastered him. Except in times of perceived crisis, people will not do what is right only because it is right. They must be prepared. And the word must then be given by a known, familiar voice. No one knew who F. S. T. might be. For that matter not many would have known who S. B. was.

To be Financial Secretary at fifty and stay Financial Secretary till fifty-four is no great thing; and though the House was beginning to appreciate his lucid expositions of finance, it is certain that at this time neither Bonar Law nor Austen Chamberlain had any real confidence in Baldwin's capacity as a minister in charge of a department. Still, he had done well enough to be made President of the Board of Trade, when ill health forced Bonar Law to withdraw, Chamberlain became Leader, and Horne followed him at the Exchequer.

On his appointment Bonar Law wrote :

> You have what I am told was one of my defects, too much modesty ; so my advice to you is to get rid of that defect as soon as possible.

Some of his friends were disappointed—they would have preferred to see him Speaker of the House in succession to Lowther. Baldwin himself had no inclination that way. He had some of the gifts the Chair demands: good sense, good humour, an unexpected firmness and a deep devotion to the House of Commons. But two he lacked, attentiveness and industry. His mind would all too often have floated away from the Chamber, to be recalled by some sudden outbreak, some demand for a ruling, requiring rather more than a genial placation. A Speaker must know his procedure as a conductor knows his score.

Baldwin made his first appearance as a Cabinet Minister on May 9th 1921, when he introduced the Resolutions under the Safeguarding of Industries Bill in a speech described as pleasant and skilful, with a remarkable slip which no one noticed—he ascribed Sergeant Bothwell's last words, "and fearing nothing," to his slayer, Balfour of Burleigh. Baldwin's economics were at all times very simple and easy to expound. The world was in a state, as Mansfield said of the French Revolution, "without precedent, and therefore without prognostic." Our industries were menaced from all sides by the cheaper production of foreign countries; the exchanges, rocketing and collapsing, made forward calculations almost impossible; and the new States that had risen out of the ruins of three Empires were wholly given up to the creed of economic nationalism. Free Trade against Protection was under these conditions an exhausted issue, and we must go into the jungle not with the axe, a discredited weapon, but with a tank. Let the State keep the ring against unfair competition from without, and within the ring let experience, aptitude, instinct and craftsmanship have free play and fair reward. It is the creed of the Late-Victorian ironmaster when the evening chill was in the air. Business men felt that the President was one of themselves, and left off baiting his department with deputations. And Labour, watching the curve of unemployment rising and the curve of wages falling, could not close its ears or its mind to anything that might promise relief. That August 1¾ million men were out of work, 400,000 of them soldiers of the last war. And 7,000,000 had had their wages cut down.

Patience, good humour and an unexpected readiness in answering questions are gifts to which the House of Commons always responds, and by the end of the session Baldwin was better liked than he had ever been before. Liked and trusted, and in that ugly, angry, ragged Parliament, where would-be revolutionaries confronted "the hard-faced men

who looked as if they had done well out of the war,"* to be
trusted was a rare accomplishment. But close on the passage
of the Bill followed a gentle rain of questions on Vacuum
Flasks, Dolls' Eyes, Camphor Anomalies and Magic Lan-
terns : and his officials noticed that in these matters his pleasant and skilful ways seemed to end in a humorous detachment
from the whole business. Not always humorous : one of them
would describe "the bewildered resentment" with which
the Minister received instruction on technical points. Indeed,
the Act failed to yield quick results because the industries
would not learn to put their cases properly. "Still," he
said, "I am a very patient man," and he was always inclined
to think that, with reasonable common sense, an Act would
administer itself. But it was coming to be known that,
patient and silent as he might be, in Cabinet he could
be stiff. Once, some Budget adjustment being under consideration, Lloyd George said, "But we have not heard
what the President of the Board of Trade has to say."
"Perhaps," said Baldwin, "you will not like what he is going
to say. He feels as if he were the director of a fraudulent
company engaged in cooking the balance sheet." No more
was heard of the adjustment. The first commodity to enjoy
the benefit of Safeguarding was Fabric Gloves. Vehement
opposition developed and it looked as if the Cabinet would
overrule the Board of Trade. Baldwin made it clear that if
they did, he would resign. Feature by feature, he was building up the picture of himself as a Parliamentary figure : that
mysterious process by which the House selects its coming
men was already at work.

At the end of the session the Baldwins made the first of
many visits to Aix-les-Bains. He spent a day looking at
Geneva, his only visit to the sacred city of the League. These
holidays were his charging time. At fifty-five he was almost
youthfully active in body—indeed, some years later he
stepped out for the hills so smartly that his French body-
guard had to jump on a tram to overtake him. Leaving Mrs.
Baldwin to perform her cure, he would tramp and brood
for hours on end, and his broodings after five months of

* It seems impossible to determine whether Baldwin or Keynes said
this first.

Cabinet office were far from happy. We often went over the ground together—the nature of party, the justification of party, the relations of a Prime Minister with his colleagues, and of a Cabinet with the House of Commons. At every point he maintained that the administration under Lloyd George, the Coalition born of the Infamous Election (his own words) of 1918, was charged with mischief. All the relationships were wrong; and the Inner Ring, Lloyd George, Churchill, Birkenhead and Beaverbrook, were at odds with the official, prescribed policy, and were irrepressibly vocal at awkward moments.

"But," I once said, "in the end you won them round, and on your own terms. Churchill served under you; Lloyd George offered to serve; Birkenhead became your devoted friend. All but Beaverbrook. What was between you?" "Bonar Law," he answered. "We fought for the soul of Bonar Law. Beaverbrook wanted to make him a great man after his own fashion. I showed him there were better things to be." At another time: "I like everything that is good of its kind. I like Lloyd George. I like Beaverbrook!"

Certainly, to a man with Baldwin's high sense of party, the outlook in the later months of 1921 was ominous. The Liberal Party, fatally divided by personal discords, seemed near extinction. The Conservatives retained some self-identity, but they in their turn showed signs of fissure along the line which separated those who were attracted by Lloyd George and those who were repelled: in other words, those who were willing to remain in the Coalition and those who might prefer to leave it and take their chance when the General Election came. Birkenhead and Austen Chamberlain would stay; Balfour was incalculable, Curzon restless; Bonar Law doubtful, and failing in health. Yet his was the commanding voice, and, when the time came, it would be for him to give the word—Coalition or Independence. And Baldwin set himself to make sure that Independence it should be. Whether he had looked farther into the future than that, whether in those long walks he ever reckoned how many steps were between him and the highest place, I sometimes asked myself. He liked a phrase I once quoted to him of a colleague whose ideals were thought to be too high for

this low world: "there is a great deal of red earth in him all
the same." It fitted Baldwin too. Later, he was to set the
world wondering whether a man so obviously good could
really be so clever, or a man so amazingly lucky really be
so simple, as he appeared. But in that autumn of 1921
neither his virtues nor his abilities were of very high or
decisive account. He was popular; he was competent. But
he was no great name in the party, to the public barely a
name. He knew it: and he was content to let time work. "I
should like to be Chancellor of the Exchequer," he said;
"that is the limit of my ambitions."

He believed in his party: he thought that, fairly and
honestly presented, the Conservative case could win, and
hold, the country. But the party must be detached from its
unhappy association with Lloyd George—detached and perhaps purged. And in office it must conduct itself with such
moderation as would give Labour no excuse for unconstitutional ways. In a word, we must revert from the
powerful influence of the Inner Ring to responsible
Parliamentary government: which, whatever Clydeside and
the Shop-stewards and the Socialist intellectuals might say,
was what the Trade Unions really preferred because it was
what they really understood: and, understanding it, would
make it work. But what the Conservative case would be—
that also time would reveal. In spirit it would be the old
Disraelian Toryism; in body, whatever the needs of the day
might require.

The old Disraelian Toryism? Or was it the old Disraelian
day dream? "The Conservatives can't talk of class-war:
they started it." This gruff judgment introduced one of
Baldwin's favourite themes—the gross and almost irreparable
error which, under the vehement guidance of Lord Chancellor Halsbury, the Conservative Government had made in
1901. Down to that date, the Courts on the whole had
inclined to interpret the Trade Union legislation of the
Seventies in a sense more favourable to the Unions than to
the employers: to secure equality of status between masters
and men in combination, by tilting the balance, when the
law was silent or unclear, to the weaker side. In 1900 there
was a strike on the Taff Vale Railway in the course of which

things were done by some of the Union men which in the
view of the Company were not lawful under the governing
statutes.* The Company prosecuted two officers of the Union
for incitement, and sued the Union for damages. The Union
claimed that under the Act of 1871 it could not be sued, and
on appeal its claim was upheld. Then in July 1901 the Lords
reversed the decision of the Court of Appeal and with it
the whole trend of judicial interpretation for thirty years.
The Union found itself cast in heavy damages, and the
alarm in Union circles was sharpened by the open exultation
of the employers and of their representatives in Parliament
and the press. And that, Baldwin always maintained, was
the moment for the Tory Party to strike in, and restore the
position intended by the Tory legislation of 1875. They
missed their tide, and in 1906 they met their punishment.
The Liberals willingly did what the Conservatives had failed
to do, and so created an opposition between Conservatism
and Labour which was not inherent in the history or policy
of either. Not that the Liberals had in the long run profited,
and their forlorn and broken state left the Conservatives to
figure alone as the representatives of property and the employing class.

But 1906 was far away and long ago. In 1921 and 1922,
with nearly a million young lives gone and treasure past
counting, the Spirit Ironic was asking, as it asks Napoleon
in Hardy's drama,

> Ajaccian Bonaparte,
> Has all this been worth while?

Indeed, the years following Waterloo furnish the best parallel
to our state in the days of the Coalition, because just as the
French wars masked the consequences of the new industrial-
ism until they were almost unmanageable, so the war of
1918 effected equally deep-seated changes, the outcome of
which was visible only when the war was over. At Washington we surrendered our naval supremacy—the first sign that
our standing as a Great Power was shaken. In Europe it

---

* The Trade Union Act of 1871 and Cross's two Acts of 1875: the
Employers and Workmen Act, and the Conspiracy and Protection of
Property Act.

looked as if we had substituted the hegemony of France for
the hegemony of Prussia. At home it seemed to many that
the better world so liberally promised at the Election of 1918
was unlikely to be realized by any Government the old parties could form, perhaps by any Parliament. And there, to
Baldwin, was the root of all trouble and the seed of all danger..
The Two Nations of Disraeli were arming against each other,
and only a renewed Conservatism, resolute and sympathetic,
could save our Parliamentary Constitution, and avert a
social war. "If you rattle the sabre long enough, you are
bound to draw it some day." Therefore there must be no
provocation, no sabre-rattling on the Tory side: no
Churchill, no Birkenhead. So, and so only, if the forces of
subversion got the upper hand in the Labour movement,
could they be crushed—by the common sense of the English
people, directed by a Conservative government. Whether
Baldwin knew of Trotsky's saying that a policeman's
truncheon on the head of an English workman would mark
the beginning of the social revolution, I cannot say. But I
think he might have agreed.

Meanwhile those forces had only too much matter to work
upon. When the United States entered the war in 1917, an
English official, asked privately to summarize his experience
of relations with Labour, replied that wages, prices and
profits should be held in a rigid triangle: if one got loose,
the rest would follow, and the consequence would be certainly economic, and possibly social, chaos. It is in the nature
of things that employers should think more of profits, their
workfolk of wages, and the housewife of prices; and by the
end of the war all three had got fantastically out of relation
with one another and with the economic situation as a whole.
Within a month of the Armistice, the Railwaymen were demanding an eight-hour day and better pay for overtime; in
January 1919 the Miners' Federation declared its policy to
be a six-hour day and a general wage advance of 30 per
cent. The returning soldiers could not be absorbed in industries which had not yet regained their foreign markets:
by February a million men were on Unemployment Benefit;
and Clydeside had warned the Government that if the
employers did not accept the men's demands the Unions

would have recourse to "any other methods" which they might consider likely to advance their cause.

Such a threat, or such a warning, coming from one district or one trade was not perhaps very alarming. The danger lay in combined action by two or three great Unions acting in alliance: and the alliance was there, the Triple Alliance of Transport, Railways and Mines. The demands of the Transport workers were industrial only—more wages for shorter hours. The Railwaymen added joint control with the shareholders in the industry. The Miners were firm for nationalization. And now together they were claiming some measure of control over Government policy in other matters too—the blockade of Germany, relations with the new order in Russia, the coercion of Ireland. But for whatever reason, and the main reason perhaps was the habit of constitutional action on the part of the Union leaders—a habit Baldwin was fond of associating with the Wesleyan order in which, like some of his own ancestors, those leaders had often been trained—the Alliance did not use the power which it seemed to possess. In September 1919 the Railwaymen struck, but they struck alone. For nine days the public was put to great inconvenience; a million men were idle. But the Supply and Transport organization formed in the war still worked: the necessaries of life were distributed; and the revolution did not come.

Meanwhile, on June 22nd 1919, the Royal Commission appointed to consider the future of the mining industry, the Sankey Commission, had laid its report, its four reports in fact. The members were divided chiefly on one issue—nationalization—recommended by the chairman and, with some reservations of detail, supported by the miners—or district amalgamations in the interest of efficiency. For a year and more, negotiation and agitation proceeded together, and in October 1920 the Miners' Federation, believing, or at least hoping, that the allies were ready to follow, declared a strike. It lasted no more than a fortnight and ended with a concession on wages, silence on other issues and fresh negotiations. On March 18th 1921 the owners made their offer. The Federation refused to accept it and the second coal strike began. But the allies, the Railwaymen and Transport

workers, stood aloof. At the end of three months, on June
28th, a settlement was announced. Wages were fixed at
the pre-war rate with an increment of one quarter: and
profits at 17 per cent of wages. Any surplus was to be
divided, 83 per cent to the men and 17 per cent to the
owners. The distribution was to be applied by district
boards acting under a national board, masters and men having equal representation. The poorer districts were to receive a subsidy from the taxpayer.

With this settlement, it might be said, the immediate post-
war period comes to an end—an end reached rather by
the exhaustion of the contending parties than by any solution
of the problems over which they were contending. The
Labour movement had shown itself not revolutionary, not
united; it was long before the Miners forgot or forgave the
desertion of the Railwaymen and the Transport workers in
the spring of 1921. Cool heads, on whichever side, did not
fail to observe that a country struggling to its feet after the
costliest of all wars, a country burdened with a foreign debt
without precedent, simply could not afford to waste millions
of working days on strikes and lockouts in one year. The
public—and the public included every working man
who found himself standing idle and hungry because in some
remote trade his fellows had laid down their tools—was
growing fretful under this continual disturbance of daily life;
fretful and, in politics, apathetic. "At this moment," Baldwin
said at the end of the session of 1921, "any party would be
returned if they promised to do nothing." On their wedding-
day he gave his wife a pot of pâté de foie gras. "It is all I can
afford," he said; "these strikes!" The desire for tranquillity
was at work before Bonar Law selected it as the watchword
of his party at the next election.

Perhaps a brilliant and popular foreign policy might have
saved the Coalition from the disrepute into which it was
manifestly falling, if the materials of such a policy could
have been found. But the ancient pattern had been distorted,
if not torn; and, by ourselves, disarmed as we were, had we
the strength to frame a new one? Memories are short, and
time in these late years has moved swiftly. It is difficult, but
it is necessary, to realize that in 1921 war meant a French

air fleet raining death on an undefended London. Or something worse perhaps : a gas-attack in a low-lying fog. Baldwin, who delighted in Balfour's graceful and toying precision, once wrote down in Cabinet while Balfour was speaking—always searching for the right word as he went—his summary of a situation with which he was commissioned to deal.

> I think I understand. I am to try if possible to induce the French to agree to a very small battle fleet so as to leave us free to accept American proposals without modification. Having persuaded them to deprive themselves of this form of naval defence, I am then to persuade them that they really require no submarines because a war between France and England is unthinkable. This task being successfully accomplished, I am then to ask them to reduce the number of their aircraft seeing that we cannot sleep securely in our beds lest in a war with France London should be burnt to the ground. For a task so complex as this I fear a trained diplomatist is required. But I will do my best.

That was where victory, and three years of peace, had brought us. Our island story was told. These are Baldwin's own words.

In a Government so constituted as the Coalition, the President of the Board of Trade had hardly more influence on Foreign Policy than the President of the Board of Agriculture. And it was a matter in which Baldwin could never really interest himself, never keep his attention fixed. Of one thing only was he from first to last convinced—that party divisions on foreign policy or defence could work a deadly mischief. Unhappily, the divisions were there. What, in 1922, was to be done with Germany? Was Russia to be readmitted to the comity of nations or kept outside? Was the League of Nations a dream, an ideal, a nuisance, or the living form of a new order? These, perhaps, were the three main issues of the time, and on each of them men equally thoughtful and sincere might find themselves at odds with one another. For a hundred years and more, English ministers of all parties, Castlereagh and Canning, Aberdeen and Palmerston, Salisbury and Grey, had reiterated to foreign Governments the sobering, and sometimes exasperating, truth that in England public policy is dictated by public opinion. But in

1922, and for many years afterwards, it might be truly said
that there was no public opinion, no common settled attitude
of mind: but, in its place, an immense variety of sentiment,
often quite uninformed, but not, for that, less passionately
entertained. The largest measure of agreement, perhaps,
might have been secured for the thesis that the victors had
broken faith with the world by disarming the vanquished
and not disarming themselves. In truth we had disarmed
beyond the limit of security. The rest of the world had not.
That is the governing clue to the history of England in the
years between the wars. No one knew it better than Baldwin,
or affirmed it with more energy than he did, years later, on
the eve of the crisis of 1931.

In Ireland murder reigned on a scale which might
almost rank as civil war: first the war between Sinn Fein
and the forces of the Crown—in the summer of 1920 the
Army of Occupation numbered 60,000 men: and thereafter between the Republicans and the Free Staters who had
signed the Treaty of Peace with England on December 6th
1921. Baldwin liked Irishmen. He would relate with glee
a story of the Ulster leader, Sir James Craig, visiting de
Valera in the mountains under safe-conduct. After three
hours' discourse, de Valera had reached Poyning's Law of
1487, and Craig had to leave, still under escort. As they
crossed the British lines, the sentinel saluted. Craig and the
escort turned and winked at each other. They had tricked
the Englishman. But Baldwin was deeply affected by the
tragedy of Ireland, and it was his dark memories of the
Cross Times there that sustained him in the great battle
over the Indian Settlement ten years later. He was fond
of quoting Balfour: "I will not be a Peel to split the Conservative party." "You came near it," I once said, "over
India." "No," he said, "not really. I knew they would
see reason. And I was quite determined that India should
not be another Ireland."

But in the end it was on its foreign policy that the Coalition
was wrecked. The United States had refused to join Great
Britain in guaranteeing the security of France, and the
only alternative for France was to guarantee her own security
by holding Germany down. England was not afraid of a

German revival in arms, was ceasing to expect very much from German reparations, but was looking to the re-opening of a valuable market. The discord between the two allies was growing more audible every month. And on August 1st 1921 Balfour, as Foreign Secretary, published a note on war debts which was, later, to concern Baldwin gravely. The note said that our indebtedness to the United States had been incurred largely in the interests of our European allies. That was plain truth. The undertaking which followed, to collect no more from the Allies than was necessary to meet our American obligations, sounded generous. But the effect on American opinion was unhappy. "Of course we shall pay. But we think you are cads to ask us," is hardly the language for a debtor to use. But that is how the Balfour note was read throughout the States.

Meanwhile it seemed as if another war might at any moment break out in a quarter to which the public had paid little attention. Turkey, under Mustapha Kemal, had come suddenly to life again. Here again the Allies were at odds : the position of the British forces occupying Constantinople was precarious; and the Turk, no inconsiderable diplomatist, was well aware that England was in no mood for war, and that if war came the Dominions would stand apart, while France and Italy might be ranged on the Turkish side, if not as allies at least as more than friendly neutrals.

It may well be asked whether any Government could in fact have mastered the chaos of 1922 : settled our debts, restored our markets, revived the Alliance, overawed the Turk and put life into the young League of Nations—lamed from birth by the abstention of America. But that is not how an electorate judges its governors : and by the middle of 1922 the situation, in Baldwin's view, was charged with a danger of a new and subtle kind. The ultimate justification of party is that it provides an alternative government when the constituencies are dissatisfied with the men in office. And there is much truth in the well-worn saying, that the people never vote for a party, only against one. But against whom were they to vote in 1922? The only answer was—against Lloyd George. But if Lloyd George carried the Conservatives with him, where was the alternative Government to be

found? Could Asquith form one out of Liberal fragments and
mutinous Conservatives? Or Labour, inexperienced and
untried? All meditations ran the same way, to the same end,
or the same issue. The Conservatives must make up their
minds between the continuance of personal government
under Lloyd George, and the restoration of Parliamentary
government without him. The electoral omens were on
their side—if Bonar Law could be got to read them right.
There was much to think about that summer in the hills
above Aix. All that time on holiday he read no English
papers. On September 29th he was recalled to London.
The Turkish crisis has suddenly become acute.

An influential and independent school of thought deplored
the prospect of a Greek capitulation, and would even have
regarded hostilities as a lesser evil. On August 4th
Lloyd George had delivered a speech which was, in effect,
a call to Greece to strike. But the Turks struck first; soon
the Greek army was in flight, soon Smyrna was in flames.
The occasion had come. A meeting of the Conservative Party
was summoned to the Carlton Club for October 19th. In
less than a month Baldwin was Chancellor of the Exchequer
in a Conservative Government with a majority of 73 over
all parties combined. The Coalition was shattered. Lloyd
George had fallen beyond recovery.

"Does little Baldwin think he can turn us out?" Lloyd
George had asked. Popular memory, always inclining to the
dramatic, came to think of the Carlton Club as a field where-
in a stripling, known to few, had with his own arm brought
down the Goliath of Europe. In fact, Baldwin since his return
from Aix had been very carefully making sure of his ground
and gathering supporters. But till the morning of October
18th he was still doubtful on which side Bonar Law would
alight. He saw him several times that day and by the evening
he knew that all was well. It was not Baldwin's resolution
alone, but Baldwin acting on Bonar Law's sense of public
duty, that brought the Coalition to an end. The Conservative
Leader was stricken in health: his advisers could not promise
him more than two years of active life—he himself doubted
whether he could carry the burden for more than one. In
fact, he carried it for no more than six months. But he had

placed his party in power, and very early in the new Parliament he made it plain that the era of personal government was closed.

"Ministers," he said, "are not servants of the Prime Minister. They are responsible Cabinet Ministers. It is essential that the people should understand that it is under the ordinary method of constitutional government that the work has to be done." After dangerous oscillations, government had swung back to its natural centre, in Parliament. More than fifteen years later, in almost the last words he spoke in the House of Commons, Baldwin reiterated the true doctrine. He was being pressed to take certain negotiations out of the hands of the departmental Minister and conduct them himself. "His Majesty's Ministers," he answered, "are co-equal." Then, as he sank back on the Treasury Bench, he added, "Luckily they are not co-eternal."

What the Carlton meeting did disclose—though few realized it then or for some time afterwards—was that this countrified business man, who seemed to have reached the Cabinet by accident, was the master, and the unequalled master, of a new eloquence: direct, conversational, monosyllabic: rising and falling without strain or effort, between the homeliest humour and the most moving appeal. At the Carlton meeting he first struck the note which a vaster public was so often to hear from him and could never hear too often—a simple earnestness, which brought the issue, whatever it might be, within the moral comprehension of the common listener. Here is the speech:

My Lords and gentlemen,—Mr. Chamberlain has called this meeting, as he has very clearly, and with his accustomed felicity of speech, told you, to put before you the views of the majority of the Unionist members of the Cabinet; and it is my duty at this moment to put before you, very briefly and very clearly, the views of the minority in the Cabinet—that is, of myself and of Sir Arthur Boscawen.

I have long been aware that there was a good deal of discomfort (let me leave it at that) in the ranks of the Tory Party, and when, a short time ago, a conference of the Unionist members of the Cabinet was held to consider the political situation, there were only two courses open before me—one, an easy one, to keep silent; the other, a very difficult one, to say what I felt. I will put my views to you as I put them to my colleagues.

I will preface this by making one remark. It seems to me, from what Mr. Chamberlain has said, that it is a very easy thing to enter into a Coalition, but that, having entered into it, it must be permanent, because at any moment that you feel you ought to leave that Coalition, you open yourself to charges of having deserted, because you wished to escape the responsibility for the acts of that Coalition. I am quite sure, speaking for myself, I have no desire of that kind. If I stand as an Independent Conservative at the election, I shall make it perfectly clear to my constituents that I accept full responsibility for everything up to the moment when I had to separate myself from my colleagues. But, after all, the essence of coalition is voluntary association, and you cannot compel people to coalesce in any particular form; and it seems to me that a fatal mistake was made in agreeing to go to an election without consulting the party as to whether they were willing or not to continue the arrangement which they entered into in 1918.

As I am only going to speak for a very short time, I will not beat about the bush, but will come right to the root of the whole difficulty, which is the position of the Prime Minister. The Prime Minister was described this morning in *The Times*, in the words of a distinguished aristocrat, as a live wire. He was described to me, and to others, in more stately language, by the Lord Chancellor, as a dynamic force, and I accept those words. He is a dynamic force, and it is from that very fact that our troubles, in our opinion, arise. A dynamic force is a very terrible thing; it may crush you, but it is not necessarily right.

It is owing to that dynamic force, and that remarkable personality, that the Liberal Party, to which he formerly belonged, has been smashed to pieces; and it is my firm conviction that, in time, the same thing will happen to our party. I do not propose to elaborate, in an assembly like this, the dangers and the perils of that happening. We have already seen, during our association with him in the last four years, a section of our party hopelessly alienated.* I think that if

---

* On this sentence, Churchill's words are the best comment, "The Irish Treaty and its circumstances were unforgivable by the most tenacious elements in the Conservative Party."

the present association is continued, and if this meeting agrees that it should be continued, you will see some more breaking up, and I believe the process must go on inevitably until the old Conservative Party is smashed to atoms and lost in ruins.

I would like to give you just one illustration to show what I mean by the disintegrating influence of a dynamic force. Take Mr. Chamberlain and myself. Mr. Chamberlain's services to the State are infinitely greater than any that I have been able to render, but we are both men who are giving all we can give to the service of the State; we are both men who are, or who try to be, actuated by principle in our conduct; we are men who, I think, have exactly the same views on the political problems of the day; we are men who I believe—certainly on my side—have esteem and perhaps I may add affection for each other; but the result of this dynamic force is that we stand here to-day, he prepared to go into the wilderness if he should be compelled to forsake the Prime Minister, and I prepared to go into the wilderness if I should be compelled to stay with him. If that is the effect of that tremendous personality on two men occupying the position that we do, and related to each other politically in the way that Mr. Chamberlain and I are, that process must go on throughout the party. It was for that reason that I took the stand I did, and put forward the views that I did. I do not know what the majority here or in the country may think about it. I said at the time what I thought was right, and I stick all through to what I believe to be right.

The man who delivered the speech is thus described in the prints of the day. He was fifty-five. He was short and stocky, rather pale, with a humorous mouth that could close with a snap, blue eyes under shaggy brows and hair inclining to red. His voice: crisp, musical, far-carrying: with a harsh note in reserve if a topic was to be ended, an intruder silenced, or a suggestion dismissed.

At the time of the Maurice debate in 1918, Lloyd George and Baldwin were walking to the House together. "You know, Prime Minister," Baldwin said, "this is a very remarkable occasion. For years they have been trying to catch you deviating from the line of strict veracity. And now they have caught you—telling the truth." Lloyd George shouted with laughter and told the tale everywhere. To Baldwin he said, "That is the difference between Bonar Law and me.

Poor Bonar can't bear being called a liar. Now I don't mind." Speaking at an Oxford dinner, Baldwin once said that the election of 1922 had been won on six words of Lloyd George.

> There is a vast new electorate in the country. There are millions of voters unattached to any party, and up and down the country they were wondering what they wanted and for whom they were to vote. One morning they opened their papers and read that Lloyd George had said of Bonar Law that he was "honest to the verge of simplicity." And they said, "By God, that is what we have been looking for."

CHAPTER III

IN OFFICE

On taking office Bonar Law made Baldwin Chancellor of the Exchequer. The former Chancellor, Sir Robert Horne, had actually been due to leave for Washington on October 18th. But the rush of events—the Carlton Club meeting and the resignation of Lloyd George—carried him from the Treasury to the Board of Trade. Thus it fell to Baldwin to redress the mischief of the Balfour note and negotiate the settlement of the American debt, hampered by the knowledge that in a private letter Austen Chamberlain had spoken of a settlement at 5 per cent as not only just but generous.

The American commissioners proposed that the debt should carry interest at $3\frac{1}{2}$ per cent and should be extinguished in 61 years by a sinking fund of $\frac{1}{2}$ per cent. The principal was then 4,075 million dollars and unpaid interest at 5 per cent brought the capital amount up to 4,686 million. The proposal therefore meant an annual payment of 187 million dollars for 61 years. Baldwin could not accept the offer. What he had contemplated was a payment of 140 million dollars for 50 years, but he had warned the American authorities that he doubted whether even this figure would be acceptable to the Cabinet.

They then produced a second project, reducing the interest to $1\frac{3}{4}$ per cent for the first five years, thus helping the United Kingdom over the trying time of conversion from war to peace, but carrying forward the balance and adding it, with interest, to the principal. This offer, telegraphed to London, elicited a firm refusal from Bonar Law. No reasonable banker, he argued, would exact such terms from a solvent debtor. If we were not solvent, then no settlement was of value. If we were—as the negotiations assumed—why should the guarantee of the British Government be rated at more than 2½ per cent? The Prime Minister did not understand American feeling or the figures of interest in which Americans thought. Accustomed, as our Ambassador pointed out, to interest at 4 or even 5 per cent, the Americans could not understand why the British Government should be let off with 2½ per cent.

Between those two telegrams, the English negotiators had glimpses of a possible compromise—interest at 3 per cent and extinction in 66 years. Baldwin hoped, moreover, by reducing the interest in arrear from 5 to 3½ per cent to lower the annual payment still further to 156 million dollars. He so proposed, and after his offer had been made a second telegram arrived from the Prime Minister, evidently unhappy over the line his colleague was taking, repeating his preference for 2½ per cent, and hoping rather than expecting that the arrears of interest would be remitted. The Americans then made their third proposal—interest at 3 per cent for 10 years; thereafter 3½ per cent; arrears of interest to be 4½ instead of 5 per cent. The total effect was to require of Great Britain a payment of 161 million dollars a year for 10 years and 184 for 52—a burden greatly in excess, it will be seen, of what Baldwin had at first declared to be the maximum which his colleagues would accept. But, our Embassy insisted, there was no room for delay: no time to return to England with the latest offer and there seek a Cabinet decision. The necessary measures had to be taken before Congress rose on March 4th, not to meet again till December. But by December the Presidential campaign would be in sight, and a Presidential election fought on British debts was not a prospect to be faced with equanimity by those charged with the maintenance of good relations between England and the United States. And the cost of the settlement, £33,000,000 a year, could not be said to be beyond the capacity of Great Britain. Fourteen years later J. P. Morgan, a good judge of American conditions, declared that Baldwin did right to close, and that no better terms could have been had. Horne was not less emphatic. But it is evident that he closed on his own authority and so confronted his colleagues with the alternative of disavowing their Chancellor or accepting the accomplished fact.

Keynes had written, while the negotiations were in progress,

> I hope on the whole we refuse the American offer, in order to
> give them time to discover that they are at our mercy as we
> are at France's, France at Germany's. It is the debtor who
> has the last word in these cases. We could reply quite politely
> that we have made the best offer we can in the present cir-
> cumstances of uncertainty and, if they want more, they must
> wait till the general position clears up and we know what we
> are going to get from France and Germany. We will therefore
> reopen the matter in two years' time and meanwhile we have
> no objection to the interest mounting up on paper at 5 per
> cent although of course we can't pay this.
>
> P.S. These pure finance people are interesting. Hawtrey
> says, "Jump at it."

Where such high authorities differ, the common man will
abstain from judgment.

On January 29th 1923 the *Olympic* docked at South-
ampton. A swarm of reporters rushed on board, to find
Baldwin at breakfast. He first tried to send them all
ashore, but good nature, the pleasure of being home again
and, perhaps, a certain exaltation of spirit over a mission
well performed, made him relent. What he actually said
is not clear: it is admitted that he was badly reported.
But he said enough about the ignorance of the American
public to make certain sections of the American press,
especially the Western sections, exceedingly angry, and to
throw political circles at home into most unwonted excitement. The King was startled, and wrote to the Prime Minister asking, reasonably enough, how Baldwin had come to
publish any statement before it had received Cabinet approval. "I am sorry," the Prime Minister replied, "that
Your Majesty should have noticed that paragraph." "And
why," returned the King, "should I not notice it? I read
the papers." By the afternoon of that wet and gloomy Sunday it was known that the Prime Minister was strongly
opposed to the settlement. "I should be," he was reported
to have said, "the most cursed Prime Minister that ever
held office in England if I accepted those terms." For two
hours on Sunday evening, the Prime Minister and the

American Ambassador debated the matter in all its bearings. Baldwin sat silent. "I never felt so miserable in all my life," he afterwards said. But what other terms were there? The Cabinet at least could think of none, and on Tuesday, the 31st, the settlement was approved.

The Carlton meeting and the American settlement had brought Baldwin into the focus of attention. His speech on the Address, February 16th, showed to those who were nearest to him that, if he was not aiming at the succession, he was ready to accept it. Broadly, quietly, courteously he marked out the course his party was taking—for peace, for the sanctity of contracts, for the rebuilding of the industrial and financial fabric on which our prosperity depended. And he ended on words which startled the House, long unaccustomed to such an appeal in such language.

> The English language is the richest in the world in mono-syllables. Four words, of one syllable each . . . contain salvation for this country and the whole world, and they are Faith, Hope, Love and Work. No Government in this country to-day which has not faith in the people, hope in the future, love for its fellow-men, and which will not work and work, and work, will ever bring this country through into better days and better times, or will ever bring Europe through or the world through.

The Carlton speech was for party consumption: the speech on the Address was intended for a wider audience, which it reached. The Dean of Bristol made it the theme of a sermon to business men. Haldane and the aged Halifax united in praise. The Vice-Provost of Eton wrote:

> Just one line of thanks for the very lovely close of your speech. The little more and how much it is—the addition of the fourth monosyllable, work. I do not think anything quite like that has been said before. It was dangerous to add to the perfect trinity "love, faith, hope" but you dared, and you were justified in your daring.

And an old Liberal member, Gerald France, gave voice to a judgment which was rapidly forming:

> For some things I do not regret having left politics, but to read of fine ideals being set forth with courage and manliness

makes me long to have been there again last night. At one
time I could not have "placed" the Prime Minister's successor
in your party. Now it is different, and I am more glad than
I can say that character as a foundation for ability with an
added grace of humour are so conspicuously revealed in his
successor.

On April 17th the Chancellor opened his first and last
Budget. Chamber and galleries were packed—more from
curiosity about the man than from any expectation of financial surprises. Budget speeches have a form and sequence
of their own from which Chancellors rarely deviate. But
what surprised friends and strangers alike was the vivacity
and point with which Baldwin spoke.

From Paris, Bradbury, Chairman of the Reparations
Commission, wrote:

> A more or less profound study of a couple of dozen budgets
> has led me to the *constatation* that popular Budgets are nearly
> always bad budgets and that good budgets are almost always
> unpopular. Your effort goes far towards re-establishing that
> faith in human nature which was so gravely jeopardized by
> my Treasury experience.

The Chancellor was safe, he was sound, he was orthodox.
No one had expected him to be brilliant too, and the qualities
he showed that evening needed only one thing more to make
him a leader of the Commons. Had he authority as well?
Authority in his own party first? Could be bring them together? Balfour, Curzon, Chamberlain, Birkenhead—inside,
could he control them? Outside, would not the high standing
of some and the superb capacity of others be more than a
Government of mediocrities with an untried chief could con-
front? So the lobbies buzzed. And the Prime Minister was a
dying man. On May 19th he sent his resignation to the
King.

By constitutional usage an outgoing Prime Minister cannot proffer advice on the choice of a successor, but he must
give his advice if asked. Bonar Law was not asked. "If I
were," he was reported to have said, "I am afraid it would
have to be Baldwin." To Curzon he wrote: "I understand
it is not customary for the King to ask his Prime Minister
to recommend his successor in circumstances like the present

and I presume he will not do so." These words were enough to relieve the writer from any obligation towards Curzon or any other of his colleagues. The King's first intention, it was believed, was to send for Curzon. But two of Baldwin's friends, meeting the King's Secretary by accident in the Park at night, pointed out the difficulties that might arise with a Prime Minister in the Lords where the Opposition was unrepresented. Balfour was consulted. He acknowledged that the objection, or perhaps the excuse, was valid, and that it overrode Curzon's eminent claims to the Premiership. So the decision was taken. Early in the afternoon of May 21st, the King's Private Secretary called on Curzon to explain that the Prime Minister must be in the Commons. The shock to Curzon was terrible: he had been summoned to London—he had been photographed by an active press, smiling in serene triumph, the one Englishman who had reached the two great offices, Viceroy of India and Prime Minister. And after no more than five years of office Baldwin had been preferred, Baldwin, "a man of the utmost insignificance." Curzon expostulated vehemently. He believed that the Conservative Party must be reunited. He was confident that he could reunite it. And he was not alone in doubting whether any other man could. For the moment it certainly looked as if the Royal decision would end in a break-up of the party on the threshold of office, and the return of Lloyd George. Apart altogether from the personal humiliation, there were good grounds for Curzon's distress.

In accordance with constitutional practice, Ministers placed their resignations in Baldwin's hands and their offices at his disposal. The chief places to be filled were the Foreign Office and the Exchequer. To Curzon Baldwin wrote:

> There never was a time when foreign affairs caused more anxiety than they do at present, and your unrivalled experience is to-day one of the greatest assets of the Empire.

And Curzon answered :

> As my retirement at this moment might be thought to involve distrust in your administration, which would be a quite unfounded suspicion, I will for the present continue at the Foreign Office.

Baldwin had expected a refusal, but "there was a vein of pure gold running all through Curzon," he would say, and it was Curzon who, on May 28th, proposed the election of Baldwin as leader of the party. And Curzon, masterful, delightful, querulous and gay, was the most entertaining of correspondents.

> Poincaré, [he writes] whom I had hoped to elude, was in Paris! Crowds of pressmen were dogging me about, and I felt sure that if I did not even leave a card on him, every paper in Paris would denounce me for rudeness, and proclaim the final rupture of the Entente (which I admit is not in very robust health). So down I went to the Quai d'Orsay to leave my card. But—confound it—he was in! So in I went and talked with him for twenty minutes about the style of Renan, his methods of work, the temperament of Mussolini— anything but the Ruhr. Then I escaped.

Nor could the proconsul abstain from an occasional reprimand for official proprieties neglected.

> Crowe has sent me an enquiry from your Private Secretary as to what you can say about a separate Rhineland state. The only source from which the P.M. can obtain such a statement is his Foreign Secretary, and the F.S. can only speak if he has the authority and backing of the Cabinet.
>
> But I must confess I am almost in despair as to the way in which Foreign Policy is carried on in this Cabinet. Any member may make any suggestion he pleases and the discussion wanders off into helpless irrelevancies. No decision is arrived at and no policy prepared. Do please let us revert to the time-honoured procedure. I am at any time at your disposal for discussion. I have no fear we shall not achieve harmony. But we must act together and the P.M. must see his F.S. through.

It would have been better for Baldwin if he had taken this friendly censure to heart.

The Exchequer proved a difficulty. McKenna, recovering from a dangerous illness, was forbidden by his doctor to accept office until his health was restored, and Baldwin kept it in his own hands until Neville Chamberlain succeeded in August. Balfour had allowed it to be understood that he would accept a place in the Cabinet, but without departmental responsibility. There remained Austen Chamberlain and his friends, Birkenhead and Worthington Evans in chief.

Austen was staying at the Paris Embassy with Crewe. Summoned back in haste, he had a long conference with Baldwin at Chequers on Saturday May 26th. There he learnt that Baldwin "did not propose to hold any communication" with him (the formality of the phrase is characteristic), but he had already in a private telegram authorized his friends to accept any offer that might be made to them. So the new Cabinet was formed. "No one (except Birkenhead) would not shrink from the task that has fallen to you," one friend wrote, "and you would not be what you are if you did not feel this more strongly than most. But we may surely feel pretty comfortable that, after all we may do or not do, the ultimate direction and disposition of human affairs lies with Him who is able to give, to one whom He calls to difficult work, that right judgment in all things without which the task cannot be accomplished."

To a journalist who offered his congratulations on the steps at No. 10, the new Prime Minister answered, "I need your prayers rather." To his mother he wrote, "I am not a bit excited, and don't realize it in the least."

•

CHAPTER IV

PRIME MINISTER

I feel a want of many essential qualifications which are
requisite in Party leaders. Among the rest, personal gratifica-
tion in the game of politics, and patience to listen to the
sentiments of individuals whom it is equally imprudent to
neglect and an intolerable bore to consult.

Peel, 1830

WHEN Asquith retired from public life, in 1926, Baldwin
wrote,

My dear Oxford,
  I have wanted to write to you for several days but I have
been more than usually busy and it is not easy to express what
I feel.
  I don't think that anyone who has not been a Prime
Minister can realise the essential and ultimate loneliness of
that position: there is no veil between him and the human
heart (or rather no veil through which he cannot see) and in
his less happy moments he may feel himself to be the repository
of the sins and follies of the whole world. You can understand then how my heart has often gone out to you during
these last years. I had admired without reserve your courage,
your dignity, your self-restraint: you have set an example in
circumstances of cruel difficulty that I hope we younger men
may have the strength to follow when such trials come to us.
  And I shall never forget the kindly courtesy which you
showed to me in the House of Commons.
  The position of leader came to me when I was inexperienced, before I was really fitted for it, by a succession of
curious chances that could not have been foreseen.
  I had never expected it: I was in no way trained for it.
You forbore to take advantage of these things and you gave
me a lesson by which I hope I shall profit in the years to come.
  I hope you will not feel that I have broken unduly through
our English reserve in saying so much. But if I cannot speak

now, the opportunity will never come, and so I have taken my courage in both hands.

Secure in the respect and affection of your friends, indeed of all Englishmen whose respect and affection are worth having, may you have as many years of peace and happy rest as you desire and not one more!

Asquith replied:

I have received many kind and not a few moving letters, but none that has touched me more deeply, or that I value more highly, than yours.

There is, as you say, an unshareable solitude in the position of Prime Minister, who has to bear the burden not only of his own sins, and his colleagues', but at times it almost seems those (whether inherited or newly invented) of the whole world. It was certainly so in my experience. It was no doubt a sense of this that made the younger Pitt, in his later days, declare, that one essential quality which a Prime Minister could not do without was Patience.

I am most grateful to you for what you say of my demeanour in Opposition. That is a less searching ordeal, in normal times; but since the close of the War neither times, nor persons, have been normal. My difficulties have come (as you know well) not so much from the natural quarter—the opposite side of the House; but from my own political household.

Out of regard to many loyal and devoted friends both in and out of Parliament, I have been slow to seek release from an intolerable situation. But I shall never regret the step which I have taken.

In regard to yourself, let me say that I have never found, and could never desire, a more straightforward and scrupulously honourable opponent, or one who more completely satisfied my ideal of an English gentleman.

Here is a theme to which Baldwin constantly recurred. The Prime Minister is a person apart. He has no colleague of equal rank: no one to share his responsibilities: all his decisions are his own. But most men rise to this solitary eminence after years of discipline in lower offices; of controversy, within their party and without; of alternations in public favour; of hard-fought elections and temporary eclipse. Looking back, Baldwin could see no predecessor who had reached Downing Street with the same unexpected ease that had attended his own progress. His name was associated with no famous law, no national debate; he had left no mark on any department; he had never really fought an election. He was Prime Minister because none better could be thought of. But of all the gifts which that office seems to require, there was one he believed himself to possess in preeminent degree. "My worst enemy could never say that I do not understand the people of England." And it was in corresponding terms that he conceived his duty. Whatever else the Prime Minister may do, or be, he must bring that knowledge into the Cabinet room, and make it tell in the deliberations of his colleagues. He need not say much or do much: indeed, the less he says, the less he interferes, so much, in Baldwin's view, the better. But his colleagues must know and feel that this lonely man does embody the force to which they owe their offices: the will of the people, the sense of the nation.

The first long conversation we ever had turned, somehow, to the character of Halifax, the Trimmer. If statesmen were canonized, it would have been Halifax to whom Baldwin's devotions would have been most often and most earnestly addressed. Somewhat earlier, Laski, fiercest of the Labour intellectuals, had written to him:

> I would not change places. But I wish you could have that year free for thought and talk. For I wonder then if you would not discover that the things in you which make me wish that you were in my party would not lead you to that re-assessment of ultimate doctrines to which academic observers, like myself, are being driven. I rarely escape the conclusion, especially when I read your major speeches, that it is tradition rather than fundamentals that has put you among the forces of the right. For, if I may say so, there is something in you of the temper of George Savile, Lord Halifax, which tinges all principles that claim finality with a recognition that novelty is inescapable.

After which a refreshing gale from old Conservative times may be admitted:

> Do not extend the franchise.
> Give no pensions to widows or anybody else.
> Take a firm line in India and Egypt and stand no nonsense about democratic institutions.

"My party," Baldwin would say, "what is my party? Diamond Jubilee die-hards and Tory Democrats pulling me two ways at once."

But I reminded him of Macaulay's judgment that history has always been kind to Halifax because Halifax always took the side that history was to approve. "Ah," he said, "how right that is. It is much more important to know what people are going to think than what they are thinking." For the statesman, perhaps. But for the party-leader—for the Whips —for Ministers fighting a bill through Committee—for followers anxious about their seats—less so. And throughout Baldwin's career we find this division between the party-leader who must think of to-morrow and the statesman whose horizon has a radius of years. "Baldwin is a political mystic," said one friend. "Understand Baldwin?" Lloyd George once said. "Of course you can't. He is one of Us. He is a Celt." "To understand him you must have West Highland blood, he is a seer," was the judgment of another who had observed him closely in a crisis. But his descents into the lower and dustier atmosphere were for that reason all the more effectual. "The greatest party manager the Conservatives ever had," was Churchill's verdict. "When it comes to tactics," said a mutineer, rubbing the injured place, "Baldwin has us stone cold." And behind the management, controlling the tactics, was always the unruffled confidence— he understood the people of England, and they understood him.

But who are these people: how did Baldwin picture them to himself? And—West Highlander he might be, Celt he might be called—Baldwin always thought of himself, and proudly, as a provincial. Churchill, hammering out a speech for Worcester, was surprised to learn that the Malverns were in that county and that the Severn flowed through it. "I was brought up in London," he explained. London has dominated many politicians and corrupted not a few. Baldwin was immune to the metropolitan infection. Sliding without effort into the family business, he found there the cheerfulness, the goodwill, the honesty, the fine instinctive craftsmanship, which to this Englishman came to be the very meaning of England. I remember a talk we once had—the outcome can be read in one of his speeches—on Considerateness as the central virtue of the English soul: how no other language has a word for it; how it keeps in tune those other virtues which public life requires if it is to be anything more than a sterile encounter of party interests. He told me how once, misled by his advisers, he had made an appointment to which the Labour Party had good reason to object. Better informed, he revoked it. Speaking to some Labour members he said, "You could have given me a bad time over that." "Oh," they answered, "we knew it was just a mistake and so we left you to find it out." And his memory, stored with the incidents of public business and dispute, always seemed to return most naturally to examples of kindness and good feeling that he had encountered by the way. Near the end of his life, at a small local meeting, he found he had forgotten where he was, and why. "I knew I could never speak again and I told them how sorry I was to have spoilt their gathering. 'That's all right,' they said, 'we only wanted to see you among us once more.' The Englishman is a gentleman all through."

And Baldwin was an Englishman not casually, by accident of birth, but deliberately and by election. To be an Englishman was the part he had undertaken to play—and in his judgment it was the best and most honourable part that could fall to any man, gentle or simple, rich or poor. There we are all equals: there all of us are one. So when fortune raised him to the first place in the service of the King, he was ready for it: the gait, the accent, the scenery, the words—all were prepared. Within a few days this man from the provinces had become a national figure: a fond projection of everything that the common Englishman still believed himself to be. Within a few months the lonely Prime Minister was what no man in that place had ever been before, a household figure, almost a family friend. He attracted to himself that affectionate approval with which the people of England had once regarded George III. They liked to talk about him; to see pictures of him smoking one of the innumerable pipes which he bought for half-a-crown at a shop in Bridge Street—he was once found before a looking glass, getting his pipe at the right angle for a

Cunliffe-Lister   Hogg   Runciman   Gilmour

Thomas   Baldwin   Chamberlain   *Wide World*

On board the *Empress of Britain,* 1923
The British delegation to the Imperial Economic Conference in Ottawa

Smuts Curzon   Baldwin   Halifax

Picture Post Library

The Imperial Conference, Downing Street, 1923

photographer. They trusted him, they believed in him, less for anything he had done or was likely to do, than for being himself. But a friend once sent him S. Columban's warning to his successor. "In your abbacy men will either hate or love you. Either way lies danger. Hate wars on your peace: love on your integrity." And it seemed to me, sometimes, that public affection—not popularity, but sympathy and understanding—became a food, almost a drug, which he could not bring himself to forgo. He came to listen for the echo—so long friendly; and he shrank from the angry noise of a people in discord with its rulers and itself.

A public man who has been long on the Parliamentary stage cannot, when he becomes Prime Minister, be very different from what he always has been, from what he is known by long observation to be ; and he would very quickly be seen through if he tried. Men often fail, and fail unexpectedly, in lower office. There are bad Chancellors, bad Secretaries of State. It is less easy to recall a bad Prime Minister—the process of selection is too thorough. But on Baldwin the process had hardly begun to work before it was finished: he was a Prime Minister without antecedents and with no formed political habits. If there was to be a picture, it would have to be drawn by himself. And self-portraiture is a perilous art. No man is exactly what he would like to be, and few men feel themselves exactly fitted to the part they have to play. There is always too much of something, requiring to be held in ; and too little of something else, requiring to be made good.

Baldwin's excess was a certain recklessness, a sudden impetuosity which sometimes planted him where he had not meant to go. "He takes a leap in the dark," Birkenhead once said, "looks round, and takes another." His defect was even more manifest. Sooner or later everyone who knew him came round to one word—indolence. No Prime Minister, it was said, ever spent so much time in attendance on the House of Commons. And no Prime Minister ever spent so much in neglecting the other duties of his office. "I do wish," said a faithful retainer at Chequers to a visitor, "that you would persuade Mr. MacDonald not to ruin his eyesight

reading papers. Mr. Baldwin never did."* And, as party
leader too, it might be said that no man ever took so little
trouble to earn the affection which he inspired. His
friends will always remember the heavy look, of an almost
porcine stupidity, that would come over his face when an
unwanted supporter pushed some unwanted remarks at
him. "The troops, however," one loyal observer wrote,
"must fight with their tails up, and it is just the nod here
and the word there that makes all the difference between
tails up and tails down." Like a Roman noble canvassing
for the consulship, Baldwin needed a nomenclator to remind
him who these dim figures were, what they thought about
themselves, and what they wanted. And the Treasury bench
was a safe refuge from party as well as from official duties.
He would lunch at the Travellers', where no one wanted
anything. He would retire to the Cabinet room and issue
with an armful of private letters, proud of his afternoon's
work. And the rest of the day would pass, on the Treasury
bench, a little dinner with his faithful Davidsons in College
Street, a little music, and the Chamber once more.

Once a young colleague slid along the Bench to see what
his chief found so absorbing in *Dod's Parliamentary Companion*. "I think," said the Prime Minister, "if the Old
Man goes, we should stand a very good chance of winning
Carnarvon Boroughs."

* It is right to add that he underwent a slight eye-operation in 1932,
and in 1934 was advised to go abroad for three months and read no
papers.

CHAPTER V

POINCARÉ

ONE war had come near to destroying European civilization. In Russia, so far as Russia had ever been European, civilization had been destroyed. But in its place there was rising a system capable of inspiring wild hopes and not less vehement fears. The Russian Revolution had sent a seismic wave through the crust of the world, opening new fissures and widening the old, and through them what volcanic torrents might not rush, what might they not overwhelm? And here was something—the impact of foreign ideas on national unity, loosening or consolidating as might happen—that Baldwin could understand. Feel, rather: his ideas being almost always, as it were, condensed and formulated emotions. How much positive disaffection was simmering in the depths no one could say. But there was enough to call for vigilance. The Supply and Transport Service, organized to meet the possible emergencies of war, a raid across the sea or a heavy bombardment from the air, had been allowed to drop to pieces. One of the new Prime Minister's first actions was to direct that the service should be reviewed by a committee of all the departments concerned, and arrangements made for its revival or reconstitution. So quietly was the weapon forged which three years later was to defeat the General Strike.

But Baldwin never declared war on the Socialist Party. He acknowledged their good intentions; he approved their social aims; he differed from them only as to their methods. (Socialism and Laissez Faire, he once said, are like the North and South Pole—they don't really exist.) But among their methods he included the propagation of doctrines which the leaders interpreted in one sense and the followers in another, a mischief only to be countered by "deliberate, vigorous and intelligent propaganda in the right direction."

59

And to this propaganda the key was—the dominant necessity of export, and therefore the recovery of foreign markets. Let it be granted that the analogy of war held good and that the State could direct its manpower to manufacture, until every warehouse was filled with goods. If there were no buyers what would the end be but bankruptcy and famine? The structure by which we fed ourselves was so delicately contrived that the danger of interference was greater here than anywhere else in the world.

> If that machine is to be broken it matters little whether it is broken by the sledgehammer of revolution, or brought to a standstill by the crafty and insidious scattering of sand in all the gearing wheels: by excessive control damping all initiative: by reckless expenditure consuming and not replacing capital: by industrial disputes, no matter who was responsible, by lockouts not less than by strikes.

Unionists must convince the people that all that was offered by Socialism could be more securely achieved by them, "and if there are those who want to fight the class war, we will beat them by the hardness of our heads and the largeness of our hearts."

Here Baldwin was speaking with entire conviction and entire self-confidence. But events were carrying him from a field where he was a master to one in which by experience he was hardly an apprentice and by temperament not qualified to be anything more. A month before this profession of faith, June 26th, he had made his first statement on Air Defence. The Government had come, he said, to the conclusion that we needed a Home Force of sufficient strength to protect the country against an attack of the strongest air force within striking distance. This meant adding 34 squadrons to the 18 now available. But what was the country "within striking distance" against which this force was required? The Trades Union Congress, at all events, knew the answer, and two days later the annual conference resolved that competition in the air with France was the preface to a new era of war, and directed the Parliamentary Party to offer every resistance to the measure.

But, call it peace or call it war, England and France were in unconcealed opposition over the treatment of Germany;

and the opposition was reflected at home—in the press, in the public, in common talk. There was a German party and there was a French party. Both parties, and both Powers, desired to see German reparations paid. But the English Government preferred the way of reconstruction, the French of confiscation. England saw more hope in a prosperous Germany, even if prosperity meant strength; France, in mortal terror of a strong Germany, cared nothing for her prosperity and was bent on seizing such productive assets as were to hand, notably the great industrial area of the Ruhr. On January 11th 1923 the French armies had marched in. By June, when the Germans made an offer which the British Government was, on the whole, prepared to commend to its ally, France and Germany were to all intents and purposes at war again, the German weapon being passive resistance: the French, intrigue with any separatist movement they could find. And France was formidable. She had the Little Entente at her beck. She had an independent air force of 600 machines. We, by the same reckoning, had 52. France, in fact, could do what she liked with Germany. What she actually would do depended on the value she set on the English alliance, and, so long as English policy was directed by Lloyd George, the value was very small. Curzon was not distrusted; but he was impetuous, passionate and self-important. Of the statesmen of the last generation, only Edward Grey had been really trusted by French Ministers.

To say that Baldwin never understood foreign politics is to go halfway only to the truth. He could never bring his mind to bear on anything that did not interest him, and foreigners made him peevish or sent him to sleep. He could not speak their language, read their books, think their thoughts or share their emotions. In forwarding a personal message from Herriot, the French Ambassador added, "Mrs. Baldwin will translate." One transient gleam of interest shows itself in a Private Secretary's note: "The P.M. is always being asked about the situation in Russia and would like to know what to say. Not more than a page." Like all prudent Englishmen Baldwin was convinced that the reparation figures dangled before the electors of 1918 were fantastic, and that a stable, disarmed Germany would be an excellent customer for English goods. Where France was thinking of her dead, Baldwin was thinking of our unemployed. Still, a new Prime Minister—uncompromised by old associations; the mortal foe in politics of Lloyd George; the destroyer of that Coalition which the French had come so profoundly to distrust—might, perhaps, by his candour and straightforwardness, rebuild the broken bridge and re-establish the Entente as the great instrument of peace and European settlement. But first he must persuade Poincaré to quit the Ruhr, and Poincaré was not to be persuaded. On a deputation from the League of Nations Union, Lady Selborne summed up the situation with all the downrightness of the Cecil stock: "We must speak plainly to France and not annoy her. Disarmed ourselves, we must tell a nation armed to the teeth to do what we tell her. And a few easy things like that." It was not to be done. Ninety-nine Frenchmen out of a hundred were behind Poincaré, and Baldwin could not honestly aver that ninety-nine out of a hundred even of his own party were against Poincaré. "Therefore," said the Frenchman, "let the German Government order passive resistance in the Ruhr to cease: *puis, on pourra causer.* Meanwhile these charming conversations may continue; but let there be no interference by the League of Nations, and let Lord Robert Cecil keep silence."

Such was the outcome of the famous interview between Baldwin and Poincaré in October 1923. The official report might say that the two statesmen were in agreement. The truth, apparent to all the world, was that the English Prime Minister had been defeated, and indeed humiliated, by his more resolute and better armed opponent. I once asked him: "You remember your interview with Poincaré?" ("I do indeed," he answered, with a wry mouth.) "Did you ever talk to any other leading men in Europe?" "No," he said simply, "I didn't like them. Ribbentrop once lunched, and recited *Mein Kampf.*" Brüning also lunched and they were heard discussing whether Brüning and Browning were the same name. There were others, but he preferred to forget them. Rudyard Kipling made a rule for himself and recommended it to others, "When you have found out what you

can do, go and do something else." His cousin was otherwise made. He knew his limitations. Just as some men are
born with no aptitude for figures or machinery, so the
balancing and forecasting of alien forces and intentions,
out of which foreign policy has to be contrived, were outside the range of Baldwin's natural intelligence. He had
to get them up, and commonly his interest flagged halfway
through the unwelcome task. In Cabinet, he would ostentatiously close his eyes when foreign affairs were under
discussion. "Wake me up," he would say, "when you are
finished with that." He withdrew, willingly enough, into
the circle where he could brood to some purpose, on things
he understood, by instinct as much as by experience—the
future of his party; his own standing, lonely and insecure,
as Prime Minister; above all, the unemployment which
was eating away the energies of the nation and breeding
dangerous thoughts. "It deprives men of hope: it deprives
them of faith; and without faith and hope it deprives them
of love—love of home and love of country. And only a
nation united in that love can carry its full weight in the
councils of the world."

CHAPTER VI

THE DISSOLUTION OF 1923

SOME years later, speaking to me of the dissolution of November 1923, Baldwin said: "We did not know as much about unemployment then as we do now." The case for Protection was very simple. Our high taxation increased the cost of production—the foreigner could undersell us in the home market—let the balance be adjusted by a duty on foreign imports. Even the classical Free Trade doctrine had admitted that a mild duty on imported corn was permissible to counterweigh any additional burden which taxation imposed on landed property: and Cobden had never dreamed of taxation even approaching the amount now levied on land and industry alike.

The general argument was enforced by the special circumstances of the moment. Unemployment was the consequence of industrial saturation, or, as the older economists would have said, of over-population. The relief once furnished—or hoped for—by emigration was available only in a reduced and scanty measure. Meanwhile, ruined exchanges, inflation and devaluation were giving German industry a formidable advantage in the markets of the world, an advantage which American, and indeed English, finance was very ready to exploit. Without a tariff, we were helpless, and any day might bring news that the stocks of steel accumulating in the Ruhr were to be shipped to England.

The argument against was equally familiar. A mild duty would be ineffectual. A stiff duty would raise prices, lessen demand and diminish exports. If unstable exchanges were the cause of unemployment at home, then let the exchanges be stabilized. Tax food, cotton and steel—you raise the cost of production and living all round; exempt them, and what will your tariff include? A sudden dumping of steel could be met and prevented by emergency measures. The effect

64

of a tariff would not be felt for some long time, and by then the economic shape of the world would be different. It was to improving that shape, to re-establishing national credit, and so facilitating international trade, that our endeavours should be directed. In short, the League of Nations should induce the world at large to mitigate its suspicions of Russia, and France in particular to forgo her fear of Germany, and all would be well.

In solitary walks at Aix, Baldwin had meditated deeply on his own discomforts as Prime Minister and the precarious condition of his party. He was well aware that his administrative experience had been limited; that on many matters he was uninformed; and that in Cabinet he was silent and ineffectual. Austen Chamberlain and his friends had not quite rid themselves of their old associations: they were ready to make terms with Lloyd George; the Conservative Party had never really come together. The only thing that could bring it together was a General Election. Whether it won or lost was a matter of relative insignificance. But the only issue on which it could go to the country was to seek release from Free Trade pledges and deal with unemployment by means of a tariff. And Baldwin had his reasons for thinking that Lloyd George would go first and would sweep away no small portion of the Conservative Party with him.

Nevertheless it was a bold stroke for a leader who was not yet quite sure of his followers. But Baldwin could be very bold when he had taken his line and felt himself safe with his public—"an astute and relentless politician," Churchill once called him. The Cabinet was evidently uneasy, and tried to bind the Prime Minister to a personal statement, not committing his colleagues. Baldwin's speech to the National Unionist Association at Plymouth on October 26th showed to those in his confidence that he was quite ready to go on alone:

> Mr. Bonar Law's pledge, given a year ago, was that there should be no fundamental change in the fiscal arrangements of the country. That pledge binds me, and in this Parliament there will be no fundamental change, and I take those words strictly. I am not a man to play with a pledge. But I cannot see myself that any slight extension or adoption of principles

hitherto sanctioned in the Legislature is a breach of that pledge. But at any time I am challenged, I am willing to take a verdict.

So far Baldwin had said nothing that went beyond some limited safeguarding measure to deal with special cases. Then came the announcement which brought the cheers.

To me, at least, this unemployment problem is the most critical problem of our country. . . . I can fight it. I am willing to fight it. I cannot fight it without weapons. I have for myself come to the conclusion that . . . having regard to the economic environment, having regard to the situation of our country—if we go on pottering along as we are we shall have grave unemployment with us to the end of time. And I have come to the conclusion myself that the only way of fighting this subject is by protecting the home market.

Myself—for myself. Baldwin had kept within the terms of his instructions. But he was Prime Minister. The Cabinet did not want an early election, and Baldwin agreed that after the Plymouth speech the country should have a period of meditation to absorb its contents. But the reactions to the Plymouth speech altered the position. On November 7th Salisbury invited some of his colleagues to meet and consider their attitude. Devonshire, Robert Cecil, Wood and Novar were present, and Devonshire disclosed the fact that Baldwin had already spoken to the King. Their conclusions were tendered to the Prime Minister in a letter from Wood, dated November 8th:

I think [he wrote] that it is vital that we should give Parliament, and through Parliament the country, an adequate opportunity of examining the question on which they are to be asked to pronounce.

If this is not consistent with a December election, I think we should be acting both unwisely and wrongly, and should aggravate the difficulties of some of our number, if we were to attempt to snatch a verdict, and that, if this is so, the appeal should be deferred.

All this in great deference, recognizing that fixing these matters is your special perquisite.

At the Cabinet on November 9th, while December, January or spring found each its advocates, the Prime

Minister was obviously disinclined to show his hand. But the impression left on the minds of his colleagues was that he had made up his mind to dissolve: and his announcement on Tuesday November 13th made certain what, for some days, they had been expecting. The same group met at luncheon with Salisbury to consider their action. Some of them believed that Baldwin was deliberately forcing them out to make room for Austen Chamberlain and Birkenhead. That evening Wood asked him point-blank whether that was his intention: if it was not, he must see Salisbury, explain his position and make it as easy as possible for the Free Traders to stay. Then followed all the comings and goings, the conversations and letters, customary on such occasions— Sidney Herbert has taken a friendly note to Salisbury; Salisbury has had a friendly interview with Baldwin; Wood has got assurances; and Robert Cecil has prepared a draft.

The draft was delivered on the afternoon of the 14th, and handed back annotated and initialed by Baldwin the following morning. His interpretations being found satisfactory, the group decided to stay, and Birkenhead and Austen Chamberlain were informed that, though their support on the platform would be appreciated, their services were not otherwise required. Birkenhead, at least, had counted on being asked to take office, but as there were no resignations, there was no room.

The policy on which the reunited Cabinet were to go to the country was absolute freedom in all fiscal measures, with the reservation that no further taxes should be placed on essential foods; protection for particular industries; assistance to agriculture; and "a sound foreign policy based on the principles of the League of Nations."

On the margin of Cecil's draft Baldwin wrote:

> I stand by what I said as to the vital character of the League of Nations as a fundamental element in the conduct of our foreign affairs.

But fresh and sore from his encounter with Poincaré, Baldwin knew only too well that whether it was the principles of the League or its vital character by which our foreign policy was to be guided, that policy would, in truth, be determined by the real relations of the Powers, great or small, in two hemispheres. "O how I long for the days," he once said, "when, if the Japs were cheeky, we showed them the guns of the China Squadron, and no more was heard." But those days were over.

One of the most famous and ardent supporters of the League once wrote:

> It is my favourite nightmare that some leading statesman may repeat the policy of Canning and call for a strong navy and air force, and a repudiation of European entanglements.

If it was Gilbert Murray's nightmare, it was Baldwin's dream.

CHAPTER VII

FIRST LABOUR GOVERNMENT

THE returns showed that the Conservatives were beaten, but neither the Liberal nor the Labour Party had won. The constitutional position when three parties are well represented in Parliament and no one of them has a clear majority is admittedly intricate. Precedents were sought for, if not found, in 1852, 1858 and 1866. Advice flowed in from colleagues and supporters who believed that a Socialist Ministry would be a disaster to the country and the Empire, and would undermine the whole fabric of government. Lord Long of Wraxall, a man of sense and experience, advised that Asquith should be privately approached and assured that if he undertook to form a Government, he could count on Conservative support. Horne brought a message from Balfour:

> He agrees with the view which you expressed to me that the constitutional rule—although there are notable exceptions—is for you to meet Parliament. He is also of opinion that it will be a serious danger if the Socialist party is allowed to assume office at the present time and he thinks every means ought to be taken to avert the Parliamentary defeat which would bring them into office in your place. For this purpose there are only two possible courses open, (1) a coalition with the Liberals under Asquith or (2) a working arrangement. The first, in present circumstances, seems to be ruled out and accordingly the second is the only one available. This involves an approach to Asquith in the intervening period, which he thinks can be made without loss of dignity or authority. Looking to the fact that the alternative is a Socialist administration which would be equally repugnant to Liberals and Conservatives alike he is of opinion that you might say to Asquith that you have been beaten on Protection of the Home Market and that must be taken to be out of the political arena for the present; and ask him whether he would keep

a Conservative Government temporarily in power—it being understood that you would not propose anything contentious —until the country had a breathing space. If he refused, you would be no worse off. If he accepted, the trouble from Labour would be so far avoided.

In the immediate despondency of defeat, Baldwin did for a moment consider the possibility of a coalition with Asquith —it is significant that in all these discussions the name of Lloyd George does not occur. But he quickly recovered his footing and his courage. To make overtures to the Liberals would have been in direct contradiction to the principles by which he always directed his dealings with the Labour Party. Sooner or later, he knew, they must come into power, and so into office. Therefore they must be given the opportunity of acquiring the art and science of constitutional administration. In no circumstances would he have entered into any combination with Lloyd George; and a coalition with the Old Believers, the faithful remnant under Asquith, would either have been, or would have been viewed by the Opposition as being, a Party of Order to keep the working classes in their place. But, thoughts of coalition once dismissed, the constitutional position was clear. The defeated Government should meet Parliament and accept the verdict of the House whether it should continue or resign. So Baldwin decided, and, meeting him in the Travellers', Asquith said, "You have done quite right." Technically the position was complicated by the fact that the Leader of the Labour Party was not a Privy Councillor. But the constitution which creates these difficulties has means for evading them. The Cabinet agreed that, if the Government were defeated on the Address, the Prime Minister should go at once to the Palace and resign. MacDonald should be sworn in at a Privy Council specially summoned, after which he would be invited to form a Government. Parliament would then meet, Baldwin being still Prime Minister, holding office until the new administration was complete. If, in the brief interim, any matter of urgency arose, the necessary action would be taken by the new ministers and on their responsibility, even if they had not formally received the seals of office.

The Government was defeated, on January 21st, and
Asquith wrote:

> There are so many swan songs being sung tonight, to different
> and discrepant tunes, that I fear my sympathetic note may
> sound intrusive and even inopportune. But I should like—
> before the concert is over, and the "rest is silence"—to tell
> you with what regret I part from what has been, in a parlia-
> mentary sense, a real comradeship.

Nothing could have gratified Baldwin more, because, of
the elder statesmen of his time, it was for Asquith first, and
after him for Grey, that he had the deepest regard.

The constitutional problem solved, there remained the
question of party. As things turned out, Baldwin's bold forecast proved true: the election had pulled the Conservatives
together. But the fissure was not quite closed. Austen Chamberlain and Birkenhead had not rejoined the flock, and it
seemed as if neither would return without the other. But
Baldwin wanted Chamberlain: "If Birkenhead stood alone,"
he said, "I would not touch him with a barge pole"; but
to secure the older man, with his high reputation, his classical correctness of demeanour, he was prepared to overlook
the shortcomings of his younger ally. Others were not.

Birkenhead, a colleague wrote, had been openly hostile
to Baldwin and his Government for the past months. He
carried no weight in the country. His attitude towards
political questions, particularly in foreign affairs, was repug-
nant to the deepest convictions of the great majority of his
fellow countrymen. His Glasgow speech raised such a storm
of protest because it expressed in striking language just the
very point of view which the war had rendered generally
hateful. For him to be installed as a Leader of the party
without any recantation or modification of his Glasgow
opinions would be regarded as a defiance of the opinions
passionately held by large numbers of the electorate.

Then the warning:

> You may secure Austen and his following—whatever that
> means—but you will repel others. I should myself have to
> consider very carefully my own position. Apart from that, if
> you submit your judgment to Austen in this respect, what-
> ever may be the result of the party meeting, you will not

in any real sense be the Leader of the Party. There is nothing less desirable than to be nominally the Leader of a party if you have not the authority of Leadership. If you really feel that the party cannot get on without Austen it would be far better in your own interests, as well as in the interests of the party, to resign in Austen's favour. Of one thing I am quite certain—that if we are to enter into political warfare with the Labour Party, labelled as associates of Birkenhead and his like—we shall assuredly be beaten. Conservative policy must have something to offer the people, and particularly the women, beyond a mere appeal to the rights of property and the fear of Socialism.

Plain speaking: more plain than prophetic. Within twelve months Baldwin was Prime Minister, Chamberlain Foreign Secretary, Birkenhead at the India Office. And it may be doubted whether one elector in a thousand, "particularly the women," remembered that Birkenhead had ever been to Glasgow. Political memories are short, and the phrase which had excited this moral turmoil:

the world continues to offer glittering prizes to those who have stout hearts and sharp swords,

was quietly entombed in the *Oxford Dictionary of Quotations*. "Of all your colleagues," I once said, "the one whom I like better the more I hear of him is Birkenhead." "You are right," Baldwin replied: "his heart was as good as his head, and that is saying a lot. All the world knew his shortcomings: his colleagues knew his virtues too."

It might have been expected that after an election needlessly provoked and lost, Baldwin's leadership would have been challenged. But the party were well aware that in substance they had gained what in appearance they had forfeited, the confidence of the country. No folly could be greater than to part with a leader who of all figures in the public eye was unquestionably the most popular. They might chafe at his inertia, his laziness, his easy-going ways. "What can you do," one angry colleague asked, "with a leader who sits in the Smoking Room reading the *Strand Magazine*?" But what could they do without him? If the Labour Government held on, who except Baldwin could keep the Conservative Opposition together? If some

Parliamentary crisis ended in resignation and dissolution, who was so likely to win the next election as the man who in a very few months had made himself a domestic institution? The man, moreover, who had sacrificed his office rather than break a pledge. An American friend wrote: "When the *Nation* calls you the most universally popular Prime Minister on record something must have happened!" Against the fretful, the sneerers, the disloyal, might be set the devoted group of personal friends. But the instinct of self-preservation alone compelled the body of the party to range themselves under the only leader who could restore them to office. And all this Baldwin knew as well as any political calculator in the land. In a post to which perhaps he had not aspired, he found himself indispensable.

Thus it was with an assurance unusual in a leader who had done little in six months but lose an election, that he met the party in February 1924. He reminded them first of what many among them had failed to realize: that the Reform Act of 1918 had made it far more difficult to forecast the movements of opinion—the new element was an incalculable element. But there was one fixed point on the political map, and the Labour Party had calculated that the discontent engendered by unemployment would sweep them into power in 1926. The Conservatives had learnt a lesson which they could have learnt in no other way: let them take it to heart and apply it, and they would find themselves back in office at the date appointed for their overthrow. The electorate had given their verdict. It was against Protection, and it must be accepted until there was clear evidence that public opinion had changed. In the meantime the party must fight its hardest for Imperial Preference and Imperial development, maintain the Safeguarding of Industries Act, and think out a policy for agriculture—though what was to be done for agriculture without the revenue which Protection would assure, neither Baldwin nor anyone else could clearly see.

There was very little in all this that another might not have said as well. What followed was in a different strain. A friend once said that it reminded him of Hampden's talk with Cromwell on the evening of Edgehill: "You must have men with a spirit in them, or you will be beaten still."

> I pointed out yesterday two directions in which I thought the Labour Party made such an appeal to the country. It is the genuine and honest ideal that appeals to the young. That party, moreover, offers a career to the able and the ambitious, and in these days no party that cannot equally offer a career to a man who has ability, the desire for service and power inside him to render that service, can possibly compete with a party that does. Now there has always existed in our party a desire to choose a rich man as candidate. But if you must have a candidate who can water his constituency with £1,000 a year you are going to have a choice of about half per cent of the population, and if you are going to fight a party that has the choice of the whole population, you will never beat them in this world, and, more than that, you will never deserve to beat them.

Admirable advice! None the less, I find the Chief Agent ten years later complaining of constituencies which expected their member to pay all expenses and £3,000 a year to party funds. Here, as so often, a common saying of the time comes true: "Baldwin always hits the nail on the head, but it never seems to go any further."

But, if the party needed a lesson, Baldwin had had one. At Plymouth he had asked the country to meditate, to give reasoned consideration to what he put before them. But opportunities of meditation are the last thing that the public wants from a leader. "I never tell people to think for themselves," John Morley once said; "I believe in regimentation."

CHAPTER VIII

IN OPPOSITION

"I was not a good Leader of Opposition," Baldwin once confessed, and the year we have come to gave him few opportunities of developing any talents of that kind which he might have possessed. He knew, and Asquith knew, and the Prime Minister knew as well as either of them, that Labour was in office until the Liberals chose to put them out. MacDonald's first steps therefore were such as Asquith and Lloyd George were bound to approve. An interchange of sentimental courtesies with Poincaré relaxed the tension which had made the Entente little more than a misleading name. By recognizing the Soviet Union as the ruler *de jure* of the Russian territories, MacDonald opened the way to a renewal of relations whenever the Kremlin might choose to have them renewed.

But very few weeks, or even days, had passed before it became clear that the Labour Party was still most imperfectly trained in party discipline. On February 21st the representative of the Admiralty in the Commons—the First Lord being in the Upper House—announced that, for the relief of unemployment in the shipbuilding trade, the Government meant to lay down five cruisers. Consternation was visible on the Labour benches, and, leaping to the occasion, a Liberal member asked leave to move the adjournment. Many Labour members rose in their places and the Speaker granted leave. In the interim before the motion the Prime Minister administered a sharp reproof to his disorderly forces, and placated them in debate with the assurance that, though the cruisers were to be laid down, they would not be built without consent of Parliament and that, in any event, being for replacement only, they made no addition to the strength of the Fleet.

Indeed, in the early days of this shortlived administration, the issue between a profound, emotional pacifism and a rational calculation of needs and means of defence was so clearly defined that anyone who has considered the arguments on both sides can hear in advance the debates of the next ten years. The Government adhered to the formula of their predecessors—a defence force in the air sufficient to give adequate protection against attack by the strongest force within striking distance—the formula which the Trade Unionists had repudiated in 1923. And in a letter to Poincaré on February 21, MacDonald made it clear to France and the world against whom it was directed:

> The people in this country regard with anxiety what appears to them to be the determination of France to ruin Germany and to dominate the Continent without consideration of our reasonable interests and the future consequences to European settlement. They feel themselves apprehensive of the large military and aerial establishment maintained not only in Eastern but also in Western France. They are perturbed by the interest shown by your Government in the military establishments of the new states of Central Europe.
>
> Finally, they question why all these activities should be financed by the French Government in disregard of the fact that the British taxpayer has to find upwards of £30,000,000 a year in interest on loans raised in America and that our taxpayers have also to find large sums to pay interest on the debt of France to us, to meet which France has herself as yet neither made, nor propounded, so far as they can see, any sacrifice equivalent to their own.

Curzon himself had never been more emphatic. A few days later, on March 4th, the Secretary for Air, Lord Thomson, gave the Conservatives assurance that their defence policy would be carried out in full. And Haldane added the weight of his experience and judgment to his colleague's undertaking.

In matters of defence and foreign policy the Government showed itself in truth of a Liberal Imperial cast, and as such could count on the support of the Opposition in both its wings. MacDonald regularly sent Foreign Office papers of consequence to Baldwin, with whom he was at greater ease than he was with many of his colleagues. In home affairs this good understanding could hardly be expected, and the

public noticed with some concern, the Conservatives with
some satisfaction, that labour troubles continued as if there
had been no change in the Government, and that the Trade
Unions seemed in no way anxious to smooth the path of
the party they had placed in office. In January the railways
were on strike; in February the transport workers; in March
the miners were demanding a Minimum Wage Bill which
it was not in the power of the Government to pass. Employment was no better and no worse, but the bold measures
which the country had been expecting still remained a
Cabinet secret.

The labour troubles of those days were of a kind particularly irritating to the public—especially the London
public, which found itself, for ten days in March, deprived
of street transport and shortened in goods; by April the
country was beginning to ask whether a Government which
seemed unable to control its own people was really worth
keeping in power. But the Conservatives were fretting at
the mildly sympathetic, invariably cautious, attitude of their
leader towards the Government, and Churchill saw, and
very nearly won, the opportunity to come out as the leader of
a new party, a middle party neither Liberal nor Conservative, or perhaps both, with a policy founded upon opposition
to Socialism. In this role he appeared as an independent
candidate at a by-election in Westminster, supported by
Balfour and many Conservatives. He was narrowly defeated
by the official candidate. But between them, they came near
to returning the Socialist. And men wondered whether
that erratic career had come to its term.

Baldwin rarely spoke to me of Churchill. But often enough,
I thought, to disclose, certainly not an antipathy, but a
hopeless divergence of temper. Baldwin never troubled himself to study the intellectual groundwork of the new opposition; neither did Churchill. But Baldwin was at all times
sensitive to the moral challenge underlying the Socialist
creed: Churchill was not; and on the understanding of
Labour, Baldwin founded his whole policy, in opposition
or in office. If the distance between the two parties widened
so far that mutual comprehension was impossible, then
Parliamentary debate was impossible, and the way was open

to actions and reactions, measures and counter-measures, outside the scope of the Constitution framed by the experimental wisdom of the ages. Meanwhile, let Labour have its chance and learn its lesson.

Churchill had learnt it. No more was heard of the Middle Party to resist Socialism; and in May 1924 Baldwin delivered a series of speeches which might be read as the programme of the New Conservatism whenever it resumed office. At the Albert Hall, on May 2nd, he blamed the Government for refusing the modest scheme of Imperial Preference proposed by the Economic Conference of May 19th, while eagerly pressing for trade arrangements with Russia. He blamed them too for postponing the new naval base at Singapore— a gesture which was to lead to something. "If gestures are to be made, I prefer to make them to my own people." An adequate navy and army, and an air force competent to meet attack from any quarter; self-government of India within the Empire; the security of the Suez Canal; the safeguarding of industries by a considered tariff—so much was common form. But underneath it all was the question whether the restlessness of the time would issue in a conflict of classes, or could be encountered and satisfied by wise government. Nothing had done more to bring Labour into power than the promise to deal with unemployment. And what had Labour done?

In a phrase which he was not allowed to forget, the Minister of Labour had confessed that he could not bring rabbits out of a hat, and Baldwin's next speech—to the Junior Imperial League, on May 3rd—was a challenge to the Government either to be Socialists and say what they meant to do, or confess that they were only the Left Wing of the Tory Party—a party whose record from the abolition of the Slave Trade, through Sadleir, Shaftesbury and Disraeli, was one of which it need not be ashamed. Before such an audience Baldwin was in his happiest mood, and in his analysis of democracy and of the means to industrial peace, he was speaking from a full heart and a matured experience. But within a week the Government had been delivered of another unlucky dictum: "The Board of Trade does not exist to find markets for particular industries"; and speaking at Liverpool, Churchill had made proposals for co-operation among all who could support the Albert Hall programme. Unemployment was the weak place in the Government programme, and by early summer it was clear that the Government could do nothing. As Baldwin said on May 21st, "they are in the very unpleasant situation of a Government that has been found out," but his own party, not yet re-united, and not quite certain of itself, was hardly yet in a state to turn them out. Baldwin in fact about this time seems to have anticipated a sequence of short administrations, elected on promises and despatched because the promises were not kept.

> The post-war psychology of electorates throughout the world is peculiar. In every great country—here, in France, in the United States—the people have evicted the statesmen who were most prominent in the War. Everywhere, the electorates feel that the war will have been fought in vain if something does not come out of it leading to better circumstances and a better environment for the working masses. But no Government can bring to people all that they desire—very often they do not know clearly what they desire. But they want things to be different and they call on fresh Governments in the hope of getting it.

Then he spoke about himself. The war had left him a poorer man, and £3,000 spent on three elections had been met by selling capital. And, once more, if Conservative com-mittees insisted on large contributions, they would exclude from Parliament the young men who were the hope of the party. That must be changed. At the late election seat after seat, especially in the London suburbs, had been lost be-cause Conservatives confined their Conservatism to cursing the Bolsheviks and doing nothing for the cause. But if Socialism was to be beaten, it must be beaten by young men at street corners.

And what were young Conservatives at street corners to say? He gave them their programme at a meeting of the Conservative and Union Clubs on June 13th. They recog-nized as clearly as their opponents that not all was well with the world, least of all the industrial world. Where they parted was that the Conservatives believed that national unity was essential to progress, class hatred and disruption were fatal. And so intricate were the relationships in business and industry that a great population living largely on the export trade might find itself starving before the Socialist millennium was reached. But behind these excellent sentiments, giving body to their professions of goodwill, must be economic knowledge. Their opponents had trained men at their call. The Conservatives must meet them not only with hope and sympathy but with understanding. In gayer tones, he assured the International Advertising Convention on July 15th that he was a standing proof of the gospel of Manchester. The text-books said that nothing sharpened the intellect of a manufacturer so much as losing a market. He had lost two—and it had so sharpened his intellect that he became Prime Minister.

He could afford to be lighthearted. By now it was clear that the promises to which the Labour Party owed their success were not to be kept; and equally clear that the division in the Liberal Party was not to be closed. The prospect of office was bringing the Conservatives together. By August political calculators were busy forecasting the date of the election, the Whips were watching for an occasion which would bring Asquith into the field. It soon came.

Since April an Anglo-Russian Conference had been sitting in London. Its proceedings were as dilatory as the world has more lately learnt to expect when Russians are at the council board. On June 18th the Prime Minister assured the House that on no account would the Government guarantee a loan to Russia. On August 5th, after a twenty-four-hour sitting, sustained on sandwiches and whisky, the Government announced that the Conference had broken down. Four members of Parliament undertook to put it together again, and on August 6th Parliament learned that the Treaty had been drafted and would be signed the next day. Most of it was common form. But to the astonishment of the world one article provided that outstanding claims should be thrown together in a separate treaty, in connection with which the Government would ask Parliament to guarantee a Russian loan.

On August 5th, the day of the breakdown, Campbell,

the Editor of the *Workers' Weekly* was brought before the
magistrate on a charge of inciting members of the armed
forces to mutiny. He was remanded for a week. On his second
appearance the Treasury counsel withdrew the charge. The
incriminated paper announced in triumph that the withdrawal had been ordered by the Government under pressure
from Socialist members. The Conservative Opposition gave it
to be understood that the matter would be raised when
Parliament reassembled.

An abortive conference, an abortive prosecution, and in
both cases a sudden capitulation to the extremists of the
Labour Party, these things together made it certain that
not housing and not unemployment would be the issue of
the election which could not be much longer delayed. The
question put to the electors would be—how far may a
British Government go, how far are you prepared to go, in
the direction of Socialism undisguised? Lloyd George was the
first to take up the challenge implicit in the Russian loan.
A week later Grey spoke in the same sense. And on September 20th, ten days before the assembly of Parliament, Asquith
gave voice. He was, he said, willing to reach by negotiation
an adjustment of claims and a resumption of trade. But the
projected loan provided no security worth the name either
for the just treatment of our claims or any advance of our
credit. It was a crude experiment in nursery diplomacy.
This phrase MacDonald resented. But in describing Bolshevism as "an interlude in Tsarism" he showed himself, as he so
often did, much nearer to his opponents, Liberal or Conservative, than to the Left Wing of his own party. Out of these
exchanges one clear idea emerged. It was certain, now, that
the Liberals meant to put the Government out. But it was
equally certain that the electors would not put the Liberals
in. The traditional lines of division, obscured since 1918,
were coming to light, and Churchill took the occasion to
sever his associations with the Liberal Party and transfer
his energy and eloquence to the Conservatives.

At a mass demonstration in Newcastle on October 2nd
Baldwin opened his campaign. He began with kindly
references to the crusted Tories on the Labour benches—
and not the back benches only! He went on to congratulate

the Prime Minister on the success of the London conference
on Germany and the Dawes Plan. Then, somewhat to the
bewilderment and not wholly to the satisfaction of his ex-
pectant audience, he indulged himself in a placid analysis
of the Russian Treaty and the guaranteed loan. Did the
Government really believe that Parliament would endorse
the pledge they had given to Russia? Had the Dominions
been consulted? Had the interests of France been considered?
Did the Chancellor of the Exchequer really approve? Could
anyone suppose that Russia would ever be a great market
for British goods, comparable with the Dominions, with
South Africa, with the East? Leave that market rather to
Germany: there let her send her exports and with the profits
pay her reparations. Then with a few sympathetic sentences
on the fallacy of internationalism—a promise to make no
promises—and a welcome to the returning Churchill, the
speech came to its quiet end.

The truth was that Baldwin had not quite made up his
mind how to handle a somewhat complicated situation. The
Conservatives had put down a motion of censure on the
Campbell case, the Liberals an amendment referring it for
investigation to a Select Committee of ten. The debate was
on October 8th. Horne spoke for the Conservatives and was
answered by the Attorney General. Simon moved the Liberal
amendment and the Prime Minister replied. Asquith followed in support of Simon, and then after a few more
speeches, Baldwin, who had been observed in busy con-
fabulation on the front opposition bench, rose to announce
the decision of his party. The Government hoped, indeed
calculated, that Liberals would vote against the Conservative motion and Conservatives against the Liberal amendment. But they had miscalculated. The Conservatives went
into the Lobbies with the Liberals. The vote against the
Government was decisive—364 to 198—and Ramsay Mac-
Donald advised the King to dissolve Parliament. The election was fixed for October 29th. At Bewdley Baldwin was
unopposed.

In his first election speech, at Queen's Hall, on October
15th, he analysed the condition of the Government. What
had made Conservatives anxious, he said, was the appre-

hension—almost the certainty—that in a crisis the policy
of the Government would be settled by those extreme forces
which seemed to control it. Sooner or later, the Prime Minister must destroy those elements or they would destroy him.
The burden was too great for any man: the burden of dis-
unity and distrust in his own Cabinet; and he took the
plunge, he decided to stand or fall by the Campbell motion
in order to avoid debate on the Russian treaty* and on
the growing unemployment. They had come into office on
promises and emotions, not on any accurate study of the
facts; now they aspired to office on a programme of projects.
For the moment electrification was the blessed word, the
Mesopotamia of the Labour programme. But to persuade
an ignorant electorate that unemployment could be relieved
by harnessing natural powers which we did not possess was
no better than a cruel fraud. Had they made the situation
easier for the unemployed? They had made it harder, by
repealing the McKenna duties and ignoring his own arrangements for Imperial Preference.

Campaign speeches run as true to form as Budget speeches.
If Baldwin's show any personal quality it is rather in their
quietness, their reserve, their understatement. On October
16th he delivered his first broadcast. By common consent
King George V and Baldwin stood apart in their mastery of
this new device: and Baldwin could speak unrehearsed,
without a script, from a few notes. To the immense, unseen
audience he talked with an ease that brought him into each
family group, and if the Conservatives voted one way because they were Conservatives, the Socialists the other
because they were Socialists, the middle multitude voted for
Baldwin because he was Baldwin. And close observers were
aware of the effect on the man himself. His diffidence
dropped away: a note of authority came into his voice when
he spoke of progress and stability and ordered freedom; a
note of contempt, confident and outspoken, for the doctrinaires of the Labour Party, their obsequiousness to the Kremlin, their meaningless talk of Constitutional rebellion. That
there was a rift in the Cabinet was common knowledge,

---

* Baldwin was speaking with authority. A Labour minister's wife
had confided this to Mrs. Asquith, who passed it on to Baldwin.

and Baldwin took good care to wedge it open. "It makes my blood boil," he said to a great meeting at Southend, "to read of the way in which M. Zinoviev is speaking of the Prime Minister of Great Britain to-day. At one time there went up a cry 'Hands off Russia!' I think it is time someone said to Russia 'Hands off England!'" This was on October 20th.

CHAPTER IX

THE RED LETTER

On October 10th, Sir Eyre Crowe, Permanent Secretary to the Foreign Office, had been handed a copy of a letter, purporting to be signed by Zinoviev, Head of the Comintern, and addressed to the Central Committee of the British Communist Party. It contained instructions—of, it must be admitted, a most feeble and platitudinous character—for the development of subversive activities in Great Britain. On the following day evidence was received that the original had reached England. The document was studied in the Northern Department of the Foreign Office, which was satisfied of its authenticity. On October 15th Crowe minuted to the Prime Minister proposing that the Government should address a protest to Rakovski, the Russian Ambassador, and communicate the facts to the press. The Prime Minister approved—provided there was no doubt at all that the letter was authentic—and directed the Department to prepare a note to Rakovski, which should be published. These instructions reached the office on the evening of the 17th October.

On October 21st the draft dispatch was sent to MacDonald and returned on the morning of the 24th, largely rewritten. That afternoon the Foreign Office learned that another copy of the Zinoviev letter was in the hands of the *Daily Mail* and would be published the following morning.* The Department decided to expedite their own publication and so informed the Prime Minister. He was dumbfounded, having fully expected that the rewritten draft would be sent to him for final approval.†

---

* It afterwards appeared that both copies were given, to the Foreign Office and the *Daily Mail*, by a well-known business man, who had them from a friend in touch with Communist circles.

† As subsequent events (in no way connected with the Zinoviev affair) cast doubts on the good faith of the official chiefly concerned, it is right to say that MacDonald accepted "without reserve" the explanation

The Foreign Office note to Rakovski appeared in the London papers on Saturday, October 25th, and Rakovski's reply in the Sunday papers. It was sent to the Prime Minister, who minuted that on his return to London "information would be at hand to carry the matter further." A second reply, written under direct instructions from Moscow, followed, and was seen by the Prime Minister on Monday 27th. It declared that the letter was a fabrication and demanded "the punishment of official persons concerned in the forgery." This insulting paper was shown to MacDonald, who decided that His Majesty's Government could not receive it. It went back to the Embassy. On the 29th, the day of the General Election, Rakovski sent it in again. It was returned. On November 1st it was once more delivered at the Foreign Office, and on November 2nd MacDonald saw the Ambassador, explained why he could not receive it and believed that he had sent him away, if not satisfied, at all events convinced. On November 4th, he approved a dispatch to the Ambassador "assuming that you will address him further before he replies to your note of November 1st." Meanwhile a Cabinet Committee had decided that they could not pronounce on the genuineness of the letter—thereby, it will be observed, questioning Crowe's statement of October 15th that it was undoubtedly authentic. But, in view of that finding, the Prime Minister felt himself bound to withdraw the dispatch already published, and then, having cleared the ground of all doubtful issues, "launch out." The Department was to tell the Russian Government that he was thoroughly dissatisfied with their propagandist activities and could not allow their pretence that the Third International was unconnected with the Soviet Government.

On November 4th, MacDonald resigned. The new Ministers had before them a letter from Rakovski dated November 8th complaining that the late Prime Minister had quite misunderstood their conversation of November 2nd. He therefore stood by his letter of October 27th which, however, the Foreign Office "could not find in their

---

given him. A Minister correcting a draft does not always initial the paper, his corrections being taken as authenticating it as a whole and approving what is not altered.

records," as it had been returned, for the third and last time, on November 1st. The only documents before the Cabinet were the old letter published in the Sunday papers of October 25th and the new letter of November 8th: and what degree of authenticity the original letter really possessed was never established.*

Later it became the fashion in Socialist circles to maintain that the election of 1924 was won by a trick, not to say a forgery.

> But [MacDonald wrote to Baldwin four months later] I have never been able, as yet, to reduce the very heavy clouds of suspicion which surrounded the whole of that disgraceful affair to definite proofs and charges.

And a subsequent debate carried matters no further. In truth the Red Letter, as it was called, did little more than add a certain excitement to what both parties knew to be a foregone conclusion. Twelve months had been enough to show the electorate, first, that the Socialists were no more competent to deal with the malady of unemployment than their opponents; second, that their internal discords were incompatible with a steady policy in any direction; and third, that a Socialist victory would mean another short Parliament and another General Election at no distant date. Baldwin offered stability, the very thing which he seemed to embody, in face, in build, in the accent of his voice. And to the new electorate, personality counted for more than policy. Asquith's happy comparison of MacDonald to Johnson's Poll Carmichael—"she was wiggle-waggle: I could never persuade her to be categorical," may have been above the heads of a popular audience, but it expressed exactly what the electors were feeling. No one knew what a MacDonald government would do or not do next. What for years had been their favourite nostrum, the Capital Levy, had disappeared from the programme. The Russian loan was referred to a future Parliament. The one thing

* My own belief is that it was "authentic" in the sense that it correctly expressed the opinion and attitude of the Russian Government or the Comintern—so far as they could be distinguished; and that it proceeded from one or other of them. I do not think it was necessarily "genuine" in the sense of being personally composed or authorized by Zinoviev.

certain—Red Letter or none—was that powerful elements of
the Left had transferred their allegiance to a foreign power
which was working, not silently and secretly but loudly and
ostentatiously, for the subversion of English institutions.

The results of the election showed the usual discrepancy
between votes cast and parties returned which our electoral
system makes inevitable. The Conservatives came back
413 strong—a majority of 211 over all parties combined;
Labour had 151 seats, the Liberals 40; eleven odds and ends
completed the total. With one exception, all the Labour
Leaders were re-elected, but in spite of Conservative support,
Asquith lost Paisley. Yet it was not unobserved that while
the Conservative vote had increased by over two millions,
Labour, fighting in adverse circumstances, had increased by
more than one.

On November 4th, Baldwin became Prime Minister for
the second time. The reunion of the Conservative Party was
made manifest by the inclusion of Austen Chamberlain,
Birkenhead and Worthington Evans in the Cabinet. But
nothing showed more clearly that Baldwin at last felt
himself master in his own house than his choice for the
Treasury. He sent for Churchill and asked if he would serve
as Chancellor. Of the Duchy? Churchill asked. No, of
the Exchequer, said the Prime Minister. Tears came into
Churchill's eyes.

The Duchy went to Cecil, and Curzon saw himself
Foreign Secretary with Cecil making League of Nations
speeches by his side. But the outcome was even more
painful than the prospect.

> I am informed [Curzon writes on October 31st] that you have
> it in mind in the formation of a new Government to make a
> change at the Foreign Office. I cannot believe that you would
> put so terrible a slur on my administration, which was con-
> ducted amid extraordinary difficulties but not without success,
> in the closest and pleasantest cooperation with yourself and
> your predecessor. It would be too much to expect me to
> accept such a situation.

Baldwin replied:

> When you left the Foreign Office you had successfully over-
> come the great difficulties surrounding a number of questions

At Chequers, 1924

of varying degrees of gravity. A fresh start can now be made, and in the present condition of public affairs I regard it as of the first importance to have the Foreign Secretary in the Commons.

Loyally Curzon accepted his leader's decision. Austen Chamberlain went to the Foreign Office, and Locarno.

CHAPTER X

SECOND ADMINISTRATION

WHATEVER else might be said or thought of the Conservative victory—whatever part had been played by Zinoviev or Campbell, or the Attorney General or the *Daily Mail*—one thing at least was clear. In both senses of the word it was a popular victory: far more working-men and women had voted for Baldwin than for MacDonald. It was plain too that the Liberal Party was no longer to be reckoned with and that the field was set for a direct encounter in the party field, where, if the Die-hards of Conservatism could be paired against the Doctrinaires of Socialism, the revived Disraelian Toryism and old trade-union Labour could hammer out such a compromise as Labour, when it came back to power, would not be disposed to upset.

But just as Disraeli in 1880 had forecast all the troubles of his successor in the one word Ireland, so his ghost might have breathed in the victor's ear the one word Coal. On the miners' picks depended the prosperity of every industry in the country, not least of those exporting industries which, as Baldwin had said, were the dominant feature in the economic scene. And the mining industry was unhappy, the miners discontented, the owners stubborn: neither of them noticeably intelligent. "I should have thought," Birkenhead once remarked, "that the miners' leaders were the stupidest men in the kingdom if I had not met the owners." And what did the doctrine of Ordered Progress mean to Durham and Nottingham; to West Cumberland and South Wales; to Arthur Cook and Sir Adam Nimmo? What did the whole mining industry mean to those millions of electors who had never seen a pit, and only thought of coal as something to put on the domestic fire?

What this Government will not do is to attempt to control the industries of the country. We believe that by any change in the basis of our system we should fall into a pit of misery and poverty hardly to be visualized and never experienced. The people have repudiated Socialism. They have repudiated nationalization. They have repudiated the goal of a Britain controlled whether from London or Moscow. They have repudiated the idea of employing violent material remedies to ancient spiritual wrongs.

This warning was uttered on March 3rd 1925 in a speech at Birmingham. When Baldwin spoke he had in mind a private member's bill put down for second reading on Friday three days later. On the face of things it was not fair that a trade unionist who might be Liberal or Conservative should be compelled to contribute to the funds of the Labour Party, and this injustice Mr. Macquisten and Mr. Greaves Lord, a Conservative trade unionist, proposed to remove. The Cabinet was divided: a vote might have shown a majority in favour of the Bill. But Baldwin made it clear in Cabinet that he would oppose it, and Birkenhead passed a note across—on a House of Commons envelope:

> I think your action shows enormous courage and for that reason will succeed.

Doubtfully and reluctantly the Ministers yielded to the fixed resolution of their leader.

The mover handled his bill with good taste and good humour, the seconder was harsh and long. They could not fail to be provocative, and Labour was in a noisy mood when Baldwin rose. After a few sentences about the awkwardness of legislating on a Friday he opened his case in tones so quiet that the House stilled itself to listen.

> In some ways this is a very difficult speech for me to make. The matter of the Bill itself digs right into one of the most difficult and fundamental questions in the country to-day, and it touches . . . questions which have interested me during the whole of my working life. I have thought so much about them, I feel I have so much to say about them, that my difficulty will be in choosing the little I can possibly say to-day, and in finding words to express clearly to the House what is in my mind.

It must be remembered that outside the Cabinet no one

in the House knew what the Prime Minister was going to say. He had an amendment:

> That this House, while approving the principle of political liberty embodied in the Trade Union (Political Fund) Bill, is of opinion that a measure of such far-reaching importance should not be introduced as a Private Member's Bill.

But how he was going to reach it, the House could not even guess. What he had in store for them was a history of industrial evolution as seen by the head of an old family business:

> where the fathers and grandfathers . . . had worked, and where the sons went automatically into the business. It was also a place where nobody ever "got the sack," and where . . . a number of old gentlemen used to spend their days sitting on the handles of wheelbarrows smoking their pipes. Oddly enough, it was not an inefficient community. It was the last survivor of that type of works which ultimately became swallowed up in one of those great combinations towards which the industries of to-day are tending.

He had learnt his lesson years before, when a coal strike in which they had no concern put Baldwins out of action and he paid his unfortunate workpeople an allowance out of his own pocket. There was no conscious unfairness— business was inevitably tending to amalgamation—so were the labour unions, and then—God help those who stood outside! He came nearer to his theme.

> Those two forces . . . are enormously strong, and . . . throw an immense responsibility on the organisations themselves and on those who elect them and . . . there are a great many on both sides who have not got the requisite qualities of head and heart for business. There are many men with good heads and no hearts, and many men with good hearts and no heads.

Both these organizations must in a certain sense be uneconomic. The Trade Union restricts output to protect the weaker man. So does the employers' organization. One forces the workman to join the union; the other prevents any new man from starting in that particular trade. And,

> Progress can only be obtained . . . by those two bodies of men, so similar in their strength and so similar in their weaknesses, learning to understand and not to fight one another. . . . Trade

unionism has its weak spots. My honourable and learned friends have laid their fingers on three points which trade unionists themselves know are their weak spots [hence the interruption from the Labour benches]. . . . The whole tradition of our country has been to let Englishmen develop their own associations in their own way. With that I agree. But there are limits. . . .

As these associations . . . become more and more powerful, on whichever side they are, there may come a time . . . when they may directly injure the State. It is at that moment that any Government should say that, whatever freedom and latitude . . . may be left to any association in this free country, nothing shall be done which shall injure the State, which is the concern of all of us and far greater than all of us or our interests.

Then a little nearer still:

I do not know whether the House will forgive me if I speak for a minute or two on a rather personal note. For two years past, in the face of great difficulties, perhaps greater than many were aware of, I have striven to . . . breathe a living force into my great Party. . . . We find ourselves, after these two years in power, in possession of the greatest majority our Party ever had . . . how did we get there? . . . It was because, rightly or wrongly, we succeeded in creating the impression that we stood for stable Government and for peace in the country between all classes of the community. That being so, what should our course be? . . . I have not myself the slightest doubt.

I want my Party to-day to make a gesture to the country . . . and to say to them: We have our majority; we believe in the justice of this Bill . . . but we are going to withdraw our hand, we are not going to push our political advantage home. . . . Suspicion, which has prevented stability in Europe, is the one poison that is preventing stability at home. . . . We, at any rate, are not going to fire the first shot . . . we believe we know what the country wants, and we believe it is for us in our strength to do what no other Party can do, and to say that we at any rate stand for peace. . . .

I know . . . that that will be the feeling of all those who sit behind me. . . . I have equal confidence in my fellow-countrymen throughout Great Britain. Although I know that there are those who work for different ends from most of us in this

House, yet there are many in all ranks and all parties who will re-echo my prayer: "Give peace in our time, O Lord."*

By universal consent the speech was placed at once among the few masterpieces of Parliamentary eloquence which that generation had heard. It was the subject of an admiring article in the *New York Times*. Some members spoke of Asquith in 1914, older members spoke of Gladstone, one aged peer recalled Disraeli. Haldane sent a message of gratitude for a speech "which has lifted public affairs to a higher level and recalled to me things that happened fifty years ago." Birkenhead was triumphant over the fulfilment of his prophecy.

> You have shown the greatest and the rarest form of political courage and I told you that it would succeed. I believe this will mean a permanent strengthening of your position in the House *as a whole* which is of immense importance to a Prime Minister.

One faithful watchdog reported the judgment of the lobbies: "He has won the leadership for years to come," and Curzon wrote:

> Let me congratulate you on your wonderful speech. It was a sure instinct that persuaded you to make it: and the reception it met with must be as welcome to you as it was delightful to your colleagues.

It was his last letter.

In old age Baldwin looked back on the speech he made that day with more satisfaction than on anything else he ever said, in Parliament or on the platform. Particularly did he treasure a letter, fourteen years later, from David Kirkwood, once the firebrand of Clydeside.

> This evening in the gloaming I was taking a walk in the country and my mind turned in the peace and quietude of a perfect twilight to the dreadful things that are taking place in Europe. Naturally, I thought on the beginning of the War in 1914. It was then that I realised what leads me to write this letter.

* It may be necessary to tell a younger generation that these words were taken from the Anglican liturgy, not, as one journalist averred, from Neville Chamberlain.

In 1914 there was a powerful minority opposed to the Government, but a deeper antagonism in the industrial field between the employers and the workers. It seemed then and for long afterwards that no power could eradicate that antagonism. I was, as you know, always in favour of the dilution of labour to meet national danger, provided the dilution was not used to reduce the standard of the working people. You may remember that, holding those views, I was in opposition to my own and other Trade Unions.

To-day I find an atmosphere completely different. The Unions have agreed spontaneously to dilution of labour and extension of overtime. The Employers with equal spontaneity have accepted as reasonable the terms suggested by the Ministry of Labour to protect the workers from exploitation. I asked myself how it came about that so marked a change had taken place during the last few years. I tried, with a friend who was walking with me, to trace the development back to some point of time. We went back to a speech you made in the House of Commons when Fred Macquisten introduced a Bill which would have affected the Trade Unions. Your speech was made in opposition to the Bill. You set down the fact that relationship between Employers and Employed had deteriorated, that each section had become impersonal in the great associations, and you ended with a phrase usually associated with war: "Give peace in our time, O Lord."

I remember the occasion so well, because we on our side of the House were on the edge of our nerves and mighty gritty when you began. Yet in a few minutes you were speaking to a House quiet through interest and appreciation. It is one of the few occasions in my experience in which the word has become flesh. You will remember that Abraham Lincoln at Gettysburg said: "The world will little heed nor long remember what we say here," yet Gettysburg is remembered because of what he did say there.

It seemed to me, this evening, that in your speech you made flesh the feelings of us all, that the antagonism, the bitterness, the class rivalry were unworthy, and that understanding and amity were possible. You would not accept it from me, if I said that the speech caused the change. I prefer to say that it expressed the inarticulate feeling for a change and so materialised an ideal thought into a living reality.

It may be that in your retirement from the turmoil of public life, you have been already reminded of that occasion in association with the present atmosphere of harmony in the nation, but I thought I should like you to know that one, who did not accept all your views, remembered you and your words while he was thinking of one of the few happy developments of this time.

May I add that, though you see little of us nowadays, your name is often on our lips and thoughts of you in our hearts.

The comparison with Lincoln should be noted. It will recur. But when the emotion had subsided, in the House and in the country, critics on both sides did not fail to observe the tactical brilliance of the Prime Minister's intervention, and the one theme on which Baldwin ever showed some personal vanity was his Parliamentary skill. With one stroke he had quelled his dissidents, mastered his Cabinet and projected on Parliament and the country the picture of himself as the kindly reasonable head of the national family, a family which if only it would refrain from foolish tantrums was much better able to manage its affairs than anyone else could manage for it. By managing its own affairs Baldwin meant applying to the mining industry, sulky, distracted and suspicious, the methods which had carried the firm of Baldwin placidly through the changes and upheavals of a generation. But as one Labour member said to him, the tears running down his face, "It was true, Prime Minister, every word was true. But those times have gone."

The third speech of this group was delivered at Leeds on March 12th, in the glow of his Parliamentary triumph. Millions of the newly enfranchised, he said, were enlisted in the Labour Party. In that party there was a section which aimed at ending the industrial system as we knew it, and in that section was a smaller group which would end it by violence. That was the challenge. It was answered at the election. But that verdict was not final. Conservatives must earn their return to office by their conduct in office. The industries by which we live were created by skill, employing capital, that is the savings of the people; while, to exchange the products of the world, we had further devised the marvellous mechanism of finance. In many ways we were paying the penalty of priority—in congested towns, ugly factories and smoke-laden air.

What remedy did the Socialists propose? That the State should become the common owner of the means of production. So, by direction exercised through bureaucrats and committees, we should be rid of unemployment, in short achieve equality of opportunity, freedom and fraternity. But men were not born free—or equal—or fraternal (I ask any mother in the audience if she does not agree). Then after some mild banter about South Wales and the inevitability of gradualness (which reminded him of the candidate in Dickens who won his election by aiming at the illimitable perspective), he swooped on the revolutionaries, Wheatley and Cook, regaled his audience with a few quotations from Trotsky, and ended with his perpetual plea for confidence and the abatement of suspicion.

The response was not encouraging. Under directions from the Labour Party the rural workers refused to meet the farmers and landowners in a conference on the problems of the land. Experiments in a new type of steel house produced a rash of strikes all over the country. In the mining industry there were indeed signs that owners and men were coming together in a joint enquiry. But simultaneously busy heads were building a new Triple Alliance of coal, transport and engineering, for united action in case of any trade dispute. Early in May the results of the miners' conversations with the owners were made public. They showed that the existing agreements could not be maintained. But at least the two sides had met, and at Welbeck on June 1st Baldwin was able to speak in language of some confidence and some censure. He was growing impatient with the owners in more industries than one, and for the workpeople he had gifts in his hands.

One of his first acts as Prime Minister in 1923 had been to set up a Committee under Sir John Anderson to study the future of National Insurance. After more than a year's deliberations the Committee produced a sheaf of reports. During the MacDonald interim the Conservative Shadow Cabinet continued the enquiry and formulated a project of their own. The two findings, official and unofficial, were brought together, and within a fortnight of the great victory Chamberlain and Churchill had received from the Prime

Minister full authority to proceed. In February the Ministers of Agriculture and Labour were brought in. In March a Cabinet Committee of the four ministers, with Lord Salisbury and Worthington Evans, approved the scheme down to the last detail. Churchill's report glows with triumph. The Bill is ready: the actuary's report will follow: Insurance will appear as an integral and inseparable part of the Budget: we are near the battlefield and I cannot conceive that hesitation and division should now appear. "You are lucky," he suddenly adds, "in having a temperament on which cares sit mildly."

But mine after mine was closing down, and the consequences of our return to the gold standard were visible throughout the exporting industries. At the last sitting of the Joint Enquiry the mine-owners made their decision known. Wages were higher than the industry could carry, and the shorter working day was reducing production below a profitable level. They proposed therefore to give a month's notice on June 30th terminating all existing agreements. A deputation of the Trades Union Congress found the Prime Minister well aware of the gravity of the situation, but quite determined not to intervene until every hope of direct agreement had proved vain. On July 1st the owners made their new proposals. By a unanimous vote the miners' delegates refused to entertain them. Breaking-point had been reached. Mediation by Bridgeman proved ineffectual, and on July 10th the Government set up a tribunal to enquire into the causes and circumstances of the dispute. Somewhat late in the day, it might be thought. The tribunal sat for eleven days and on July 28th the report was issued. In effect it threw the issue, undecided, to the Government to do as the Government thought best. On July 31st—public anxiety growing keener every hour—a thousand delegates, assembled in the Central Hall, Westminster, pledged their Unions to the defence of the miners' cause, while instructions went to the railwaymen not to handle coal after that midnight. A Cabinet was hurriedly summoned for 6.30. It met in gloom. The alliance of railwaymen and miners meant, in effect, the General Strike, so long expected, so often averted or evaded. It might mean revolution. This was the end, then, of those reiterated appeals for industrial peace.

I often noticed in talking to Baldwin that an indirect approach seemed to put him on his guard, a direct question always elicited a direct reply. "Why did you give that subsidy in 1925?" I asked. "We were not ready," he said. And that was his one answer to an anxious and distrustful Cabinet. He was not quite sure that the General Strike would come: at a Royal Garden Party one of the Labour leaders had told the King's secretary that Thomas would keep the railwaymen at work. But the danger was there, and the organization to meet it was not. So, after the Cabinet, Baldwin saw the miners and asked if they would join in a further enquiry—the condition being that wages should not be reduced. They agreed, and he then announced the decision he had wrung out of his colleagues—a subsidy, of unknown amount, to keep the mines working till the spring. In effect the taxpayer was to make good the difference between the wages provided by the agreement of 1924 and those offered by the owners now. The cost? Anything from 7½ millions if trade was good to 24 if it was not. But one thing at least was unhappily certain. The Budget was knocked to pieces.

It is about this time that reading the newspapers of the day we become aware of a new curiosity about the Prime Minister. The first Baldwin, the business man run by business men, had soon disappeared. The Baldwin of the unlucky election in 1923, frank, honest, impetuous, but not very clever in his politics, that picture could hardly be taken now as a faithful likeness of a leader with four hundred votes in the House. Yet on the morrow of victory Birkenhead had written to a friend:

> It is of course a tragedy that so great an Army should have so uninspiring a Commander-in-Chief. But this cannot be helped and I think he will be well under control.

The friend passed the letter on to Baldwin. The picture of Birkenhead controlling Baldwin is not without its humour, and in a very few months the artist was at Baldwin's feet overflowing with the affectionate reverence of an Undersecretary hoping for advancement and bent on deserving it.

"Your personality," he wrote some years later, "converted a Cabinet, which assembled on the crater of some recent and bitter memories, into a band of brothers." But, just as his face had baffled the cartoonists, so the Prime Minister's character provided journalists and the more exalted breed called publicists with a puzzle to which no key could be found. An ordinary man raised to eminence by a series of extraordinary chances? Then when would he be found out? Or, conceivably, a remarkable man after a new pattern? Then what would he make of himself, of his party, of his office?

One thing at least was clear. Baldwin was of the Liverpool stock, not a Peel, far from a Pitt. Very early in his Second Administration a cartoonist had detected the truth. Austen Chamberlain is shown advancing to report the menacing approach of a Sphinx, Zaghlul Pasha of Egypt. "You are Foreign Secretary," is the Prime Minister's bland response. Sooner or later every one of his colleagues could report the same experience. "Why come to me? I have perfect confidence in you." Letters laying some problem of administration before him for decision are answered, always promptly, but not so helpfully: "Go ahead as you propose in your letter just received." Or, not infrequently, "The P.M. has no time to study these papers, and leaves the matter to Mr. A.'s discretion." But, as one good and close observer wrote:

> Team work presupposes constant leadership; not only good fellowship and supervision. Is it in his character to be firm in those daily details which if neglected may produce the crisis which more effective control might have averted?

And the answer is assuredly that it was not.

The party then? Of necessity the larger the majority the more likely it is to develop internal strains and discomforts; and throughout his public career Baldwin was harassed by a group—always forming, always quelled, always re-forming—demanding something more than a continuous parade of good intentions garnished with quotations from Disraeli; a group which could not be persuaded that the chief function of a majority was to teach the Opposition how to be a majority when its turn came, and which suspected, not without ground, that in his heart Baldwin was more at home

with the Trade Unionists across the floor than with the great
industrialists who furnished the funds of the Conservative
Party.

And himself? At the end of the session *The Times* published an article, signed "Back Bencher," in which the
Leader's character was analysed with notable skill.

> Mr. Baldwin is doing a remarkable work. He is restoring
> the whole tone and quality of British politics. He has brought
> into public life a pleasant savour, freshness and health. It is
> the fragrance of the fields, the flavour of apple and hazel nut,
> all the unpretentious, simple, wholesome, homely but essential
> qualities, suggestions and traditions of England that Mr.
> Baldwin has substituted for the over-charged, heavy-laden,
> decadent atmosphere of post-war days. . . .
>
> In his shrewd and deep simplicity of character, his patience,
> his passion for the community and its welfare, his refusal to
> treat his fellow countrymen as enemies, perhaps too in an
> occasional gaucheness, and in an essential loneliness of spirit,
> it is Abraham Lincoln whom Mr. Baldwin recalls. Like
> Lincoln he has that rarest and finest quality of a leader, the
> power of liberating and calling in aid the deeper moral
> motives in the hearts of men. . . .
>
> Faced with elements on both sides clamouring for class war,
> he is calling to aid the English spirit of which he is incom-
> parably the most complete representative to-day, with the
> hope, in his case fair, which in Lincoln's case was forlorn,
> that peace will triumph. The Englishman will be happier
> in his lot than the American. Peace will triumph and Mr.
> Baldwin's character and qualities will ensure that result.

Neville Chamberlain wrote:

> Really the outstanding feature of the session is the develop-
> ment and growth of your own position. I do wish I knew
> who wrote that astonishingly shrewd, subtle and pene-
> trating study in *The Times*. He knows you well, it is clear.
> His comparison of you to Lincoln in your "essential loneliness
> of spirit" shows that he has got below the surface . . . Lincoln
> had at all costs to preserve the unity of the North. You have
> got to preserve the unity of the country. Lincoln was in-
> experienced and full of oddities which at first sight did not
> impress. He used to hesitate long before deciding, he was
> accused of weakness and vacillation, many thought him a fool.
> But he did decide on momentous occasions, often against

the advice of his friends, and his Cabinet, and he generally turned out to be right because he had an extraordinary faculty for understanding the view of the ordinary man.

Well, that's your strength and it is gradually becoming apparent to a wider and wider circle. I rejoice at the growth of your influence because I believe it wholly good for the party and the country that they should prefer to trust a man of your character before the superficial brilliance of an essentially inferior nature like Lloyd George.

The crisis over, England went on holiday and the Baldwins went too. The subsidy—the surrender—the improvidence—the vacillation—these were wounds to be healed. But there were gains as well as losses to be reckoned up. "Never once has Mr. Baldwin tried to mislead us," so Cook, the "hysterical Messiah" of the mining world, avouched. Old Ben Tillett added his word: "After forty years' experience of Premiers and Cabinet Ministers I can safely say his conduct was the most businesslike I have known in the handling of a trade dispute." And MacDonald's Chief Whip:

> Friend and foe are agreed that the Prime Minister's strength lies in his integrity. He brought into public life not a showy scintillating genius: but a mind richly stored with the best in literature, a developed sense of fairness and a soul sweetened by natural contacts.

With all this in hand, the Prime Minister could take his holiday with some satisfaction, and return in good cheer. On November 1st Churchill wrote:

> It is a year almost to a day since you asked me to work with you. We know each other better than we did then and I have been happy under your leadership. I am sure that you have a winning hand to play if only you have the firmness and patience to play it regularly through. Gradually but surely the nation will recover its strength and be conscious of an increased well-being. Time will vindicate all the principal actions we have taken, whether it be your forbearing attitude on Labour provocation or the Widows' Pensions or the Gold Standard. The Rothermere-Beaverbrook attack will be repulsed, not by speeches, not by disdain, but by events. What about that Roman—Fabius Maximus Cunctator—was there not some famous quotation about him? Did he not give his

country a chance to pull round and realize its mighty strength and let the deep long forces work for him—instead of being lured into desperate and premature struggles?

Two years later Baldwin wrote to Irwin in India:

I still think we were right in buying off the strike in 1925, though it proved once more the cost of teaching democracy. Democracy has arrived at a gallop in England and I feel all the time it is a race for life. Can we educate them before the crash comes?

CHAPTER XI

CLASSICAL INTERLUDE

In 1923 Salisbury had been asked by Baldwin to consider the storage of food supplies against the eventuality of war. In his memorandum he assumes that war can only mean war with France, Japan or the United States. The Common Observer had hardly ever thought of Japan; conflict with America did not enter his mind; and though a poll might have shown a greater measure of good will towards our late enemies than towards our more recent friends, no one in 1925 had any apprehension of armed strife with France. The war had been wound up, the loose strings knotted and tucked away: no new war was in sight, and the Locarno treaties seemed to have re-established the balance of Western Europe, so long disturbed by the collapse of Germany and the ambitions of France. That in the fears of France and the humiliation of Germany lay the seeds of another war, the Englishman did not, could not, see.

Ireland, so long the grand exasperator of British politics, was fading into the background of past times and things best forgotten: and out of that past there came from Hawarden to Mrs. Baldwin one of the most touching pieces in the Baldwin correspondence, a letter from Gladstone's daughter, Mary Drew:

> I am venturing (as a former dweller in Downing Street) to write a line of heartfelt congratulations on the two miracles, the Irish and the European pacts. If *we* had passed the Home Rule Bill in 1886 or in 1893 I could not have felt greater joy than yesterday's news brought me. I am sure that after thanking God we must thank Mr. Baldwin and I will beg you to tell him so.

The settlement was not without its humours, too, as related by Mrs. Baldwin. On November 27th Cosgrave telegraphed to Baldwin asking him to receive O'Higgins,

McGilligan and O'Byrne. They lunched at Chequers on
the following day. The Secretary of the Boundary Commission arrived in the afternoon with maps and the party
amicably moved into the drawing-room for tea and talk.
At five o'clock they settled down to business. Baldwin set
out the alternatives before the negotiators. One was—to
follow the existing boundary, a course to which the Free
State would agree only if the Catholics of Ulster were restored to full civil rights. The other—to impose the independent award, which meant the downfall of Cosgrave.
This exposition was delivered without comment from the
hearers and in twenty minutes the representatives of the
Free State were on their way to London.

On Sunday the talks were resumed, Craig now being
present, and at half-past one the party adjourned for luncheon. Mrs. Baldwin was between Craig and O'Higgins;
"but, understand," she said, "I am not the bone of con-
tention: I am too plump." Conversation was laboriously
maintained and at half-past two the exhausted hostess went
to her boudoir for a little rest. There she found a solitary
man eating a solitary meal, "'It's the assassin,' I said;
'there always is one.'" It was Feetham, the independent
chairman, observing even at mealtime his impartial remote-
ness from both sides. By five o'clock agreement had been
reached on the Boundary and the party broke up. Baldwin
would relate with glee the last words of one of the delegates.
"We had better travel separately, Prime Minister. To be
seen arriving in London together would not be good for
either of us." He always enjoyed his Irishmen, and never
gave way to the exasperation which that race,

> gens ratione furens et mentem pasta chimaeris,

at times provokes in nearly all Englishmen. But tragedy was
waiting too. "The happiest day of my life," O'Higgins said,
"will be when the Lord Mayor of Belfast is received by the
Lord Mayor of Dublin. But they will get me first." They got
him.

Nearer home the usual mixture of good and evil. The coal
strike and whatever else it portended or implied had been
evaded. The Pensions Act was coming into operation;

housing was going well. But time was passing; Communism, still called Bolshevism, was growing, and what was being done to remove or even relieve the unemployment on which Bolshevism fed? Here was Baldwin's own field of action—and what was he doing or preparing to do? Churchill indeed was ready with his plan, heroic but cautious. The subsidy had unbalanced the national finances—and so, farewell to the grand project of National Insurance so boldly conceived, so triumphantly expounded. Now he would reduce all public salaries and wages, from highest to lowest, by five per cent—but then, might not the resentment of the Services be awkward, dangerous perhaps, if things came to an open conflict with the Unions? Or—reduce all Government establishments by 25 per cent and work down to that figure by not filling vacancies? Reduce the staff of the Admiralty and the number of battleships and cruisers in commission? Hold up the expansion of the Air Force—or fix the establishment for two years and let the staff do what they could within those limits? Cut down the Cavalry? Above all, cease to pay subsidy to the ungrateful and greedy Arabs of Iraq. And at home, bring to an end the uncovenanted benefit called the Dole. Certainly there was much to think of here. But that Baldwin thought about it I can find no evidence. "Then comes Winston with his hundred-horse-power mind and what can I do?" he once asked. And again: "I wish I had more energy; then I might have done something, and I have done nothing. But one must not expect to see results. I am always telling Winston that."

At least he could speak. I suppose that since Gladstone no Prime Minister has delivered so many public speeches as Baldwin, or spoken so often with such general acceptance. A journalist once wrote of his "insatiable conquest of the English heart," and not the English heart only. "I always told my party that Scotland is Conservative," and be it Glasgow or Aberdeen or Dundee, the Prime Minister was sure of his welcome, most sure when he took holiday from public affairs and spoke of Walter Scott or the Scottish character, or, more boldly, to the students of Edinburgh on Truth in Politics, or Why are Politicians Distrusted?

The party system . . . has its advantages, its team work, its loyalties. . . . To our sporting countrymen it appears as a game, and . . . its rules . . . for the most part are honourably obeyed. . . . But the party system does put an embargo on complete frankness of speech. . . . The political audience is not dishonest . . . nor does it desire or approve dishonesty . . . but it is . . . only imperfectly prepared to follow a close argument. . . . It is easy to see how this may lead to depreciation of the verbal currency and to the circulation of promises that cannot be cashed. . . . Let us aim at meaning what we say and saying what we mean . . . let us seek to moralise our public intercourse, and reduce the area of casuistry and duplicity.

And in December of this year 1925 he annexed a new province.

In the hall of the Middle Temple, ablaze with academic robes of every colour, Baldwin stood up to address the Classical Association. He spoke of Rome, and how shy traffickers from wild fastnesses must have shaded their eyes to watch the Roman road passing into the horizon, and thought with awe of the great heart beating at the end of the giant artery. Of Rome, and the virtues on which the Empire was built, *pietas* and *gravitas*: and the warning that Rome had left to us:

Who in Europe does not know that one more war in the West, and the civilisation of the ages will fall with as great a shock as that of Rome?

Then of Greece, and the tragedy of civic dissension, "which throws into more radiant relief the debt we owe to her in art." And then of ourselves, the *ultimi Britanni*, the youngest child of the West, the latest runner in the race, and what we may still learn from the form, the reticence, the exactness of the Classics.

The possession of a sense of proportion, of a standard of values, and of a respect for the truth of words proved an inestimable aid to political judgment. So far as I have a sense of proportion it has helped me to assess the personal equation of the individuals, distinguished and undistinguished, who form the House of Commons. So far as I have a standard of values, it has helped me to estimate speech and the written word, and has saved me many a time from bowing to the idols of the market-place.

Then after words of praise for Asquith's Roman felicity and the labours of Gilbert Murray for the League of Nations, "redeeming the failure of those Greeks whom, more than any man, he has helped the modern world to understand," Baldwin drew to his conclusion:

I remember many years ago standing on the terrace of a beautiful villa near Florence. It was a September evening, and the valley below was transfigured in the long horizontal rays of the declining sun. And then I heard a bell, such a bell as never was on land or sea, a bell whose every vibration found an echo in my innermost heart. I said to my hostess, "that is the most beautiful bell I have ever heard." "Yes," she replied, "it is an English bell." And so it was. For generations its sound had gone out over English fields, giving the hours of work and prayer to English folk from the tower of an English abbey, and then came the Reformation, and some wise Italian bought the bell whose work at home was done and sent it to the Valley of the Arno, where after four centuries it stirred the heart of a wandering Englishman and made him sick for home. Thus the chance word of a Latin inscription, a line in the Anthology, a phrase of Horace or a "chorus ending of Euripides," plucks at the heartstrings and stirs a thousand memories, memories subconscious and ancestral.

The Prime Minister of Canada wrote:

I shall always feel that what, more than aught else, the Dominions owe to the Motherland, and what will keep them one with her at heart and in spirit, are "the qualities of character" which, carried across the seas by proconsul and peasant alike, constitute the real expansion of England. The inheritance is the richer when we are made to feel that the character of England herself has been moulded in no small measure by the traditions and culture of ancient Rome and Greece.

I was glad to read the tribute your address pays to the Earl of Oxford. If you will permit me to say so, whatever may be your differences politically, you both present the similarity of being first and foremost an Englishman, one who embodies the qualities and characteristics of his country as they are portrayed by history—and which, it seems to me, are not very far from "the *pietas*, the *gravitas* and the truth of the spoken word" of the Romans.

But Baldwin's excursions into the field of literature had

not always such happy sequels. Often and ruefully would he acknowledge that Mary Webb had been the bane of his life. The consequences, indeed, of his casual but laudatory reference to her masterpiece were little short of tragic.

My family [wrote a "proud Salopian"] made many miles of roads: one over Shelve Hill and thence to Sliperstones. This is *the* Mary Webb road. It was dedicated to the public on condition that the five gates should be kept shut. So they were till the Mary Webb public began to arrive. Their mind was concentrated on Mary Webb and could not reasonably be directed to closing of gates. Limited to time, the chara patrons had no minute to spare in which to close a gate, still less to open it. So the chara crashed through the gate to the intense hilarity of the passengers. The Grasping Landlord—myself—put up new gates, one a specially forbidding looking object at which the chara driver blenched. Fortunately there was at hand a County Council steam roller, and the driver, for what was really a very modest sum, undertook to charge the gate (and successfully) and a further sum was raised to induce him to charge the gate-posts. It is much to his credit that he was able so to loosen them that the charabanc party were able to uproot them and throw them into the valley below. Meanwhile the farmer—one knows how unreasonable farmers are—summoned to the scene, pulled the driver from his perch and inflicted on him personal violence which to one of his sedentary habits may have been beneficial.

The upshot was that the Grasping Landlord had to reduce his rents, his tenants pleading that they farmed for a living and could not spend their time searching for sheep on the other side of the Sliperstones.

CHAPTER XII

THE GENERAL STRIKE

THE General Strike of 1926 may be interpreted in either of two ways: as a revolutionary movement to overawe Parliament and coerce the Government, or as a sympathetic action in support of the Miners' Federation in their negotiations with the Employers and the Cabinet.

Since he first took office—perhaps before taking office—Baldwin had been convinced that sooner or later the Trade Unions would have recourse to the General Strike, and, as we have seen, one of his first acts as Prime Minister was to recall into being the Supply and Transport Committee which had run down after 1921. Some of the Ministers in the Labour Government of 1923 knew of its existence, but looked the other way. By 1926 its arrangements were complete and Baldwin sat quietly waiting on events.

The subsidy of 1925 had purchased an armistice. That was all, unless another enquiry could find a remedy for a mischief which seemed incurable. The enquiry was duly held. But once again the Trades Union Congress forestalled the findings of any enquiry by declaring, on February 26th 1926, that "it would stand firmly and unitedly against any attempt to degrade further the standard of life in the coalfields." There was to be no increase in working hours, no reduction in wages: and all agreements between Owners and Miners must be national and not regional. But careful observers noticed that some six weeks later the Congress spoke with a milder voice, only "reaffirming its previous declarations in support of the miners' efforts to obtain an equitable settlement of outstanding difficulties." Minds went back to 1921 and that "Black Friday" when at the last moment the Railwaymen had stepped aside and left the Miners to surrender. It might happen again. Labour was half-hearted; the leaders were looking nervously over their shoulders to see where their

followers were going. The Co-operative Societies, who were
designated as the Commissariat of the Revolution, wanted to
know who would repay the credits they were expected to
open. And the Supply and Transport Committee went on
quietly putting the last touches to its arrangements.

Meanwhile, on March 10th, Baldwin had met representatives of the Owners and Miners and advised them to
make no public statement until they had studied the Report.
But the more they studied the further seemed all prospect
of agreement. "We do not intend," so one of the Miners'
leaders said on March 31st, "any surrender of the National
Wages Agreement. We do not intend any reduction in
wages. We do not intend any increase in hours." But this
meant a new subsidy, and Baldwin had on March 24th
used words which could be interpreted to mean that, against
the Owners and against the Commission, he might, "to save
the situation," renew the subsidy for three months after
May 1st. But, as he knew, the situation was beyond saving.
The catchword "Not a minute on the day, not a penny
off the pay" had taken hold of the Miners' Federation;
and, translated into resolutions, was in fact a refusal to treat.

This, the Miners' ultimatum, was delivered on April 9th.
They had already asked the Trades Union Congress for
assurance of support and received a less than encouraging
reply. "The Industrial Committee fully realize the serious-
ness of the present position, but they are of opinion that
matters have not yet reached a stage when any final declaration of the General Council's policy can be made." On April
23rd Baldwin made his last effort at conciliation. He invited
the Owners and Miners to meet him together and say out-
right what the reason of the deadlock was. The answer was
as plain as he could have wished. The Miners would not
consider either district settlements or any extension of hours.
The issue—district or national settlements—was not one
which the public clearly understood; to the country at large,
and to many of Baldwin's own party, the dispute was between rich owners for whom no great sympathy was felt,
and poor miners, bound by the conditions of a decadent
industry to work and live on terms which made the public
conscience uneasy.

Language used in conference by men tired, angry and excited was written down and studied microscopically for some evidence of bad faith, for assurances never given and pledges never exchanged. There is little doubt, for instance, that after the meetings on April 26th and 27th the Owners thought that Baldwin had undertaken, if they produced a national minimum percentage, to restore by legislation the eight-hour day. There is no doubt at all that he never made such a promise. And coming so late it would have been of little use. The Trades Union Congress, seeing its own leadership passing into the hands of men who were determined to challenge the Government, realizing that the preparations of the Government were complete and that the revolutionaries had no preparations at all, tried at the last moment to thrust itself into the mining negotiations and so recover control of a movement fraught with as much peril to itself as to the Government. On the 27th the Cabinet—Baldwin being absent on negotiations with the miners—advised that a State of Emergency should be declared: the Civil Commissioners to proceed to their stations, and troops to be moved to Lancashire, Edinburgh and South Wales, eight battalions being held in reserve in case the strike became general. On April 29th a conference of all the affiliated Unions "endorsed the effort of the General Council to secure an honourable settlement," words which might mean anything or nothing. On the morning of the 30th the Owners saw Baldwin and made their last offer—a uniform percentage increase of 20 per cent in return for an eight-hour day. He referred it to the Federation; their reply, delivered the same day, was a unanimous rejection of the terms and a demand for a continuance of the subsidy until re-organization had "brought greater prosperity to the industry." This nebulous utterance yielded a still more nebulous paraphrase. Ministers put the question direct: "Will you, in return for a prolongation of the subsidy, enter into negotiations on the basis of the Commission's finding?" That finding was:

> If the present hours are to be retained, we think that a revision of the minimum percentage addition, fixed in 1924 at a time of temporary prosperity, is indispensable.

Fox Photos

In 1926

The Miners replied that they could not accept reductions as a preliminary to reorganization, but added that they were prepared "to give full consideration to all the difficulties connected with the industry when the scheme for such reorganization will have been initiated by the Government."

"Initiated"—a more ambiguous word could hardly have been chosen. But it served its purpose. The subsidy was to continue until the Miners were satisfied that reorganization had been initiated, and all the endeavours of Ministers to discover what "initiated" meant were dismissed as "boggling with words." So matters were reported late on Friday night to the affiliated Unions, and on the morrow it was decided to place the future conduct of negotiations in the hands of the General Council of the Trades Union Congress. The tide was running strongly to the Left and impassioned speeches emphasized the unity of the leaders and their followers. Never, said J. H. Thomas, had any Government made so great a blunder. Bevin compared them to George III and Lord North, and warned them that he who takes the sword may also perish by the sword. Ramsay MacDonald also spoke of swords, and seemed to think that all the trouble had come from the Government's asking the Miners to say what they meant. The assembly decided to call a General Strike and adjourned singing the Red Flag.

On Saturday May 1st the General Council of the T.U.C. made it known to the Cabinet that they had taken over the conduct of the mining dispute. At the same time they offered to arrange for the distribution of foodstuffs to the population at large. The offer was ignored. That evening, conversations, friendly, informal and non-committal, were held between the Prime Minister, Birkenhead, Steel-Maitland—Sir Horace Wilson, Secretary of the Ministry of Labour, attending; and, for the Unions, Pugh, Swales and Thomas. Citrine acted as secretary. Early on Sunday morning, Wilson made the following note of the Trade Unions' position as clarified by this long talk.

Sunday 1.15 a.m. The Prime Minister has satisfied himself as a result of the conversations he has had with the representatives of the T.U.C. that, if negotiations are continued (it being

s.b.—8

understood that the notices cease to operate), the representatives of the T.U.C. are confident that a settlement can be
reached on the lines of the Report within a fortnight.*

At 2 a.m. Baldwin gave a copy of this note to Thomas, for
communication to the full Council and the Miners. Both parties
clearly understood that if it was accepted, the Council would
return authorized by the Miners to accept a reduction of wages.

The Cabinet met at noon. At once hostility to the formula
made itself heard. Some Ministers thought that it was vague
and indefinite: others that it amounted to a surrender under
threats. Birkenhead had, indeed, with Baldwin's con-
currence, warned Thomas that the formula might be un-
satisfactory to the Cabinet; and Ministers in general were
of the opinion that before any negotiations involving a
further subsidy were resumed, the threat of the General
Strike must be unconditionally withdrawn. Birkenhead insisted that the formula was neither an assurance nor an
agreement, but only a record of the impressions left on the
Prime Minister's mind. The feeling of the Cabinet was
uneasy and distrustful.

At 5 p.m. that Sunday afternoon the Cabinet met again,
only to learn that the Miners had left London and that the
Trades Union Congress could not deliver their reply before
six o'clock. At a quarter to seven the Trade Unionists reported that they were still unable to get at the Miners, but
that they desired to receive further instructions from the
Ministers as to the interpretation of the formula. The Cabinet agreed that the same trio should meet the Labour representatives at 9 p.m. and approved a Note to be issued after
that meeting if Ministers thought it desirable.

The basis of the settlement, it said, must be "a sincere
acceptance of the Report," and the essence of the Report
was that the industry needed to be reorganized and that
some interim adjustment of hours and wages was inevitable
while the reorganization was in progress. If this basis were
accepted, then the Government would resume negotiations
and continue the subsidy for a fortnight.

* The phrase "on the lines of the Report" will be noticed. So far the
Labour representatives would go. They would not bring themselves
to "accept the Report."

Then followed this passage:

But since the discussions which took place last night [*i.e.* 9 p.m. to 1.15 a.m. on Saturday–Sunday] it has come to the knowledge of the Government that specific instructions have been sent under the authority of the General Council of the T.U.C. directing their members in several of the most vital industries and services of the Country to carry out a General Strike on Sunday next. Such action would involve a challenge to the constitutional rights and freedom of the nation. The Government must therefore require from the Trades Union Congress an unconditional withdrawal of the threat before it can continue negotiations.

The Cabinet then adjourned and reassembled at 9.30. Two hours later they were joined by the trio. Their conversation with the Trade Unionists, Pugh, Swales and Thomas, had issued in another formula which Baldwin himself had written down.

We [the T.U.C.] will urge the Miners to authorize us to enter upon a discussion, with the understanding that they and we accept the Report as a basis of settlement and we approach it with the knowledge that it may involve some reduction in wages.

They also, it appeared, regarded the First Formula as no more than a general impression. As regards measures towards a General Strike, no irrevocable step, they said, had been taken and the instructions would be withdrawn at once if conversations ended in a resumption of negotiations. At about 11.30 the Trade Unionists retired to consult the Miners; the Government representatives were uncommitted.

Such was the report brought back by Baldwin and his two colleagues to the Cabinet. They were discussing the position when, a little after midnight, word was brought that the strike had already started. Printers in the office of the *Daily Mail* had refused to print a leading article. By this action the situation was changed. The Note was therefore redrafted and the Prime Minister authorized to communicate it to the Labour committee. It now read:

It has come to the knowledge of the Government not only that specific instructions have been sent under the authority of the executive of the Trade Unions represented at the conference convened by the authority of the General Council of the T.U.C., directing their members in several of the most vital industries and services of the country to carry out a General Strike on Sunday next, but also that overt acts have already taken place including gross interference with the freedom of the press.

The Government must therefore require from the T.U.C. both a repudiation of the actions referred to that have already taken place and an unconditional withdrawal of this threat before it can continue negotiations.

This document, signed by Baldwin's secretary, Colonel Waterhouse, was handed by Baldwin at 12.45 to Pugh, Swales and Thomas, who took it to the Treasury Board Room, where the Miners were waiting. The Cabinet, which was sitting at No. 11, broke up; the Prime Minister went to bed. The Trade Unionists made their way out, and the General Strike had begun.

"Is it true," a friend once asked Baldwin, "that you went to bed to avoid receiving their surrender?" "No," he replied, "I had done all I could and there was nowhere else to go." One of the staff at Downing Street thought it his duty to inform the Palace. "That's all right, my dear fellow," came the answer; "the King doesn't read the *Daily Mail*." But, whoever might, or might not, read the *Daily Mail*, those luckless compositors had lost the game for their own side. The Government was ready: the Unions were not. The Unions were half-hearted: the public was resolved.

"As soon as the strike began, Baldwin was a passenger." Such was the verdict of one colleague, which other colleagues would hardly have contested. But—"don't forget," he once said to me, "the cleverest thing I ever did. I put Winston in a corner and told him to edit the *British Gazette*." Indeed, we have only to imagine Churchill, or Lloyd George or Neville Chamberlain, in control to realize what bitterness on both sides the dispute would have engendered. Or, on the other hand, what mischief might have followed if the preparations of the Government had been less complete or less skilfully brought to execution. A very few days were enough to show that the Strike—whatever its object—could not succeed. There was no life in it. Therefore there was no case for negotiation, and well-meant offers of mediation were received with the firm but polite assurance that no mediation was desired and that nothing less than unconditional surrender could be accepted. On May 10th the leading jurist on the Labour side, Sir Henry Slesser, said in the House that the legality of the strike could only be determined by the Courts and whatever this decision, Labour would obey it. Two days later Mr. Justice Astbury had before him an application by the Sailors' and Firemen's Union, which had not joined the strike, for an injunction against its own branch officers, who had. In giving judgment he declared the whole strike illegal. Fortified by this judgment, Sir John Simon charged the leaders of the strike as lawbreakers. Eminent legal authorities, then and since, have questioned the soundness of Astbury's law. But it was the golden bridge for a routed enemy. Pugh and his colleagues came to Downing Street at 12.20 on May 12th, and in a few minutes the news flashed round the world that the strike was over.

But if the Prime Minister had done nothing, he had spoken, and with effect. On May 6th he had broadcast his first message:

> Constitutional Government is being attacked. Let all good citizens whose livelihood and labour have thus been put in peril bear with fortitude and patience the hardships with which they have been so suddenly confronted. Stand behind the Government who are doing their part, confident that you will co-operate in the measures they have undertaken to preserve the liberties and privileges of the people of these islands. The laws of England are the people's birthright. Those laws are in your keeping. You have made Parliament their guardian. The General Strike is a challenge to Parliament, and is the road to anarchy and ruin.

On the 8th he gave a guarantee that all men who returned to work would be protected against loss of Trade Union benefit. That evening he delivered his longest broadcast, a full review of the position.

> The Trades Union Congress [he said] have only to cancel the General Strike and we shall immediately begin with the

utmost care and patience with them again the long laborious task which has been proceeding over these many weeks, of endeavouring to rebuild on an economic foundation the prosperity of the coal trade. . . . The General Strike must be called off absolutely and without reserve. The mining industry dispute can then be settled. . . .

I am a man of peace. I am longing and working and praying for peace. But I will not surrender the safety and the security of the British Constitution. You placed me in power eighteen months ago by the largest majority accorded any party for many, many years. Have I done anything to forfeit that confidence? Cannot you trust me to ensure a square deal for the parties—to secure even justice between man and man?

On May 12th:

The General Strike is over. . . . I shall without delay enter into negotiations with the object of adjusting those differences between owners and men in the coal trade which were engaging the constant attention of the Government at the moment when the General Strike so unhappily emerged.

In short, the Strike was a paragraph in a long narrative of suspicion and obstinacy, which the Prime Minister would set himself to end: a great undertaking at a great moment. Rightly the Cabinet placed on record their appreciation of the part which the reputation and position of the Prime Minister in the country had played in the unconditional withdrawal of the strike notices and which they felt would be of inestimable value in the reconstruction following the Strike.

And in reply to the King's congratulations Baldwin wrote:

If there was one mission more than another which as Your Majesty's first servant it has been my dearest wish to fulfil, it was to lessen the misunderstandings which threaten industrial strife, and to prevent the possibility of such conflicts as the one from which we are emerging.

At the moment when it might have seemed that these hopes had been in vain and that amid great national and personal disappointment it was necessary to start again at the beginning, I am touched, Sir, beyond measure by the kind message of sympathy and trust which Your Majesty sends me, and am inspired with renewed confidence and strength to face the immediate problems which must arise in connection with the return of our industries to normal conditions and the restoration of peace in the coal industry.

Your Majesty's words of encouragement, supported as they are by the spirit of fair play and the inborn common sense of your people, reassure my faith in a brighter and better future leading to that final and lasting settlement which can alone secure the prosperity of Your Majesty's Kingdom, Dominions and Empire.

NOTE

It is perhaps well to put on record here the nature of the organization for maintaining supplies and transport. It rested on the Emergency Powers Act of 1920, directed against any movement which was "calculated to deprive any substantial proportion of the community of the essentials of life." In July 1923 Sir John Anderson reported on the actual state of the organization: the officials went on meeting all through the Labour interim of 1923, and in November 1924 the Home Secretary laid the results of their deliberations before the new Cabinet.

The scheme was that, under the general direction of a Cabinet Committee, each department should be responsible for some defined field of action. The Board of Trade would accumulate adequate stocks and arrange for local distribution; the Ministry of Transport for distribution at a distance and electrical supply. The Home Office would see to the maintenance of law and order; the Ministry of Labour would occupy itself with conciliation and avoid any form of recruitment which could be regarded as strike breaking. That was left to voluntary agencies; and it was foreseen that some special executive might be required for protection and publicity.

The country was mapped in eleven areas, each with a Civil Commissioner, a junior member of the Government, and an Inspector of the Ministry of Health as Staff Officer, to stimulate local activity—the eighty-eight Voluntary Service Committees under local notables—and to co-ordinate local services and the local branches of the national services. Each Commissioner had a departmental staff for Finance, Food, Coal, Transport, Postal Work and Shipping, a police officer, and a military liaison officer. These officers were to receive preliminary directions from their Departments, but on the emergency being declared they put themselves at the disposal of the Civil Commissioner, who in case of violence was to exercise all the powers of the Government. Fourteen departments in all were represented on the central co-ordinating Committee; but it was realized that if the emergency was acute the whole organization would have to be simplified down to provision for Food, Fuel and Transport; Communications; Finance; Publicity; and the protection of loyal subjects. There was some difference of opinion as to whether the secrecy which had been strictly maintained before the strikes of 1919 and 1920 should be, or indeed could be, observed. No public statement was made, but from time to time some hints were dropped, which appear for the most part to have been ignored. It seems certain that none of the Labour leaders in 1926 had any idea of the extent or thoroughness of the preparations made to encounter a general strike.

CHAPTER XIII

AFTER THE STRIKE

On the morrow of the General Strike Baldwin held in public regard a position to which it is not easy to find a parallel in English history, because it is not easy to find a parallel to the emotion which flooded the country, and indeed spread across the seas, to the Continent and America. At no time since the victory of 1918 had our name stood higher in Europe than in that summer of 1926 when, for an Englishman, a journey through Europe was a progress from one group of admirers to another. Reading the episode in the baleful light that streamed from Moscow, observers in France, in Germany, in Scandinavia saw it as a revolutionary challenge accepted by one brave, skilful man and defeated by the unanimous response which his dexterity and courage evoked. And if the challenge was a warning, the victory—I noticed this in conversations all the way across Europe— was taken, wistfully and at times almost despairingly, as one proof more of what the English could do. And for Baldwin that was enough. Colleagues busy with the next step found him indifferent and languid. The Party was calling out for guidance, and no guidance was to be had. "'Leave it alone,' I said, 'we are all so tired.'"

One at least of his younger colleagues was ready to go forward, and at once. This was Arthur Steel-Maitland, Minister of Labour. Moderate men, he wrote, both in the Trade Unions and among the Socialist intellectuals were troubled in mind. They did not want revolution but they were bewildered. Now therefore was the time to propound the terms of a genuine industrial peace, now, while the country still had confidence in the Prime Minister, and the Trade Unionists' suspicion of some reactionary "hidden hand" overbearing him had not hardened into positive hostility. To proceed with Trade Union legislation regardless of its reactions on the industrial position as a whole would stultify the Government as a peace-making influence. "We cannot wield a sword in one hand—even if it be in reality but the phantom of a sword—and at all convincingly proffer an olive branch in the other." He suggested therefore that the Prime Minister should approach Philip Snowden on one side and Montagu Norman, Governor of the Bank of England, on the other, and having secured their sympathy, draw in Pugh and Bevin, "the ablest leader in the Trade Union movement, with a combination of practical ability and imagination greater than that of any other." Who could speak for the employers was a doubtful point. But—"Shall we go on? The chances are that we shall fail. But if we succeed . . ."

To this appeal I can trace no response whatever. Yet it might well have been thought that the Destinies had led Baldwin, at the right moment, to the very place where he could act most effectually and decisively, where in fact he had only to do what he had for years being saying. Those who can recall that summer will know that by his handling of the General Strike Baldwin had won the prestige of an enchanter. Nothing seemed beyond his powers: whatever might happen, "Baldwin will think of something." And, putting the extremists on both sides out of the field, the whole country was calling out for industrial peace.

And the broadcast promise, the square deal, and even justice between man and man?

The immediate outcome of it all was, perhaps inevitably, a suspension of the Seven Hours Act by a measure which passed its second reading on June 29th. For the first time since he entered Parliament, Baldwin was the object of a personal attack. Innocent, stupid Lansbury had published in his *Labour Weekly* a statement of Baldwin's holding in the family business, from which it appeared that nearly a quarter of a million of the capital belonged to the Prime Minister. There followed a furious scene in the House. Baldwin rose, and in his quietest tones admitted that he held the shares. They were the bulk of his fortune. Had he sold them in the war, he would now be a rich man. But for five years they had paid no dividend and he expected no return for years to come. The storm broke out again on the third reading. One member was suspended for calling him a murderer. Hartshorn, a moderate man whom Baldwin liked, denounced him as the greatest enemy of the working classes in the present generation. Baldwin, quite undisturbed, suggested that if both sides would return to the Report of March they would find a way out of their troubles.

"I always thought," one critic remarked, "that the Baldwin of 1926 stood on a moral level to which I am not sure that he ever returned. He might have done anything. He did nothing. And ever after he seemed to be trading on an accumulated fund of confidence which was never replenished." The truth is rather that after the General Strike he was in one of those moods of exhaustion and collapse which followed on the hour of decision, resolve, success: on the effort to maintain his nervous balance, to suppress his natural timidity. Years afterwards I noticed how often he would recall trifling incidents of those twelve days, instances of good humour and fair play between strikers and soldiers: as if he was trying in retrospect to recover the confidence he had not really felt. He had won, true. But the strain had left him weakened in nerve and body, and to his natural languor was now added a self-protective shrinking from such encounters. "Sick in body, far more sick in mind," was the judgment of one lobby correspondent. "The heart of a tired man has gone on strike," was his doctor's verdict. Seven years later, we shall see, another unexpected shock in a very different field worked even more powerfully, and in a way calamitous to himself and to his country.

The strike, ill-contrived and ill-executed, had failed. Failed, moreover, in part from half-heartedness within, but still more certainly from public disapproval without. Conceive, however, a situation in which the Unions were wholehearted and well-led and reinforced by public sympathy against an unpopular Government. What was to prevent a second engagement? Certainly not a few lines in an Act of Parliament. Then why legislate at all? Or why not legislate equally for a General Lockout? What, for that matter, was a General Strike? How could a single definition be

framed to cover movements varying in all their circumstances? Was the upheaval of 1926 itself a general strike or,
as Clynes elegantly phrased it, a sympathetic strike on an
extensive scale? And what extension of sympathy between
two, or three, or four trade unions amounts to the coercion
of government? Baldwin, with his usual candour, acknowledged that he would have preferred a two-line bill—a
general strike is illegal, intimidation is illegal. But he explained, somewhat lamely, that such language, he was
advised, could not be put in a statute.

The debate in which these innocent words were spoken was
opened on May 2nd 1927 by the Attorney General, Douglas
Hogg, who for two hours and more battled against a storm
of angry interruptions. Hogg was followed for the Opposition
by Clynes and Slesser; by Macmillan, who gave the Bill the
approval of the younger Tories; and Spencer, lately expelled
from the Labour Party. The third day was Simon's, who saw
no difficulty in framing a short declaratory bill, and Baldwin's, whose speech was in effect an apologia for his change
of front. He had averted a collision in 1925, first by the withdrawal of Macquisten's bill, then by the subsidy. But his
trust in the good sense of the people had not been answered
by events—the extremists had forced the General Strike,
and then, sliding into one of those historic retrospects which
he always, and commonly his audience too, enjoyed, he
went on:

> Side by side with the fact that . . . the Governments of the day
> have entrusted to the machinery of trade unions certain work
> in connection with social legislation, and side by side with the
> fact that you have many trade unions . . . of whom the public
> have not heard much, because they have succeeded in com-
> posing troubles in their own industries without causing trouble
> to other people outside—side by side with these two facts
> you have the fact that in some unions you have the power
> gradually getting into the hands of what to-day is called the
> Minority Movement.

Bromley, of the Engineers, rose. Would the Prime Minister
give one instance in the whole Trade Union world where a
union was in the hands of the Minority Movement? "I am
not going to quote names," Baldwin replied. And answering

shouts of "Withdraw," he snapped, "Nor shall I withdraw."
Then the storm broke. With difficulty, and the suspension of
one member, the Speaker restored order and Baldwin resumed his speech. But he had made his point, and the wrath
with which his words had been received was proof, as he
demurely remarked, that the Minority Movement was not
popular on the Labour benches. He knew his ground. Only
a few days before, a Communist had proposed, at a conference of union officials, that steps should be taken to prepare
a general strike in opposition to the bill. He was voted down
by an immense majority, one speaker remarking that the
Communists were as much the enemies of the working classes
as the Tories. A few months of attempted negotiation with
the Russian comrades carried that same speaker one step
further. "We have different moral standards," he said. It
was Ernest Bevin.

To trust the Trade Unions; to imbue them, no difficult
task, with his own contempt for the doctrinaires; and to
keep the gap between constitutional and revolutionary
socialism wedged open, was the line which Baldwin had
steadily pursued. The Trades Disputes Bill was a deviation
under pressure. Left to himself he would undoubtedly have
let bygones be bygones. As he said in his last broadcast on
the strike: forget all recriminations, waste no time in deter-
mining the share of blame: look forward and not backward.
But he was the leader of a party, and "parties, like snakes,
are moved by the tail." Legally and materially, the new
Act made hardly the slightest difference in the relations of
capital and labour. Foreign consuls reported to their em-
bassies that it excited very little public interest either way.
But the party demanded it and so the party must have it.
Again and again messages had come from the Trade Union
side begging him at least to order an enquiry into the state of
the law before he asked Parliament to change it. He ignored
them all. With the laying of the Trades Disputes Bill, the
Disraelian make-believe rolled away like a morning mist
and revealed the Conservative Party armed and accoutred

to keep the Unions in their places and arrest the growth of
the Parliamentary Labour Party. The Conservatives were,
in fact, determined to make a party triumph out of what,

rightly viewed, was a national victory, and Baldwin put
himself in their hands.

An incident following shortly after seemed to show that
he had lost all control of his Cabinet, not to say all interest
in its doings. While the Bill was still before Parliament the
public was startled by an announcement which suggested
that the Conservative Party had taken leave of its senses.
A plan was published for a new House of Lords, part
nominated by the Government of the day, part elected by the
peers, with power to force an appeal to the country in all
cases of difference with the Commons. The Opposition at
once asked for a day to move a vote of censure. Baldwin
offered but a languid defence—the proposals were very like
those of Lloyd George five years before, they were only published for criticism and ventilation; in a word, though the
word was not spoken, they might sink or swim: the Prime
Minister did not greatly care. Then, close on this unlucky
episode, came a revolt in that quarter of the political horizon
where Tory principles had seemed inveterate. A speech in
Lincolnshire on July 21st set the farmers raging in all parts of
the kingdom. They wanted Protection. Baldwin was bound
by repeated pledges not to give it.

The situation of the Government was not happy. The
miners were still wretched, and still obstinate. When Baldwin
took his holiday, he left Churchill to negotiate. At once the
temperature rose, and a long session ended in an emphatic
refusal to treat: "We are not going to settle: we are going to
fight." The Liberal Party was preparing a midway policy for
the next election; the Conservative Party was divided and
distrustful. Yet the truth, as Baldwin's instinct told him, was
that the country liked him, and on the whole preferred
him to any alternative leader in sight and in any direction.
Labour did not want Lloyd George; the country did not
want MacDonald. And when it came to the party, under
whose name could they go down to battle? Meanwhile the
healing process was at work in industry. Let it work, work
without interference, unless the Head of the Family was
called in, to ease some stiffness or turn some corner. That is
what Prime Ministers are there for. And for that part Baldwin was fitted as much by his weakness as by his strength.

To evade all action, to avoid all decision; to give his ministers their run; to reserve himself for the moment when something more was at stake than a party victory or a Parliamentary rebuff; and that something always the same—the
unity of the nation embodied in Parliament and expressed
in the honourable conflicts of constitutional debate. And here
he could be stern, with his party and with the House. More
than once or twice followers received sharp reprimands
for some breach of courtesy towards the Labour Party. On
the other hand, no demonstration in the House would move
him from the line he had decided to take. An occasion came
in the closing days of this session.

MacDonald had moved a vote of censure on the Government, on November 16th, for their neglect of the distress and
unemployment in the mining industry. From the outset he
made it clear that the Opposition would not accept a departmental reply, and as he unrolled the story—always the
same story—of distress among the miners, it was hardly to
be denied that the matter was one which affected the
Government as a whole. Baldwin, now as ever, would not
stand between a departmental minister and his responsibilities. When MacDonald sat down, Cunliffe Lister, President of the Board of Trade, rose to reply. The Opposition
broke into a roar of "Prime Minister." Baldwin sat unmoved.
Questions, precedents, points of order hurtled through the
stormy air and the Speaker suspended the sitting till six
o'clock. But the Opposition resumed their outcries and the
Speaker, judging that they did not wish the debate to continue, adjourned the House.

On the next day MacDonald returned to the charge.
Would the Prime Minister make a statement himself on the
intentions of the Government? Baldwin replied that the
Opposition could have heard its intentions if they had
listened, and MacDonald gave notice of a vote of protest
against the Prime Minister for evading his responsibility. His
speech on moving the vote was temperate but acute, and
Baldwin took occasion not only to justify his abstention but
to give his views on the office of Leader. It was a theme to
which he often returned in conversation. Once he said that
the ideal arrangement was a Prime Minister in the Lords

and a friend whom he could thoroughly trust leading the Commons—Salisbury and Balfour for example. "And if he cannot trust him?" "Then Rosebery and Harcourt! But it is a puzzle, and I never quite saw the answer."

> The work of Leader of this House is no sinecure, and the more closely the Prime Minister attends to the business of this House the heavier the burden, because he is often taken away from work that he ought to be doing, and this makes more difficult the performance of his daily duties.

MacDonald could not carry both parts; Lloyd George could not—

> And the day may come . . . when it may be impossible for the Prime Minister to lead the House of Commons, and the actual Leadership will have to be performed by a Minister delegated for that purpose. But then the question arises, in what Debates ought the Leader of the House to participate?

As a matter of fact, this was not the question at all, because it was not for the Leader but for the Prime Minister that the Opposition had shouted. So, skating swiftly over this thin place, Baldwin settled down to one of those fatherly discourses which, if they sometimes provoked a cynical comment from the intelligentsia, always touched the conscience of the House, not least of the Opposition. But then, as Baldwin was fond of saying, "the intelligent are to the intelligentsia what a gentleman is to a gent."

> When I was a young Member of Parliament I learned that such demonstrations, instead of being, as I expected, regarded as something rather heroic in the country, did nothing to add to our popularity and tended to lose us a great many votes. . . . I think it was the realisation of that fact that led the Leaders of the Opposition to put down this motion in the hope that it would pull their party together and make the country forget that demonstration of bad manners which they copied from other parties in their less wise moments. . . . There is a precedent for everything. . . . The only novelty . . . was that as I left the House there was a sound of hissing which had been heard in this House but for once before, and which in this country has always been peculiar to a bird that walks on the village green.

Under this bland treatment, the Opposition was almost purring with affection renewed.

Disorder has never achieved its end. There is not a single man in any of the three parties who would yield for one instant to clamour.... Never, never, in this House, or in any House of our people, can it achieve what those who create these disturbances hope to achieve.

"This House, or any House of our people." I often thought, talking over occasions and incidents like these, that the ruling passion in Baldwin's intricate spirit was pride —pride in the England which had created Parliament: pride in Parliament, at once so august and so homely; and pride in himself as the leader of Parliament, the symbol and organ of national unity. To be in touch with the Commons was more than his duty, it was his delight. "He made the humblest member feel that he was Somebody." But, as I have said, it was a delight purchased by the neglect of much that a Prime Minister ought not to neglect. A modern Cabinet is a great administrative organ, and for administration Baldwin had no liking. Here his weaknesses were all too plain. His interests were narrow, his study superficial; and of those long hours which the ʟeader spent on the Treasury Bench far too many were stolen from the other and not less imperative duties of a Prime Minister.

In Henry Cockburn's *Memorials of his Time* the reader will encounter a character of Robert Blair, which, with some allowances, might pass for a study of Baldwin.

Too solid for ingenuity, and too plain for fancy, soundness of understanding was his peculiar intellectual quality. Within his range nobody doubted or could doubt Blair's wisdom. Nor did it ever occur to anyone to question his probity. . . . He had one quality, or rather habit, so marked that it was the only one by which some people knew him, and which affected all his proceedings. It was generally called laziness . . . he had certainly a great taste for contemplative repose, and . . . this of course implied a considerable extinction of vulgar labour, and a great aversion to many of the efforts that public men are often required to make, and to many of the occupations in which they are often expected to engage.... This dislike of disturbance . . . disinclined him from meddling with the thousand little teasing and degrading affairs in which men of influence get involved.... In dignity, sense, honesty and . . . in repose, he was an absolute rock.

Such certainly, or something very like it, was the picture of himself that Baldwin at sixty had projected on the vision of close observers. To the common people everywhere he was the honest man in politics, a profession not fertile in honesty. To the Labour Party a fair opponent. To impatient followers sometimes an enigma, sometimes an exasperation. But with that one gift which made him indispensable to the party: "My worst enemy could not say of me that I do not understand the English people." He had staked everything on his conviction of their ultimate, essential reasonableness. And, after all, he had been right. Late in December the Trades Union Congress accepted an invitation from twenty-four leaders of industry to confer together over the whole range of industrial organization and well-being. The times were favourable. Not for years had employment been so abundant or trade so prosperous. In spite of the Trades Disputes Act, bygones *were* bygones. At home; and abroad the spirit of reasonableness was working too, in France and Germany. And there was a place for Russia also if only Russia would answer to the liberality and good will of England. It was a contented Prime Minister that travelled down to Worcestershire that Christmas.

One unpleasant shock, indeed, his administration had received. Robert Cecil had been sitting, with Bridgeman, on the Naval Disarmament Conference at Geneva. Believing himself to be inadequately supported in the Cabinet and obstructed by the Admiralty, he suddenly resigned in a vehement and bitter letter which only reached Baldwin after his return from Canada. Baldwin, failing to placate the indignant man and unwilling to postpone his annual holiday, departed for Aix leaving an unresolved Cabinet crisis behind him. Characteristic, but assuredly most unwise; because to slight Robert Cecil was to offend that great body of opinion which he represented, and which was organized in the League of Nations Union. Years later Baldwin said that he owed his personal misfortunes to the Union; in this incident we may see the beginning of the mischief. And it is not to be forgotten that the Geneva Conference showed a profound uneasiness in the relations of England and America. "It is only by a figure of speech that war between us can be called unthinkable." In such a war, what would be the fate of the Dominion? Or of England?

Early that year, the theme being China, Churchill had written:

> Short of being actually conquered, there is no evil worse than submitting to wrong or violence for fear of war. Once you take the position of not being able in any circumstances to defend your rights against the aggression of some particular set of people, there is no end to the demands that will be made or to the humiliation that must be accepted.

It is the voice of 1934.

CHAPTER XIV

DECLINE

THE visit to Canada with the Prince of Wales in 1927 was the most timely restorative that Baldwin could have taken. Certainly it was a crowded spell—of set speeches to public assemblies and a "few words" at every railway halt. But it gave him the opportunity, as he liked to say, of interpreting England to Canada; and in return Canada ministered abundantly to that romantic appetite which was always asking for satisfaction. As a young man he had seen Montreal and thought that never had mankind found a more beautiful spot on which to build a great city; and he returned, thirty-seven years later, Prime Minister of the Mother Country. The release from London, from Parliament, from Europe, gave a new elasticity to his mind, and nowhere did he speak so lucidly, or paint his pictures with so full-charged a brush or colours so winning. He spoke of the pioneers: of Mackenzie, paddling

> northward on the great river ... until at last he saw the whales blowing in the icy seas of the north;

of Fraser,

> with his curious temper and ambitions and honest heart, boring his way through the Rockies;

and asked :

> Who was the Great White Slave who gave his name to the lake? Who was the unknown caller whose lonely voice gave the name to the valley of Qu'Appelle? Who were the strong men who named Fort Resolution, Fort Enterprise, Fort Reliance and Fort Confidence? And who was so hungry at Hungry Hall?

It was not only an indulgence of his fancy. The history of Canada, the coming together of French and English; of Loyalists from the Old Colonies and settlers from Scotland;

the gradual achievement of unity, and variety preserved within that unity; all this to Baldwin was a manifestation on the grandest scale of what he most profoundly believed —that the way to peace and prosperity, within a nation and between the nations, lay in the adjustment of individual personality, ripened in freedom, to the necessity of co-operation, without which there can be no order. This adjustment is never perfect: it needs continual modification in accordance with the common sense of those who know the value of both. And those who do will know also that, politics being an experimental science, mistakes are bound to occur, that problems have to be solved *ambulando*: that the desire for precise definitions may split a State as it split the Christian Church; that statesmen are not architects but gardeners working on such material as only nature can furnish, and that they never pull up a plant to see how the roots are doing. Governed, self-governed, on these principles a state may call itself a democracy. But democracy is the hardest of all political systems to maintain. It is always on the knife edge:

> Or, as I have often expressed it, it is a certain point on the circumference of a wheel. How often has mankind travelled on the circumference of that wheel, working its way . . . to a point that you could call democracy. Go but a little farther and democracy becomes licence, licence becomes anarchy, and then the wheel goes full circle and anarchy comes back to tyranny, and man has to fight his way back out of tyranny once again.

We stand secure. Or so we are convinced. But democracy can be maintained only if the common man and the woman and the child at school mean to make their community stronger, but also freer. And on this axis, between these poles, Baldwin's thoughts perpetually revolved. It was not a political doctrine so much as an inner experience, the certitude of the mystic interfused with the pride of the Englishman, the domestic pride of the provincial and his homely loyalties. Some years later he went, "as every Worcestershire man is bound to go," to Gheluvelt, and he told the Canadian Pilgrimage in Westminster Hall what had befallen him there.

> I remember walking along that road on which every regiment in the British Army at one time or another marched through

the Valley of the Shadow of Death. And I had a conscious-
ness there, which I have never had before or since, that the
vibrant air was full of something, and the roads were full,
and I seemed to be pushing my way along. I know that that
feeling must have been with you at Vimy, that feeling that
you are being watched by an unseen cloud of witnesses;
and those witnesses are our dead who are speaking to us to-day.

But the business man had his word to say also, and, free for
once from party obligations, Baldwin gave his Canadian
hearers a plain account, an interpretation of English industry
as he saw it. We had taken too much for granted. We had
supposed that because the constant interchange of primary
and manufactured goods and the perfect system of banking
and credit that had grown up unperceived always had existed, so it always would exist. Then came the war; markets
were broken, credit destroyed; and all our policy abroad
had been conducted to one end, to restore credit and ensure
peace. But at the same time the apportionment of wages to
the competitive power of industry had been violently disturbed, and had to be rebuilt, while in our pursuit of peace
we were bringing infinite suffering on the great armament
and shipbuilding industries.

> Put yourself in the place of the working man who remembers
> the time before the war, when things were stable, when there
> were well-marked differences in wage conditions between
> the skilled man and the unskilled . . . and you can imagine the
> discomfort and irritation which he feels in the uncertainty of
> the whole position as well as in the difficulty in many of the
> trades, which he remembers as stable and steady . . . of getting
> regular employment.

And then—a favourite theme—the war had made in four
years changes that in normal times would have been spread
over half a century. No wonder the whole fabric was groan-
ing and creaking, as the pieces came into place. The wounds
were obvious, more obvious than the signs of health.

> But the wise doctor . . . knows the meaning of those healing
> currents of life which are moving again upon their task through-
> out the body politic.

Whether or not Baldwin had interpreted England to Canada,
he had certainly interpreted himself.

But Strabo, the Geographer, tells of a native of Aeolian Kyme who wrote a history of the world in which he desired that his birthplace should make a good figure. Only, nothing had ever happened there. So he ended each book with the sentence: "Throughout this period the people of Aeolian Kyme enjoyed profound tranquillity." Following the process of Conservative decay in the years from 1927 to 1929, the historian must sometimes lift his head from his papers and ask, "What was the Prime Minister doing then?" Only once in fourteen years, Austen Chamberlain said, had he known Baldwin influence a Cabinet decision—at the time of the Political Levy Bill of 1925—and, between the Canadian visit and the election eighteen months later, the Prime Minister seemed to be little more than an amiable observer of events, at home and abroad, which, even if he had the power, he had no will to direct or control. Foreign affairs were Chamberlain's business. Finance was Churchill's, and the hundred-horse-power mind was racing. Strike £10,000,000 off the Service estimates, put £15,000,000 on the motoring public. Odds and ends make up a mass of manœuvre £30,000,000 strong—all for relief of rates, and the astonishment and gratitude of the ratepayers. And Protection?

"If you worship a mulberry bush when you are a child," Bonar Law once said, "you will worship it when you are old." There was still a great and solid body of opinion hostile to Protection in any form. There was a counter-body, well represented in the Cabinet, which believed in Protection as the sole available means of checking the decline of industry and the chronic malady of unemployment. By early conviction Baldwin was a Protectionist. But he was pledged to resist any general measure of Protection and in particular any taxes on food. And he never forgot Plymouth. Nor did he forget that the new electorate, based at last by the Equal Franchise Act on the Universal Suffrage towards which we had been moving for a hundred years, needed new handling. So—to hold the Party together while experience and reflection wore down the Cobdenite tradition; to impress on the multitude the notion of himself as the honest man who would not go beyond his pledges; to charm one audience after another not as a politician but as the most English

of Englishmen; and, more gravely and earnestly, to keep
debate on the high level of principle, and let the gutter press
froth as it liked; thus to lift the party over the next election
on a wave of confidence in himself while in the meantime
colleagues went their way as they liked—somehow thus one
may think of Baldwin in those months when to outward
seeming the Conservative Government was sliding into a
slumbrous exhaustion such as had overtaken it twenty-five
years before. But, seen from afar, there was something more.

I should like [so Birdwood, Commander-in-Chief in India,
wrote] to tell you how entirely I have admired your actions
while you have held the office of Prime Minister. I think perhaps we may come from something of the same stock—the
yeoman stock of the West of England, though I, being a
Devonshire man, come from farther west and south than you
do. My forebears were entirely rooted in Devon, and so out
of the world that it was difficult for them to get away much
from it. In consequence we have all inherited a very deep
love of the county and its people. Reading all your speeches,
I have felt that the same feelings which actuate me, live also
in you.

I can confidently state that it has meant much to us Englishmen in distant parts of the world to know that our country
is represented by a real, true, straight, brave Englishman—
without, I believe, a single thought of unkindness, malice, or
anything that could approach what might be regarded as
mean or crooked. I am using no vain words when I honestly
say that this has meant a very great deal to myself, and also
to many others who, like myself, may be regarded as vested
with but brief authority and who I hope are doing our best
to uphold the traditions of England out here.

If I might thank you specially for one of your actions it
would be your selection of Lord Irwin as Viceroy. He, I am
sure, is actuated by exactly the same feelings as you are, and
to me it has been the greatest delight to be intimately associated from day to day with such a real fine character—like
yourself, so entirely true, straight and honest. May God bless
you in your work and in all that is yet before you.

In 1928 indeed the country was, politically, in slack water.
Equal Franchise, or the Flapper Vote (another of Bonar
Law's pledges), kept the cartoonists so busy that there was

little room in the public fancy for graver matters. A bad
fall at Chequers left Baldwin in great pain, and a sympathetic
House watched him speaking with difficulty on a Ministry
of Defence in March. He recovered; and at Welbeck on
May 26th he delivered one of his most comprehensive
speeches to the largest audience he ever addressed. In
1926, he told them, we had kept our heads. We had re-
established our confidence in the eternal sanity of the
Englishman. And there were three things to which the
minds of the electors should be addressed—political liberty:
economic enterprise (a few days before he had told the cotton
industry to cut out dead wood and reorganize): and Imperial responsibility. We were not an unhappy country: the
standard of living for the employed, of maintenance for the
unemployed, was not surpassed anywhere. But the functions
of Parliament were changing from political to economic. So
—let masters and men come together to make experiments:
let voters be vigilant: let the honour of Parliament be upheld.

A week later he made a fresh conquest. "Which of my
speeches," he once asked me, "did you enjoy most?"
"The one on the Oxford Dictionary." "I knew you would
say that: so did I." Then, on July 21st, he is expounding
Agricultural Credits and Rating Reform to an immense
rural audience in Yorkshire, and, four days later, presenting
a car to Lord Balfour on his eightieth birthday, with a
balance over to pay his motoring fines. Then to Aix, and,
returning, he spoke to the Party assembled in Yarmouth,
and preparing for a not distant election.

> Mr. Snowden [he said], always cautious, and sometimes
> wise, says that the Conservative Party has never committed
> the folly of issuing a list of a few dozen items of reform which
> it proposes to carry out. Nor will it ever do so as long as I am
> leader.

But, comparing the programmes of the two Opposition
parties, he had come to the conclusion that Liberalism was
Socialism without the courage of its convictions. And, after
reciting the achievements of the Government at home and
abroad, he closed with an appeal for that personal confidence
which he was to need so sorely in the coming years.

I sprang from the rank and file, and they have trusted me in good times and bad. They stood by me after the election of 1923 when stout hearts wavered. They have followed my strategy without asking too many questions. They have trusted me. I ask you to continue that trust.

Fine and true, no doubt. But as one supporter remarked, harder hitting was wanted if the local workers were to be kept in fighting trim: more of the lion, and not quite so much of the lamb. Courtesy is a virtue: but need the Prime Minister look forward so blandly to the day when "Labour may be a great party—I hope for the sake of the nation it will"? Hobnobbing with the Socialists was a dangerous charge against more than one Conservative member. What else was the Leader doing?

A month later, at Aberystwyth, he took occasion to repay the generous language Haldane had used of him, in words which unconsciously pointed to his own demeanour in adversity:

[Haldane's] outstanding qualities were serenity, poise, sympathy. Never did he show himself more worthy of the name of wise man than when at the height of a brilliant career he fell before the most unfair and scurrilous campaign. And what would have soured most men left them, the sympathy, the poise, the serenity, unimpaired.

Finally, in the October of this well-spent year, he was induced to address the League of Nations Union.

Our descent [he said] is not only from the ape; it is from the tiger . . . the tiger instincts which are still there . . . are ready to be summoned from their hidden lair in a moment, and there are not two bodies of persons more potent to summon these ancient impulses than the politicians and the Press. . . . To make a vow . . . to sign a covenant . . . it is not enough. It savours of crying "Lord, Lord". . . . If this vow of renunciation is to be kept, it means a daily struggle until you fall into the grave. It is exactly the same in these old tiger instincts of human nature. You can only save yourself and the world by a constant daily fighting . . . and in time you will win. . . . Let me submit that from to-night onwards no member of the League of Nations Union shall add one drop to the fœtid stream of insinuation and suspicion and the attribution of low motives to statesmen of your own country or other countries. . . . The statesman who makes an observation doubting the good faith of . . . a foreign country for the sake of a cheer, the newspaper which puts in such paragraphs to make news—they are both of them doing the devil's work. . . .

You may think [he went on] that I have spoken much more . . . about peace at home than abroad. That is true, but . . . I believe that unless a country is at peace with itself the weight of that country's voice and influence are diminished in the councils of the world, and I think so much of the spirit and of the voice of our great country that I want it to be heard, recognised, and acknowledged. No country that is not at peace in itself can work effectively for peace outside its borders.

Then, very cautiously and briefly, he deplored the failure to reach agreement with the United States on Naval Armaments. He recalled the frankness and friendliness of his own negotiations over the Debt, and regretted profoundly the deep suspicion of England in American speeches and papers. "There is no echo here." At the Guildhall banquet a few days later it was noticed that in his review of affairs he said nothing of America. But at a Thanksgiving Dinner soon after he was as cheerful as a lark on tobacco and liberty, Mark Twain and Anna K. Greene. Certainly no speaker has ever commanded such a variety of manner and phrasing so variously apt. This very session he had fallen flat and heavy in a debate on Unemployment: the House was almost in tears of boredom. A few days later he was being pressed to explain certain differences of opinion disclosed in speeches of the Chancellor and the Home Secretary. Which of them was spokesman for the Government? One of them, the Prime Minister replied, stated, more eloquently, but less tersely, the policy I laid down myself. The other stated no policy at all. And then, memory casting up a phrase of a famous judge, "I am struck, not so much by the diversity of testimony, as by the manysidedness of truth." The House was in ecstasies—not least the Labour member who had elicited the reply. "How can you be angry with a man like that?" he said.

So we move to the dissolution of 1929 and the General Election. Baldwin fully expected to be returned to office, and was thinking how places were to be filled. Neville Chamberlain had certainly earned the Exchequer if he

cared to take it. Then where was Churchill to go? Birkenhead's dinner-table judgment was not far from Baldwin's:
"He is often right, but when he is wrong—my God!" It
would be a startling move—Churchill at the India Office.
And on the whole too dangerous. He might go right—but
if he went wrong! Nor, Baldwin found, was Birkenhead
to be tempted from the India Office to the Woolsack. And
Baldwin was beginning to think much of India: how to keep
it out of the seething pot of English politics: how to discharge
our pledges—a long series of pledges culminating in the
promise of May 1927:

> In the fulness of time we look forward to seeing her in equal
> partnership with the Dominions.

How to discharge those pledges, and yet not abandon our
trust, and the simple code—security without, security within,
clean government, protection of the depressed, and observ-
ance of the law? Here was indeed a problem for democracy,
the greatest perhaps that history had ever set.

But on the eve of the Election, our Ambassador in Paris
wrote to him:

> You have shown a far greater confidence in the people than
> either Liberal or Socialist.
> You have given democracy the finest opportunity of proving
> its worth when the Parliamentary régime is generally at a
> discount. You have taken the democratic horse to the best
> water that has yet been offered to it, but nobody, not even
> you, can make it drink!

His words came true. "Torpid, sleepy, barren," Lloyd
George called the Government, and the swing of the pendu-
lum was not to be checked by any recital of Conservative
achievements: hundreds of new schools, thousands of free
places, nearly a million houses, cheap electricity, untaxed
tea: our whole system of Local Government recast, six
hundred thousand more men at work: and the peace of the
world made more secure at Locarno. The electors, quite
simply, were tired of the Conservatives: the party was tired
of Austen Chamberlain, far too friendly to France: too
little friendly to the United States. On the whole, the Socialist
candidates were better briefed and better trained than their

opponents, and the distressed areas were still, and, as each
month passed, more bitterly, distressed. Nothing more is
needed to account for the Conservative reverse in 1929.

But one incident deserves to be recorded. Simon was
sitting for Spen Valley. The Conservative party had invited
one of the ablest of the new Tory generation, Maxwell Fyfe,
to stand. Baldwin intervened. Simon's duties, he pointed out,
as Chairman of the Statutory Commission on India were
most onerous. On its findings hung the destiny of India and
the Empire. He had allowed no considerations of fortune
or career to stand in the way. Let the Conservatives be no less
patriotic, no less generous, and withdraw their candidate
and their opposition.

An incident: but the highmindedness it reveals is not
common in political life, and not always appreciated in the
lower ranks. "Baldwin," it was sometimes said, "never
realises how bad people can be," and, listening to him when
he talked of old battles and old antagonists, I felt in him a
great unwillingness to think ill of any man—or, at least, if he
could not think well, to speak ill. Spinoza says somewhere
of the man "who knows virtues and their causes, that he will
never desire to contemplate the vices of men, to disparage
men, or to delight in a false show of liberty." Baldwin would
have satisfied this standard. He never disparaged a man,
and always found praise more congenial than blame. And
in the past year, 1928, he had delivered what by universal
consent was regarded as the noblest of all his commemorative
pieces, on the death of Asquith. He spoke of his eloquence,
his close reasoning, his judgment, so rarely at fault: his
integrity, his loyalty, a loyalty that wrought no evil and
thought no evil: his magnanimity that never harboured a
mean thought. And then:

> The deterioration of character which is so often seen in this
> world is more obvious to mankind when men have to face bitter
> and cruel disappointments. In the last years of his life he had to
> face such, and he faced them without bitterness, without blame,
> without self-pity, with no attempt at self-justification. He faced
> them with a dignity perfect and restrained, and towards
> the closing years of his life, as throughout his life, but never
> more than in those closing years, he conferred distinction on

the public life of this country and distinction on this House
which he had known so long. . . .

We turn aside to-day for a moment from controversy and
from business, and, as we leave this Chamber, we shall leave it
for this afternoon to darkness and silence. Into that darkness
and that silence we must all go when our time comes. May
it be our lot to leave behind to our friends as fragrant a
memory as Lord Oxford, and to our country a light, however
faint, to lighten the steps of those who come after.

CHAPTER XV

INDIA AND THE LEADERSHIP

THE political situation on the morrow of the defeat was very like that in 1923. The Liberals with fifty-nine seats held the balance between Labour with 287 and the Conservatives with 261. Baldwin was disappointed and hurt. Gratitude is not a political category, and the new women voters had on the whole inclined to Labour in the boroughs and to Lloyd George in the counties. Which was particularly ungrateful of them, because, as a certain pamphlet issued from the Conservative Central Office had reminded them,

> When you put on your very best pair of artificial silk, with extra-strong toes and double cotton tops, does it ever occur to you that not only are you clothing your shapely legs in beautiful silk stockings, but you have also found one of the many things for which you should say thank you to the Conservative Government?

Baldwin's personal popularity was unaffected. He was still "the most generally trusted and acceptable personality in public life." But his party had been defeated, not on any clear issue, but on an accumulation of grievances and misgivings, against which the Conservatives had little to set by way of reassurance. Yet on votes they had a slight majority (8,666,243 against 8,360,883), while the Liberal Party with a poll of over 5,000,000 had less than 60 seats in the new house.

Many years later a lively Socialist summed up the relative positions of the three parties in the phrase—all Tories are Socialists, all Socialists are Tories: the people are Liberal, but they take Liberalism for granted and will not vote for it. In domestic affairs Liberalism was the party of moderate reform. But those who laid the emphasis on moderation felt safer with the Conservatives, those who wanted action naturally moved leftwards to the party which at least was untried. The Socialists might make a difference, the Conservatives certainly would not. And if Safety First was the word, even Conservatives might in secret hold that the national finances at least were safer in the hands of Philip Snowden than of Winston Churchill. But the relative position of parties made it certain that there would be no organic change in the social or economic structure of the country. Disarmament would be pursued more actively; Public Assistance would be administered more humanely: that, really, was all that the change from Baldwin to MacDonald meant. And it was hardly a secret that MacDonald and Baldwin were much nearer to one another than either was to certain elements, certain persons, in his own party. Rarely have the leaders of two parties lived on such terms of political intimacy and regard. The warning not to write history backwards is never more needed than in the years which closed with the catastrophe of 1939. But a moderate infusion of the prophetic gift might have led an observer in 1929 to speculate on the possibility at least of a union between Snowden, MacDonald and Baldwin to heal the disorders of the State.

If, indeed, Baldwin was still Leader of the Conservatives when their time came. He had lost two elections, and lost them in two different ways: one by his impetuosity; the other by—and here the whisperings became vocal—by his languor, his lack of fighting power, his too well marked sympathy with the other side. "If," said one exasperated supporter, "if he is a Gladstonian Liberal let him lead the Liberals. If he is a Socialist, Labour would no doubt be glad to have him. But he can't lead the Conservatives as a mixture of both." Those who thought thus did not always reckon with a vein, not often displayed, of tenacity in Baldwin's character—and in his wife's character too. He knew his weaknesses as well as his most persistent critics knew them. But he also knew that, in the crude language of the Whips' office, he was the greatest electoral asset that the Party had ever had. There he was without equal or second. If fate had removed him from the scene before the election, under what leader would the Conservatives have fought?

And what would the outcome have been? How many votes would Neville Chamberlain have lost, and how many Winston Churchill?

Of not less consequence to his party, of far greater consequence to the country, was Baldwin's unchallengeable ascendancy in the House of Commons. I asked him once how he prepared his speeches. He said, "There is a cloud round my mind, it takes shape, and then I know what to say."* Sometimes, when he was tired, or the material too bulky to absorb, it would not take shape, and then the speech would be toneless and lifeless. But when the mood and the occasion met, few speakers have ever had the Commons so completely in hand.

His deliberate, patient courtesy—deliberate, because he chafed under bores, and most members of Parliament can be bores sometimes and some of them bores all the time—is only part of the secret. It was said, "When you listen to Churchill you think of the speaker; when you listen to Baldwin you think of the speech." Of all the great orators in our history, it is to Baldwin that a Greek would have awarded the palm for *charis*—grace, ease, charm: alluring listeners to agree with him if they could, and, if they could not, at least to listen. Very rarely did he have to encounter an unfriendly reception, and if there was some noise or disturbance when he rose, he would drop his voice—never try to outshout an interruptor, was another of his rules—so that members hushed themselves, and one another, to hear. To this add—a steady irradiation of humour, never unkindly, sometimes flippant, and flippant perhaps more often than a fastidious taste would approve or an impatient judgment endure; and a modest bearing which saved his earnestness from the least shadow of the homiletic, and which was in truth the outward expression of what at all times he felt most deeply, the immense significance of statesmanship and the immense insignificance of politics and politicians.

To Baldwin the ultimate aim and object of English statesmanship was plain and unalterable—the unity of the

---

* The Highland seer ! " His Lordship mauna speak to Allan now, the cloud is upon his mind."

English people in a changing and difficult world. And in that
autumn of 1929 there was one theme—not unemployment,
not disarmament—a theme to which we may be sure not one
voter in a thousand had given a thought, for which

> it is essential for our country and essential for the Empire
> that we face the world as a united Parliament. For that we
> shall want the best work that this House can give: that, more
> than anything else we shall have to face, will be the supreme
> test of how fit we are for the democratic conditions under
> which we have to work.

This theme was India.

The India Reform Act of 1919 provided that at the end of
ten years a Royal Commission should be appointed to enquire into its working. On November 8th 1927 Baldwin told
the House that the term would be anticipated and the Commission appointed forthwith. The necessary bill was passed
through Parliament, the Opposition lending their support,
and the Commission, Sir John Simon and six colleagues,
left for India early in the following year for a preliminary
tour. A second visit was made in the autumn of 1928. But
the prospects of an agreed Constitution for India were so
unpromising that the Viceroy came home to consult with
the authorities in England. The Act of 1919, following on
the Declaration of 1917, had spoken of British India
attaining "its due place among our Dominions," but
Dominion was a term which had not then been precisely
defined. By 1929 the idea had taken a positive shape, the
name a concrete meaning. On October 30th 1929 the Viceroy on behalf of His Majesty's Government

> stated clearly that, in their judgment, it is implicit in the
> Declaration of 1917 that the natural issue of India's con-
> stitutional progress as there contemplated is the attainment
> of Dominion Status.

The Viceroy's statement was published at once in London,
and, very naturally, the question immediately asked on all
sides was, "Has the Simon Commission been consulted? Are
they recommending Dominion Status?" On the following
day, October 31st, a Friday when the House met at eleven,
Lloyd George made himself the spokesman of an inquisitive public. The answer was clear—the Commission had

not been consulted. Then, Commander Kenworthy asked, has anyone in the house, besides members of the Government, been consulted? "I can add nothing to the answer which I have already given," the Secretary for India replied. Baldwin rose. His attention, he said, had been called to an article in that morning's *Daily Mail*.

> It is sufficient for me at the moment to say that every statement of fact and every implication of fact contained in that article is untrue, and in my opinion gravely injurious to the public interest, not only in this country, but throughout the Empire.

Rarely, if ever, had any man of high rank in the State administered a reproof to the press so stern and so unqualified. Never before had Baldwin taken notice of anything personal to himself, good or bad, that appeared in any paper. Month after month the *Daily Express* and the *Daily Mail*, the organs of Lord Beaverbrook and Lord Rothermere, had pursued him with a vehement pertinacity, which, simply by its pertinacity, was undoubtedly loosening his hold on his party and his public. And he had not said one word in reply. Indeed, there was nothing he could say. But now Rothermere had left the safer ground of invective for the more dangerous arena, where the encounter was between plain truth—which nobody could array more skilfully than Baldwin—and invention. He spoke again on November 7th.

The story for which the *Daily Mail* had made itself responsible was on this wise. In September Baldwin had met the Viceroy at Aix. Then and there he pledged himself and his party to support the promise of Dominion Status. Thereupon, learning what had happened, his principal colleagues, the Conservative Shadow Cabinet, had required him to write to the Prime Minister withdrawing his promise of support.

As a study in the growth of a myth the tale is not uninteresting. Baldwin was in France on the 20th September. But he was at Bourges, not at Aix. He did receive a communication on India. But it was from the Prime Minister, not from the Viceroy. The Prime Minister did ask him to concur in the issue of the statement, on the understanding that the Simon Commission would be consulted and the consent of all parties obtained. Baldwin did agree, on those conditions, and dismissed the matter as of no further interest. Not till a month later, on October 23rd, did he learn that the essential condition had not been fulfilled. The Simon Commission had not assented to the publication. Thereupon, after speaking to a few colleagues, he wrote to Snowden, as Acting Prime Minister (MacDonald being in America), that in the circumstances now disclosed he and his party could not support the publication. That was all. But not quite all. Another paragraph in the article said that:

> I bear a responsibility which I shall find it hard to explain to my followers in recommending the appointment of Lord Irwin as Viceroy. Let me tell the House that . . . it is a most anxious and grave responsibility when any Prime Minister has to find a Viceroy of India. It was only when we had considered many names that he [Birkenhead] suggested Mr. Edward Wood. My first answer was, "I cannot spare him." He is one of my most intimate friends, not only politically but personally, a man whose ideals and views in political life approximate most closely to my own, a colleague to whom I can always tell my inmost thoughts. On reflection I felt that India must have the best that we could send. That was the reason why I agreed.

The House was tensely still, and the voice fell a little lower.

> I will only add that if ever the day comes when the party which I lead ceases to attract to itself men of the calibre of Edward Wood, then I have finished with my party. . . . A friend of mine has told me that the article was only a journalistic stunt . . . . I agree. I am glad to think that the word stunt is as little English in its derivation and origin and character as the whole of that article.

But—"let us pass from this rather sordid subject," and for half-an-hour Baldwin gave the House, now thoroughly in hand, a speech charged with romantic idealism and speculations on the mystery that after so many thousand years had brought the hard-bitten Aryan of the North to labour with and for the meditative Aryan of the tropic zone. The history would, perhaps, not endure much probing, but the House was in a mood to be enchanted, and in the closing sentences Baldwin rose to the mood.

> We politicians . . . so much of our fighting is in the twilight, or in the mist—pass away before we know the result of our work. We are cumbered with many things, and occupied with the problems of daily life which press with greater or less severity on the multitudes of our own people, but here in this problem, we have a great ideal set before us, and we cannot hope to live to see it realised. Our work must be done in faith, but let us build for the future with the same faith that we work for the present, so that when, perhaps, in long generations to come, there are men who will be putting the coping-stone upon this building, they may, haply, not be unforgetful of those of us who build in faith among the foundations.

Balfour wrote :

> I am very unnecessarily troubling you with a letter intended to express the feelings which I cannot keep to myself, of intense admiration for your great utterance yesterday. You treated the greatest of political themes in a way and with an inspiration which will give you for all time an unchallenged position among the orators of the English-speaking race. No more can be given even to those who are greedy of posthumous fame, and it is a delight to me to think that on a subject which has so greatly occupied the thoughts of my declining years, it has fallen to you, as Leader of the Party, to give utterance in fitting language to great thoughts on the greatest of subjects.

When he spoke Baldwin was well aware that his tenure of power was precarious; that his hold on his party was relaxing; that his followers in the House and their agents in the country were losing faith in a leadership which seemed to do anything but lead; looking to Churchill, looking to Chamberlain; afraid of Beaverbrook, afraid of Rothermere; spinning combinations, alliances, understandings: anything to put into the party life enough to wear down the Government and build up the picture of itself as the better alternative. And, with Baldwin as leader, it could not be done. He would not decide. He could orate on the unity of the Empire. But when it came to taxes on food and whether the electorate should be asked to decide at the election or after the election—programme or referendum—Baldwin could not, would not, make up his mind. And this was where his chief antagonist had the advantage.

Beaverbrook had made up his mind. At the annual conference of the party on November 21st 1929 Baldwin had said:

> We stand once more at the cross roads . . . Our progress depends on our capacity to visualise the Empire, the Dominions and Colonies alike, as one indestructible unit for production, for consumption, for distribution, for the maintenance and improvement of the lot of all who under Providence are dwellers in the confines of our Commonwealth. I think we owe a word of gratitude to one—not always a supporter of our party—Lord Beaverbrook—for bringing before the country the idea . . . of a United Empire.

Baldwin had seen Beaverbrook before he spoke—and on Armistice day, he gaily remarked. Certainly his language sounded like the overture to an understanding, and letters poured into the Central Office asking for guidance. The reply was ambiguous. The proposals of Beaverbrook's Empire Crusade would be examined, with others; meanwhile the Party should say nothing, but its members might do what they liked. Baldwin suggested another interview. The outcome was a second speech, on February 5th. Beaverbrook found it "quite thrilling." A third interview was suggested, but with an ominous limitation. Rothermere expressly stipulated that his approval went no further than Empire Free Trade.

> He wishes to make it clear that he does not commit himself to support you at the next election, as he may be at variance with you over India and other issues.

With this in mind Baldwin spoke to the Central Council of the party on March 4th 1930. His experience had convinced him that while Free Trade within the Empire was an ideal, Freer Trade was a practical policy. Therefore the first business of the party would be an Economic Conference of the Empire.

> What may emerge I would rather not conjecture. It is not for us to dictate. If there should emerge an agreement involving a tax on food the issue should be put to the people and they should judge for themselves.

In fact, Baldwin and Beaverbrook were at one, and the reconciliation was gracefully announced in a speech ten days later.

I am glad to pay tribute to his public-spirited action and the initiative he displayed, which led to the happy result we all know.

The terms of the concordat clearly implied that Beaverbrook should cease from personal criticism of Baldwin. But the terms did not include Rothermere, and so the attacks on Baldwin persisted. Nor did speeches reiterating his economic faith—safeguarding, consultation with the Empire, the referendum on food taxes—do much to consolidate his position. On the other side, just as in 1924, it was plain that the Labour Government was in no position to realize its election promises. Unemployment was not better but worse. Public expenditure was increasing. There was uneasiness in the City. The situation was developing on lines which Baldwin had anticipated in 1922, an election with, if the Conservative Party split, no alternative Government in sight. But he remembered the Carlton Club, and in June 1930 he summoned a meeting of members and candidates. A message came from Bridgeman—"Show them that you can be angry: be strong and of good courage: remember that you are trusted by all who know you and thousands who don't." But Baldwin had no need to be angry, because in his pocket he had a letter which was quite enough by itself to enrage any assembly that still held by the canons of constitutional propriety and had some respect for Parliament and the Crown.

It is not easy at first sight to bring into one picture Baldwin's indolence in council and his energy as a speaker. In one month he spoke at Middlesbrough, Nottingham, Bury, Leeds (he was making sure of the North); at Cambridge, where he had been elected Chancellor in succession to Balfour; in Suffolk, at Inverness, at Aberdeen, and twice in London—all by way of preparation for the Caxton Hall; and his reception at each place was warm enough to satisfy him, and to warn his enemies that whatever the lobbies might say, whatever preparations might be in hand for his removal, neither public confidence nor public affection was cooling. On the eve of the meeting he received a letter from Harold Laski.

I hope [he wrote] you will not consider it an intrusion for one who is not a member of your party to send you a word of good wishes for your party meeting. I should like you to feel that, outside the Conservative ranks, there are many Socialists who, like myself, not only feel grateful for the quality of the human directness you bring to our political life, but also recognize gladly that the spirit you represent has made the peaceful evolution of English politics much more certain than it would otherwise have been. We resent, not less than your own friends, the effort to usurp a leadership the distinction of which has been, if I may say so, an honoured feature of our time.

Please forgive this letter if it seems out of place. But I should be happy if I could make you feel that there are those on the other side in politics whose respect for you is angered by the insolent challenge to your leadership.

So fortified, Baldwin met the assembly on June 24th 1930.

We are told [he said] that there is a crisis in the Party. . . . There will be a crisis if you cannot make up your minds what you are going to do. I have made up my mind, but you have got to make up yours. You have been told . . . that we have no policy. . . . We have a policy which I have been explaining up and down the country.

Then he settled down to the economic unity of the Empire, and the referendum on food taxes. But "Lord Beaverbrook has changed his mind, and I have not. And what would be said of the party if it changed its view at the bidding of two newspapers?"

Cheers warmed the air. Baldwin came nearer to his target.

The British Press, take it as a whole, is the best, the fairest and the cleanest Press in the World. But there are exceptions. Now Lord Beaverbrook has appealed to-day in the papers to avoid personalities. . . . When you think of his papers during the last seven years and up to a week ago, when you think that even members of the Carlton Club have written for payment and worked and done all they can to destroy my position, and, with me, the Party, to talk about avoiding personalities will not deceive a soul. . . .

There is nothing [he went on reflectively] more curious in modern evolution than the effect of an enormous fortune rapidly made and the control of newspapers of your own. The three most striking cases are Mr. Hearst in America [he had asked Baldwin to write for him, Baldwin refused, and was honoured with a vicious attack], Lord Rothermere in England, and Lord Beaverbrook. . . . On January 4, this year, he [Rothermere] said: "I am against food taxes." On February 19 he was for them. In May, as I shall show you, he does not like them. To-day I am told he is supporting them. You cannot take your politics from a man like that.

The desire to dictate the policy to a big Party, to choose a leader, to impose Ministers on the Crown: the only parallel to that was the action of the T.U.C. in 1926. . . . We are told that unless we make peace with these noblemen, candidates are to be run all over the country. The Lloyd George candidates at the last election smelt; these will stink. The challenge has been issued. . . . I accept as I accepted the challenge of the T.U.C. . . . I am all for peace. I like the other man to begin the fight, and then I am ready. When I fight I go on to the end, as I did in 1926.

Never had Baldwin spoken in such tones. But more was to come.

Here is a letter from Lord Rothermere which I have permission to read. . . . "I cannot make it too abundantly clear that, under no circumstances whatsoever, will I support Mr. Baldwin unless I know exactly what his policy is going to be, unless I have complete guarantees that such policy will be carried out if his Party achieves office and unless. . . ."

In his last years, I noticed that Baldwin was fond of living through this moment again: "the Lord had delivered him into my hands."

". . . unless I am acquainted with the names of at least eight, of ten, of his most prominent colleagues in the next Ministry." . . . Now those are the terms that your leader would have to accept, and when sent for by the King he would have to say: "Sire, these names are not necessarily my choice, but they have the support of Lord Rothermere." A more preposterous and insolent demand was never made on the leader of any political party. I repudiate it with contempt, and I will fight that attempt at domination to the end.

That afternoon as Baldwin entered the Chamber, an equal

thunder of applause broke out from both sides, but it lasted longer on the Labour benches. Letters and telegrams of praise, thanksgiving, and delight poured in from every side, not least from journalists who felt that their profession had been vindicated. From first to last Baldwin could always count on fair treatment by the better elements in the press, especially the old and sober provincial papers, and what those elements thought of Beaverbrook and Rothermere was best summed up by the editor of *The Times*, Geoffrey Dawson:

> I sometimes think that *character* is what these people most dislike, and that this is the real motive of their attacks on you and Edward [Wood] and others of that sort. Someone ought to deal seriously with the complete abdication by the popular press of their first function of supplying news. . . . Northcliffe who believed at one time in educating democracy, and created the *Daily Mail* as a first class summary record of the news of the world, would turn in his grave if he could see his offspring to-day.

And another friend told a story of Asquith:

> I was once sitting with him in his study when a message came from Beaverbrook offering the support of all his newspapers on certain conditions. Asquith refused to see the messenger, but when pressed for an answer said, "Tell him I will give him half-a-crown for the lot," and resumed a discussion of Jane Austen.

Baldwin was always happy to be paralleled with Asquith. But Asquith had lost the leadership, and so might Baldwin. The Caxton Hall engagement was a victory. But some concessions had to be made to the Die-hards. Four days later Irwin was warned that the party could not at this stage accept any responsibility for repetition of the words "Dominion Status." But Irwin was resolute, and on July 9th he affirmed the Declaration of October, with Dominion Status as the natural completion of India's constitutional growth. A few days later, Baldwin followed Gladstone and Balfour into the French Academy of Moral and Political Science.

The campaign went on. On the whole, the provinces were faithful. But London and the South were wavering under the steady bombardment, morn, noon and night, of the hostile press. Yet personal enmity must have some ground to

work on, some weakness to probe, if it is to influence the
multitude, even at a by-election: and the contrast between
ardour and placidity was making itself felt on younger minds
and more militant spirits. After all, Beaverbrook seemed to
offer them an opportunity of doing something, something
clear, tangible, visible: here it seemed was a Cause, not only
a Programme; and a man who knew very precisely what he
was after and where he was going, which Baldwin did not.
And Baldwin, as we know, instinctively flinched from
dynamic forces and live wires. A referendum taken on personality would have given Baldwin a hundred votes to
Beaverbrook's ten. Taken on policy, taken in the party—
the numbers would be nearer even.

Summer passed and Baldwin, as usual, retired to Aix. On
his return, Neville Chamberlain made what might well have
proved a last effort to keep the leadership in Baldwin's
hands, knowing all the time that if he failed, he himself was
marked for the succession: knowing too that in the inner
ring there was no unanimity—none on Food Taxes, none on
India. "Strong currents," Churchill wrote, "of feeling and
even of passion are moving under the stagnant surface of
our affairs."

A party meeting was demanded, and the issue would
be whether to go on under Baldwin or another leader. It was
to be held on October 30th 1930. On the day before, a report
was circulated that forty-four members had lodged a memorandum with the Chief Whip demanding Baldwin's resignation. The report was a fabrication—perhaps a hoax;
many of the supposed signatories knew nothing of the memorandum till they saw it in the papers. "I never knew,"
Baldwin once remarked, "what a gangster was till I went
into politics." And a letter from Kipling (who knew something of journalism) expressed the feeling of thousands:

> There isn't much use in saying anything but, at this present
> damnable juncture, I *do* want you to know how much I am
> thinking about you and how I have tried to help untangle
> people's minds on the issues. It's serious for you and it's
> very serious for the country and the Empire (incidentally
> my hobby for the last 40 years).
> And all I see they can get out of it is the recognition for

the future of "gangster" journalism and putting men "on
the spot" if they don't happen to suit the political racketeer.
An exact parallel to Chicago. I hope and pray you'll be able
to down 'em and, after that, to keep 'em in their places.

Certainly, Chamberlain was no gangster. But he was his
father's son, and the vision of a United Empire meant more
to him than to Baldwin, so much more as to incline him
always to seek at least a tactical co-operation with Beaverbrook. At heart they were Imperialists: Baldwin, in their
sense, was not. But it was once said, "Chamberlain has no
antennæ—Baldwin has nothing else." Knowing them both,
I always felt that, of the two, Chamberlain had the clearer
mind, Baldwin the larger vision; Chamberlain, within his
own circle, the warmer heart, Baldwin the wider affection.
Instinct, insight, the most sensitive response to what others
were feeling or thinking—as dimly perhaps as he did himself:
all that was Baldwin; and to Chamberlain all that was at
times exasperating. Yet there were heights to which Baldwin
could rise and he could not; while, on the other hand, Chamberlain could carry burdens—departmental burdens, party
burdens of organization and research—which Baldwin was
only too willing to devolve on any other man's shoulders.
Nothing in that world of murk and disloyalty is more honourable than Chamberlain's bearing to a leader whose departure
he would have viewed with immense relief. He drafted the
resolutions for the meeting, where by a majority of 462 to 116
the party confirmed Baldwin in the leadership.

Once more the flood of congratulations poured in. Once
more Laski wrote:

> I do hope that you will feel that we who are academic Social-
> ists rejoice in your great victory today as though it were
> that of a personal friend. It is not only that you yourself
> hold a quite special place in our affection. We realize as keenly
> as any on your side how vital a victory it is for the forces
> of sheer decency in public life. *Macte antiquae virtutis.*

The second encounter had ended like the first. But the
victory was still to win. The Round Table Conference on
India opened on November 12th 1930. On December 10th
Winston Churchill delivered a speech in which he dismissed

the Indian claims as "absurd and dangerous pretensions," a sentiment with which no few Conservatives heartily concurred. Between the two dates Baldwin had moved a vote of censure on the Government for failing to formulate any proposals for the extension of Empire Trade and refusing to consider the offers made by the Dominions. But Samuel, speaking for the Liberals, declared the Canadian offer to be unacceptable; Thomas, more outspoken, called it Umbug. Snowden challenged the Conservatives to go to the country on Food Taxes; and it was not unobserved that Baldwin's indictment was something less than vigorous. Doubts, covered rather than suppressed at the Caxton Hall, were becoming vocal once more. The drift had set in again. Dissatisfaction was spreading. And so, on February 25th 1931, the Chief Agent wrote to Chamberlain:

It would be in the interests of the Party that the Leader should reconsider his position.

Here was open mutiny at last.

After consulting some of his colleagues, Chamberlain passed the Chief Agent's letter, some wounding phrases omitted, to Baldwin on Sunday morning, March 1st. He read it as a death-warrant. Indeed, his first reaction was to consult with Mrs. Baldwin as to their future—to quit politics, sell their London House—retire to Astley. Then he asked Chamberlain to call. He told him of his decision. But late that night, by a good omen, Bridgeman, who had sent the message before the meeting in June, blew in "like an admiral in a gale," and Baldwin recovered his fighting mood. "Tiger Baldwin, Tiger Baldwin," his wife would murmur at such times. He asked Chamberlain to call again on Monday morning. There was a by-election in St. George's, Westminster. The Conservative candidate had withdrawn on the ground that he could not defend his leader. An Independent candidate, vigorously backed by Beaverbrook and Rothermere, was on the spot. Baldwin told Chamberlain of his revised decision— to apply for the Chiltern Hundreds and then offer himself at St. George's. The gesture, too dramatic perhaps to be quite sincere, was enough to still the mutiny for the moment. The demand for his resignation was withdrawn or postponed.

By another good omen, the Viceroy was able to announce an understanding with Gandhi: Duff Cooper took up the defence at St. George's.

The Round Table Conference had been wound up on January 19th 1931; Parliament met on January 22nd and plunged at once into a debate on the Trade Union Bill, designed to remove the grievances and uncertainties left over from the measure of 1927—the uncertainties being more conspicuous than the grievances. As nothing came of it, nothing need here be said. Of far greater consequence was the debate on India of January 26th. Certain principles, the Prime Minister said, had been agreed upon: would the House give the Government the authority to continue the work in consultation with representative Indians, and so reduce the principles to practice? Churchill, prophesying doom and severance, found himself alone. Baldwin was emphatic in his support of the Government. The breach was open and unconcealed. Before the end of the month Churchill had left the Committee which directed the affairs of the party, and the soldier of fortune, as Baldwin used to call him, was free to offer his sword elsewhere.

In its remoter consequences, his departure was lamentable. But it was inevitable. Churchill was an Imperialist, Baldwin was not. To Baldwin the launching of a federated continent on its predestined and promised career of self-government appeared as the final achievement of English political genius. Merely to rule India, to govern India, holding that marvellous assemblage of races, languages and religions together in peace and increasing prosperity, made no appeal to him: the spectacle was one to which his imagination was blind. But that Churchill, and Kipling for that matter, belonged to an antiquated world, of that he was sure. And when Baldwin was sure, sure of himself and his cause, no consideration of place or popularity could hold him back.

> Break up the unanimity of parties on India, and no man in this House, no Prime Minister, no Secretary for India, has any chance of coping with the government of that country.

That was said on January 27th. On March 6th, speaking to a large enthusiastic meeting at Newton Abbot, Baldwin

gave his support to the Government and the continuance of
the Round Table Conference. On March 9th Reading and
the Viceroy elect had spoken hopefully of the situation in
India and the excellent results of Irwin's policy. Duff Cooper
had defended Baldwin's approval of the Conference. But, late
on the evening of March 9th, the India Committee of the
Conservative Party published their resolution :

> welcoming the decision of Mr. Baldwin that the Conservative
> Party cannot be represented at any further Round Table
> Conference to be held in India.

All the world wondered. But one interpretation was all
too obvious. Whether or no Baldwin had been pushed by
his Shadow Cabinet, in October, into disavowing Irwin's
declaration, it seemed clear that he had been driven by
Churchill and the Imperialists into eating his own words.
St. George's rang with his surrender, the luckless Duff
Cooper being left to defend a leader who had suddenly
turned round and was walking the other way.

Exultation, bewilderment, despair—all the political
emotions were chasing one another in the lobbies of the House
and the offices of newspapers. Mrs Baldwin's diaries rarely
concern themselves with politics. But three notes in succession
sum up the passions of three days.

> The St. George's election causes great excitement.
> Gutter press throwing mud.
> Things are getting difficult: I wonder how much more one
> can bear.

And this on the eve of what some listeners ranked as
Baldwin's greatest Parliamentary triumph, a triumph not
unshared.

> Found the Wreckers on our doorstep. A few cold words passed.

> Women do not forgive so easily as men.

It was on March 12th after questions that Baldwin rose.
He quoted first the declaration of 1917: "the progressive
realization of responsible Government in India as an integral
part of the British Empire." He reminded his party that they
were often twitted with their Imperialism, and that they
would do well to remember that the Empire of 1931 was not

the Empire of 1887. "It is no dead matter, it is alive and in a constant process of evolution. And it cannot be supposed that in the world of evolution India alone is static." Now, the Conference having broken up, what was the next step? It was for the Government to decide. The Conservative Party would not send a delegation to a Conference in India, but they would welcome a renewal of the Conference in London.

> Everybody knows that there are differences in our party on this subject, because there always have been. . . . There was genuine anxiety, an anxiety which I respect, among many of my supporters as to whether the delegates were going out to India. I felt it only fair to relieve them of that anxiety, as I did three weeks ago, and acquaint them with my opinion. . . . But when I was asked whether I had any objection to an authentic statement going out I was in a bit of a difficulty. I would much rather no statement had been made. These conversations had been private communications between a leader and his followers, and they ought to be private.
>
> I noticed [he went on] that there was some communication between that committee of my party and that section of the Press which had announced its intention to smash us. . . . I knew the result might be unfortunate, not to myself—I do not care twopence about that—but I was afraid of the reaction in India. My fears were justified. . . . I hope that what has happened since, and is to be said in this Debate, may remove those fears. . . .
>
> I used the word "hysteria" a short time ago, and I used it advisedly. . . . I deprecate in the strongest way possible the use of such words as "victory" or "surrender". . . . There has been no victory personally. But there has been a victory of common sense . . . rare enough in India, and rare enough at home. . . . Extremism, in India, or at home, dies hard and slowly. But whatever happens enlarges the area of goodwill and co-operation and that is the one thing that is wanted to-day. . . . On that subject—

and here with one of his innocent masterstrokes he read a long passage from a speech delivered in 1920—

> "the British way . . . has always meant and implied close and effectual co-operation with the people of the country. In every part of the British Empire that has been our aim and

in no part have we arrived at such success as in India, whose
princes spent their treasure in our cause, whose brave soldiers
fought side by side with our own men, whose intelligent and
gifted people are co-operating with us in every sphere of
government and industry."

I like the ring of those sentences [he said], so I am going
to give one or two more.

Shouts of "name" from a delighted House.

Really [he replied] it is very good of me to quote them . . .
because they will make the rest of my speech sound like a
Sunday school textbook.

And so with a compliment to Churchill for his excellent
summary of the situation then and now, he turned to the
great issue of the day.

There were differences in his party. But unless there were
co-operation between all parties, the Indian problem would
be insoluble. The extremists at home, therefore—like the
aged Colonel who called him and the Viceroy "negro-
philes"—are doing their worst to create a revolutionary
spirit in India. The responsibility of a leader is heavy. It is
his supreme duty to tell the people of the country the truth,
because truth is greater than tactics. If the mutual loyalty
of leader and follower fails, then the partnership is dissolved:

What is the principal fact I see in the world to-day? . . . The
unchanging East has changed, is changing with alarming
rapidity, and there are many people who are blind not to
see it. . . . You cannot reverse the engines on the simple
ground of British honour. . . . The ultimate result depends, not
on force, but on good will, sympathy and understanding.
. . . The great work of Lord Irwin is that he has bridged the
gulf by ability and by character, and when the history of
this time comes to be written, his name will stand out as one
of the greatest Viceroys, and a Viceroy I had the honour
myself of sending to India.

Then a word to his party—a word of confidence and defiance in one.

I know the difficulties . . . in my party—difficulties of conviction and old ties. I do not believe the bulk of our party,

either in the House or in the country, will take any different
view. . . . I shall carry out that policy with every desire to
overcome the stupendous difficulties that face us. If there
are those in our party who would have forced out of their
reluctant hands one concession after another, if they be a
majority, in God's name let them choose a man to lead them.
If they are in minority, let them at least refrain from throwing
difficulties in the way of those who have undertaken an almost
superhuman task, on the successful fulfilment of which depends
the well-being, the prosperity and the duration of the whole
British Empire.

A friend who had been watching the movements in Baldwin's party and knew the trouble in his mind, wrote on the
following day:

He has been having as bad a time as ever any man has been
called on to bear, and yesterday he put his fortune to the
touch in a way that makes everyone who loves him proud to
see. His followers have been jockeying about in the most
contemptible and treacherous way, making his position more
insecure and eating into his reputation all the while because
he didn't call them to heel or disassociate himself from them.
It looked as if he might fall from the leadership through an
accumulation of petty undefined issues and not go down, if
he had to go down, with flying colours on some clearly defined
big principle. . . .

His colleagues all advised him not to take a strong line
and not to speak out, whether through treachery or cowardice,
I don't know; but this advice would have been fatal to him
if he had taken it. However, he took his own line and kept
his soul even if he loses his party. I don't think he will lose the
party now: the moment he spoke to them from the heights,
the bulk of them looked to me to be rallying to him.

Read his speech: though of course it can't give you the
impression of what it was like in the tense human atmosphere
of the House, charged with personality and passion. A most
manful speech, so touching in its courage and simplicity:
and one felt so happy for him because, after that, whether he
stands or falls, he is all right, and none of the insinuating
littleness of his political councillors or the clamour of the press
has touched him at all.

What followed is an incident unique in Baldwin's career. Commonly, as I have said, these hours of resolution were followed by periods of languor and collapse. There was no languor in his next move. The campaign against Duff Cooper in St. George's was conducted with a virulence rare in English politics. Baldwin, ignoring the antiquated convention that party leaders do not speak at by-elections, went to Queen's Hall, taking with him a phrase he had borrowed from his cousin.

Baldwin had spoken of an "insolent plutocracy," and the remark produced a savage comment:

> These expressions come ill from Mr. Baldwin whose father left him an immense fortune which, so far as may be learnt from his own speeches, has almost disappeared. It is difficult to see how the Leader of a party who has lost his own fortune can hope to restore that of anyone else, or of his country.

The first part [Baldwin said] is a lie: the second by implication untrue. The paragraph can only have been written by a cad. I am advised that an action for libel would lie. (Take it!) I shall not move. I should get an apology and heavy damages. The first is of no value. The second I would not touch with a barge-pole. What the proprietorship of these papers is aiming at is power, and power without responsibility,* the prerogative of the harlot throughout the ages.

In less than six months Baldwin was in office under Ramsay MacDonald; by October he was virtually in control of a Government with a Parliamentary majority beyond all record. The Empire Crusade was forgotten. But, to the end, 1931 was always remembered with a demure smile as "the year when my party tried to get rid of me."

He bore no malice, and these years of stress brought also one of the lasting delights of Baldwin's life—the Pilgrim Trust of which, by the express desire of the Founder, Mr. Edward Harkness, he became Chairman. The breadth and informality of the Trust and its proceedings exactly fitted his temper. To help in preserving or repairing our

---

* Actually the phrase "power without responsibility" will be found in Disraeli's *Endymion*. Baldwin had already used it of the Labour extremists.

historic shrines, safeguarding places of special beauty, opening our rich store of national records, all this was to Baldwin a pure joy, and in his last years it was the Trust that most often brought him to London. "Have you seen the Abbey muniments?" "I was there last week—they were open to show the name of Dick Whittington. Guess why." "I know—Queen Mary had taken the little princesses to see it. Am I right?"

CHAPTER XVI

THE CRISIS OF 1931

WHEN Baldwin left office in 1929, the unemployed numbered 1,100,000. By the beginning of 1931 the figure was 2,624,000. In January Ramsay MacDonald admitted to a Conservative friend that the revelations of the Commission on Unemployment Insurance were so startling that even his Government might be compelled to override the resistance of the Trade Unions and amend the law. A few days later a Government resolution in favour of the appointment of an Economy Committee was passed in an almost unanimous House. MacDonald thereupon wrote to Baldwin and Lloyd George suggesting that each should nominate two members —not in the House. Sir George May was Chairman and the Committee entered on its labours at once. Its report was issued on July 30th, advance copies having been sent to the Conservative and Liberal leaders, and the Cabinet appointed a Committee—the Prime Minister, Snowden, Henderson, Thomas and Graham—to consider its recommendations. On August 19th the Cabinet sat, with brief interruptions, from eleven to half-past ten, to study the conclusions of the Committee, and it was plain that a rift was opening which it would not be easy to close. Ministers were agreed that the deficit should be covered by taxation both indirect and direct; that unemployment contributions should be raised and benefit limited to 26 weeks. But the May Committee had also advised a reduction of benefit by one-fifth, an economy of £14,900,000. To this the Cabinet Committee were, by a majority, opposed; and the Cabinet accepted the view of the majority.

Baldwin was at Aix. On the 8th he and Mrs. Baldwin had crossed to Cherbourg and spent two days at Caen, Falaise and Bayeux. On the evening of the 11th Davidson telephoned asking him to return. Much against the grain, he yielded to a second summons on the following morning and travelled back to London. He saw MacDonald on the 13th, promised his Parliamentary support and resumed his holiday, journeying by Chinon and Bourges to Aix. The 20th was a day of violent storms, and in the evening an urgent telephone call warned him that, like it or not, he must return at once. That day—the morrow of the long Cabinet—MacDonald saw, of the Conservatives, Hoare and Neville Chamberlain; of the Liberals, Samuel and Maclean. The Conservatives insisted on the reduction of benefit; and Samuel reported that Lloyd George and Liberals generally were of the same view. And now Snowden was up and fighting. He had met the Trades Union Congress, who had failed utterly to realize the gravity or the nature of the situation. They talked of surtax and the mobilization of resources, but the only thing, he added scornfully, they were agreed on was, that the salaries of Ministers and Judges should be cut. As a compromise, the suggestion was made of a ten per cent reduction in benefit—Snowden pointing out that the movement of prices had raised its real value by thirty per cent. But a full half of the Cabinet were against even the compromise; there was no unanimity on another proposal, a Revenue Tariff; and it was difficult for those who were most concerned to discover what the opposition in the Cabinet really wanted, or what they meant to do, if by any chance they unseated their Prime Minister and formed a Government of their own. Very rarely in English history can there have been a Cabinet so incapable of handling a situation which, if exceedingly grave, was also exceedingly simple.

Later a scapegoat had to be found and a myth invented to cover the flight of the Socialist leaders from the disaster which their own ineptitude had invited. On August 20th, when the situation could no longer be concealed and public alarm was growing hour by hour, the Prime Minister saw the Deputy Governor of the Bank and learnt from him that the Bank was in urgent need of help, that help could only come from Paris and New York, and that whether it would come or not depended on the action of the Government in the matter of unemployment benefit. It was clear by now that Parliament would have to be summoned and that as soon as it met the Government would be defeated by Conservatives and Liberals acting together. But in the meantime the crisis would have come; our financial resources were measured by days; and, as Snowden said, if the alternatives were to maintain the soundness of our currency or lower the standard of living by half, what responsible leader could hesitate to make his choice?

Meanwhile, the Opposition chiefs had been brought to agree to the modified reduction of benefit, the ten per cent cut, and this was the proposal which the Prime Minister put to his Cabinet. They refused, Snowden and Thomas alone dissenting. He turned to the banks and they replied that they must consult New York. On Sunday 23rd an answer came from the Federal Reserve accepting the whole programme of taxation and economies, including the ten per cent cut, as adequate security for the necessary loan. The crisis was over: the Cabinet shattered. On Sunday evening MacDonald announced that he was on his way to the King to advise him to summon a meeting of the three leaders, and to inform him that all ministers had placed their resignations at his disposal. He left Downing Street a little after ten. In half an hour he returned, no longer Prime Minister, to a gathering no longer a Cabinet.

Baldwin had arrived in London on the 22nd, loudly cheered by a considerable assemblage at Victoria. He might reasonably have expected that he would be charged to form a Government, and he was prepared to form one. In later years we often discussed the situation in which he found himself in those days. Let it be granted that the circumstances were exceptional, that the emergency was one outside the rules, and that a Government of all parties or no party was what the situation demanded, yet there was also to be considered the respective standing of the two men, Baldwin and MacDonald, with their parties and in the country. The Conservatives now were almost solid for the one; the Socialists had revolted against the other. Baldwin was universally trusted, but a brief flush of hero-worship left MacDonald where he always had been: attractive or repellent, he was a mystery, a bewilderment, self-centred, self-devoted; and in that August 1931 a figure created by the moment, not for the moment.

But to stand aside, to serve under the man whose place he might well have taken, was a gesture of magnanimity which the country would appreciate and understand, as it always appreciates and understands an act of sacrifice. Nor was the sacrifice in fact so great as it might, to the world, appear. A National Government under MacDonald would inevitably be a Conservative Government, since MacDonald would bring with him only Snowden and Thomas; of the Liberals only Samuel and Simon were of the first rank; and it was more than doubtful whether Samuel and Snowden would for long abide with the flock. In a Coalition Government—by whatever name it is called—the first duty of a party leader is to see that his followers have their due share of office, and the party in support can usually get more than its due. When Baldwin told his immediate friends, his Shadow Cabinet, that he had agreed in their name to join the Administration, not a voice was raised against him. "They were thinking of their offices," he said. And he was probably thinking that he would be spared the labours which he always tried to evade, of mastering papers, of answering arguments, above all of giving decisions. For himself he made one stipulation. His salary as Lord President of the Council was only £2,000 against the £5,000 attached to other high offices. As compensation he went into the Chancellor's official residence at 11 Downing Street: "It was very comfortable, and I could always keep my eye on my Prime Minister."

The first division, on September 8th, showed that the new Government had a majority of no more than 59 in a House where feeling was more violent and bitter than had been known since the Irish days before the war. On September 19th—the Baldwins were staying at Trent—news came that the Atlantic Fleet was in a state of unrest over the cuts in the men's pay. The crisis had returned. All our diplomatic posts were warned that we were about to abandon the Gold Standard. On September 20th the decision was made public. There was no panic; there was strangely little interest in the announcement. The public had confidence in the National Government and were prepared to give Ministers whatever powers they asked, and, if they appealed to the constituencies, a majority beyond their dreams. Parliament was dissolved on October 7th. Only one of the old Labour Ministers found a seat, George Lansbury ; leader of an Opposition which numbered 52, he confronted a Ministerial party of 554. The votes in the country were nearly two to one: in the Cabinet there were eleven Conservatives to nine others.

Such is the story of the crisis of 1931, a crisis in which the central figure is not MacDonald and not Baldwin, but Philip Snowden. In one sense he might be said to have created it by issuing the May Report, with no preceding study, with no accompanying explanations. But the Report gave him the purchase he needed to effect the objects on which he was bent—to balance his Budgets and to arrest the flow of borrowed money. Indeed, he was reported to have said that he could have written the Report in advance. So could any Liberal reared in the Gladstonian tradition: so could any Conservative. Indeed, weeks before the Report appeared Baldwin had stated the case for the Chancellor as clearly as the Chancellor could have stated it himself; but in his own language and on the level where his mind worked most easily. The occasion was a Government motion to increase the Treasury contribution to the Unemployment Fund.

Finance [Baldwin said] has always been the Achilles' heel of democracy. . . . A large democratic electorate cannot have the experience that qualifies them to judge what may be perilous or safe. . . . They are dependent upon the honest statement of facts and of where they may lead from those whose judgments they respect. . . . We have heard so many talks of the sacrifices that will have to be made—but we have heard nothing more about them. . . . I am quite sure that if such a demand were made for sacrifices to get a solvent Budget, the country would not be behindhand in making them. . . .

And then one of his favourite classical divagations.

I remember . . . a well-known play, written in a city which was, perhaps, the most famous democracy that was ever born. One character in that play said to another that if men were to stand for a seat in Athens, and one of them said he desired to strengthen the Athenian navy because the existence of a navy was necessary to the existence of Athens, and if another man

With Lloyd George, 1929

Barrett

Central Press

The 1931 Crisis: Baldwin, MacDonald, Samuel

stood for increased doles and no navy, the man who stood for increased doles would get in every time. . . . Democracy's tendency is to concentrate on the immediate appeal and not on the ultimate reality. . . . That is where the great responsibility of leaders of all parties to-day lies. They ought, with courage, to explain to the people what is the danger of borrowing, unless you can see your way to have borrowing repaid.

And the event showed the truth to be as Baldwin saw it. The electors did respect the judgment of their leaders: the country was prepared for the sacrifices they thought needful. The education of the democracy was proceeding well.

But no man could have held that Government together, and in January 1932 the Free Traders, Snowden and Samuel, with nine others who had received minor office, offered their resignations. At the pressing desire of the Prime Minister and Baldwin they agreed to stay, with liberty to maintain their principles in the House and in the division lobbies. Ancient precedents, but none recent, might have been found for this strange liberty. It enabled them to remain after the passing of the Import Duties Bill which, from March 1st, imposed a General Tariff, and so realized Baldwin's earliest political hopes. But the Ottawa Conference created a new situation. Baldwin, who led the British delegation, presided over some eighty meetings or more in seven weeks. His charm, his even temper, his breadth of outlook did their usual work. To the actual negotiations he contributed little. But the outcome was one that the Free Traders could not possibly approve, and two letters, temperate from Samuel, fiery from Snowden, informed the Prime Minister of their impending departure.

The Delegation [Snowden wrote] went to Ottawa with the declared intention of increasing inter-Imperial trade, and securing a general lowering of world tariffs. We had their assurance that nothing would be agreed to which hampered our freedom to negotiate with foreign countries for the lowering of tariffs. They have come back after weeks of acrimonious disputes and sordid struggles with vested interests, with agreements wrenched from them to avert a collapse, and an exposure to the world of the hollowness of the talk of Imperial sentiment in economic affairs.

One almost hears the accent of Cobden castigating Peel. But Snowden was ever a Victorian. Still, right or wrong, it was done. A century of Free Trade was wound up and written off, and with the departure of the Free Traders the government was put solidly into the hands of the Conservative Party.

The letters which passed between the two chiefs are perhaps worth recording, partly for the contrast they disclose between the logical, analytic Scotch mind of MacDonald and Baldwin's habitual refusal to take politics so seriously as all that : partly because Baldwin's reply is one of the very few political letters from his pen.

My dear Baldwin,

I am unwilling to ruffle your holiday but I cannot help myself. Ottawa is to be bitterly fought and Snowden, Samuel and all the Liberals of his school to the number of about a dozen, are to resign from the Government. I have done my best with both the S.'s but they think that they do their duty by me by assuring me that I ought not to resign and that they will say so, whilst they will not go into Opposition but will sit below the gangway on the Government side giving us general support. I have not written you about this, but I now feel that the die is cast. They stand firmly upon : That the bargaining method adopted will soon break the Empire : That the five and seven year fiscal commitments are thoroughly unconstitutional and improper : That the bargain from the point of view of business is all against us, and from the point of view of politics is irredeemably bad : That it destroys the chances of a successful International Economic Conference : That it continues the influences which have brought this distress upon the world : That it is so contrary, not only in its immediate contents but in its inevitable far-reaching and more continuing results, to Free Trade and low tariffs that they cannot support it : That whilst "go-as-you-please" may have enabled us to round one corner, it cannot be repeated. These are barriers which I see no chance of overcoming.

This, you will agree, creates a situation of major gravity, requiring close study in every detail, and, unfortunately, your return to town. It will not be necessary to come back immediately on receipt of this, as I may hold back resignations for some days and maybe even for a week or two. Samuel is willing to let me choose my time provided the newspapers do not

make delay impossible on his part. I shall send you a telegram
so soon as the crisis comes and you might then come by the
first available train.

In the meanwhile, you will wish to turn matters over in
your mind. The chief considerations which give me concern
are:

1. What will the new Government be? Party. How can it be
National? How can I remain?

2. What will be the effect on the country? There must be a
return to pure party fighting and the national unity is dis-
rupted. The leader of the House of Commons under such
conditions should be a party man and so should be the Prime
Minister.

3. What will be the effect of that again upon the country
in relation to the world? Quite honestly, I think it will be bad.
It is our internal union which has produced our external
strength. When we become as other countries are, much of
our strength goes, and for one or two of us to puff ourselves
out and try to make the outside world believe that we are
the difference between a party and a national government
belongs to the order of comedy.

4. There might be a move to place the Government on
independent national support, but that means a great re-
adjustment of political organisation which, if the Liberals
draw out, will affect one party only and that the one least
likely to do it, because it is left in possession.

Many issues lie in these considerations but I shall not raise
them. They will occur to yourself, and, whether your respite
be for a day or a week, you will no doubt be ready to discuss
them when we meet.

So, gather in your hay harvest of health whilst the sun
shines. I fear I shall soon blow a cold blast with rain on your
Aix abode. Whatever you do, do not come away without
bringing Mrs. Baldwin's forgiveness for me.

Yours always sincerely,
J. Ramsay MacDonald.

My dear P.M.,

First, my sympathy is with you: I will not express my
feelings in a letter, but I shall have plenty to say. First, don't
worry. You are bound to carry on. The many questions arising
can be discussed during the autumn, but your duty is straight
and clear. You must stick to the ship till we are in calmer
waters. Secondly, something is due to your loyal supporters.

You must hold up the resignations for a fortnight. I have never bothered you about the House, but it doesn't run itself and you need plenty of vitality to face it day in and day out. I have had ten days here, my first clear holiday for two years, and if you can't give me till the end of next week, I can't guarantee the necessary steam for the job nor the calmer judgment that only comes with an untired mind. Neville, on whom the brunt of the Ottawa debates must fall, was done in when we returned: and if he can't have a decent rest you will only have him laid up with gout at some critical moment. Half the mistakes from 1918 on have been the work of tired men. Run no risk for the sake of a few days. I was going to have returned on Oct. 2. I will be with you on Sunday week the 25th. A sudden return makes everyone yell "crisis."

I see *all* the difficulties, but though the boat may rock when our allies jump off, it may well sail henceforward on a more even keel.

I will write in a few days when I have thought a bit.

Yours always,

S.B.

CHAPTER XVII

REARMAMENT

BALDWIN never whole-heartedly believed in the League of Nations as an effective force in the affairs of the world. Though he could speak beautifully about the Assembly—"Only there do you get the argument, the friendly pressure that can be brought by men constantly meeting, men deep and true in conviction "—he would never take the few miles' journey from Aix to Geneva to see it in action. But to acknowledge his disbelief was to invite political extinction. What he knew, what he felt, was that the Four Years' War had lowered the standing of England among the nations. We could no longer send the fleet to look at them. But they could send their aeroplanes to look at us. Collective punishment of the aggressor might follow, and the fear of collective punishment might deter him. And those two *mights* together made up the most senseless of all the senseless phrases in which that time abounded—collective security.*

At the Lausanne conference in 1932, German reparations were swept up and thrown away. On the morrow, the whole German press burst into a demand for rearmament. Looking for his starting-point, the historian might perhaps choose this moment for the beginning of the war of 1939. Our Government formally denied the German claim to parity in armaments, but no action, no overt action followed: we had no reason for supposing that Germany was evading her obligations under the Treaty of Versailles, and we were ourselves too near the edge of financial catastrophe to think over much of what was happening abroad. In November Baldwin spoke.

* I was told by an English official of the League that the author was Benes the Czechoslovak statesman, who wrote the words *securité collective* into a typed draft. On hearing it, a French colleague exclaimed, "Impossible; ce n'est pas français." "Peut-être," said the Englishman; "mais c'est Benèche."

I think it is well also [he said] for the man in the street to realise that there is no power on earth that can protect him from being bombed. Whatever people may tell him, the bomber will always get through. . . .

Closely examined, the phrase was fallacious. But as a working rule it was true enough, and even more dreadfully true was the sentence that followed.

The only defence is in offence, which means that you have to kill more women and children more quickly than the enemy if you want to save yourselves —

witness the cities of Germany and their state in 1945. And from this starkly posed dilemma, to accept destruction or inflict it, destruction of a kind and an extent which humanity had never had to contemplate, what was the issue? It may be remembered that among those who had reflected on the future of aerial warfare two opinions were current. Some thought that the enemy's first, and indeed sole, aim would be the destruction of our air force: that he would not, as the saying went, waste his bombs on women and children, but that, having once established ascendancy in the air, he would cut our communications by sea and leave us to surrender at leisure. The other school held the view, infinitely more alarming to the public, that the enemy would direct his attack against our great centres of population and force us to yield by the destruction of our administration and industry. And this to Baldwin's sensitive imagination was the likelier course of a war fought in the air—our cities in flames: "the bomb no bigger than a walnut": the gas attack in a low-lying fog: tortured millions in a panic flight carrying death and destruction as they fled. A Socialist, afterwards to hold high office in the War Government, once said to him, "If London is bombed three nights running, nothing can avert a revolution." And after the revolution, what?

Baldwin went on:

I certainly do not know how the youth of the world may feel, but it is not a cheerful thought to the older men that, having got that mastery of the air, we are going to defile the earth from the air, as we have defiled the soil during all the years that mankind has been on it. . . . When the next war comes, and European civilisation is wiped out, as it will be, and by no force more than that force, then do not let them lay blame on the old men. Let them remember that they, they principally or they alone, are responsible for the terrors that have fallen upon the earth.*

The last sentence was spoken almost in a whisper, and when he sat down, a faint sigh of applause passed along the benches.

The House was deeply moved: the country was deeply moved. But to whom were these words spoken? What did European civilization mean or matter to the youth of Germany, of Italy, of Russia? What but a worn-out figment which they were destined to replace? And, nearer home, what were those young men to do? Join the Royal Air Force and study how to defile the earth from the air, or join the League of Nations Union and call everybody else a war-monger? As Churchill pointedly asked, to what conclusion did the Lord President's speech lead? "It created anxiety, it created also perplexity. There was a sense of, what shall I say? of fatalism and helplessness about it"—which, indeed, we may say, shows how faithfully it reflected the trouble in Baldwin's mind. He believed—partly because he took no interest in the scientific developments which the new weapon was stimulating—that under the death-rain from the air the nations were helpless. And he knew that in face of the surging tide of pacifism, he was helpless too.

Tell the truth, [Churchill said] tell the truth to the British people. They are a tough people and a robust people. They may be a bit offended at the moment, but if you have told them exactly what is going on, you have insured yourself against complaints and reproaches which are very unpleasant when they come home on the morrow of some disillusionment.

Baldwin was to suffer more than complaints and reproaches. But what was the truth which he was to tell? That the Labour Party at its conference a few months earlier had declared its unqualified hostility to the arming of any country in any circumstances? Everyone knew it, and everybody knew that the resolution was at least in key with a vast body of emotion throughout the country. The Peace Letter of

* One hearer wrote: "That mill-race of monosyllables between *civilization* and *remember*! And now say that Baldwin is not an orator."

December 1927 was still the gospel of many ardent, many powerful, spirits:

> Convinced that all disputes between nations are capable of settlement either by diplomatic negotiations or by some form of international arbitration, we solemnly declare that we shall refuse to support, or render war service to, any Government which resorts to arms.

To all forms of popular emotion, Baldwin—I need not repeat it—was sensitive, perhaps unduly sensitive; and when Churchill spoke of the people being perhaps a bit offended at the moment if they were told the truth, Baldwin's mind shot ahead to troubles far graver while they were becoming accustomed to the truth—troubles in industry, perhaps a general strike, the collapse of his carefully built vision of national unity, and the leadership of a defeated and broken party passing into hands that could not be trusted to rebuild it. Against the horror of war, which he understood because he shared it, he set his own fear of disunion if ever war came. "There was one thing more than anything that I was afraid of—party division on foreign policy." In 1932 policy still meant diplomacy. From January 30th 1933, when Hitler became Chancellor, policy meant arms. And party divisions on defence might leave us defenceless.

By April Hitler was master of sixty million Germans and, what was of far greater significance, of an administration, civil and military, which had survived the overthrow of 1918. The Allies had slashed at the branches: they had laid the axe to the root of German power and there left it while they had quarrelled over the fallen fruit. In August 1933 Hitler was probing into our attitude towards his preparations and his Ukrainian ambitions. In October he left the Disarmament Conference, and the shock of dismay was felt throughout Europe. The lesser states looked to their defences: the Kremlin made approaches to Paris. Belgium asked for a renewal of guarantees. In Italy, in Scandinavia, in the Baltic States, everywhere except in pacifist England the significance of the new situation was realized at once.

But at this point comes an incident of tragic consequence to Baldwin and his memory. He spoke of it within the first few minutes of our first meeting. It came to his lips in an unlucky hour in the House. It constantly recurred in his conversation till his last days. On October 6th 1933 the annual meeting of the Conservative and Unionist Associations, at the instance of Amery and Churchill, recorded its "grave anxiety in regard to the provisions made for Imperial defence." They had good cause to be anxious.* But within three weeks, at a by-election, East Fulham, an old Tory stronghold, was submerged and lost in a wild flood of pacifism. The Conservative votes were down by 9,000; Labour up by 10,000. Other by-elections showed the same trend. And it seemed to me that the shock had broken Baldwin's nerve. "It was a nightmare," he once said, speaking, for the only time, of the past with passion. Such was his ascendancy in Parliament, in his party, in the country— Beaverbrook and Rothermere back in their cages and the mutineers on the penitents' form—that he had come to believe that, given time, he could sway opinion this way or that. But what could be done with a people in such a mood? Fulham reiterated the lesson of 1922 and that precipitated election. The people of England cannot be rushed. They are slow to answer the helm; they must be reasoned with and given time to think. But the weather in that autumn of 1933 did not favour quiet thinking.

The pacifism with which Baldwin was confronted was of a composite kind. At the root, mixed with all the disillusionment that had followed 1918, was an intense, elemental horror of war as the worst of all possible evils that might befall the human race: generating in turn a vigilant distrust, a quivering suspicion of any step that might seem to lead to war—unless, indeed, it was war fought under the auspices of the League, at its instance, and in its defence. To such tempers every strengthening of our defences except by agreement within the League meant a race in armaments, and it was an article of faith that such a race could only have one end. Certainly our Air Estimates in the spring of 1933 were

* At that date, Russia was the leading air-power with, it was supposed, 1,890 machines; France second, with 1,665; the U.S.A. had 1,186, Italy 1,071. The Japanese figure was doubtful. But the United Kingdom was certainly sixth with 844, that is, slightly below the combined figure for Poland and Yugoslavia.

still pacific, not to say pacifist: the total force was still ten squadrons behind the programme of 1923. At Geneva we offered to support the universal abolition of fighting craft, except for police purposes, provided there was international control of civil aviation. We laid the draft of a Disarmament Convention before the Conference. What more could any Government, any party, do? But lurking in the corners was the old distrust of Tory policy, the old memory of intervention in Russia; the fear, professed or genuine, that the Tories were bent on the overthrow of the Soviet Government; and that weapons could not safely be placed in the hands of a party still unpurged of Imperial ambitions, still doubtful of the efficacy of Disarmament Conferences; still unconverted to the sacred doctrine of Collective Security.* And that Baldwin shared this infidelity, his resolute absence from Geneva might be taken to prove. Here, then, was a mass of emotion and distrust, only to be shifted or deflected by slow persistency: by sober, well spaced exhortations, with professions of faith in the League, which went, perhaps, so far beyond what he really felt that they might almost be called insincere. A Roman Governor watching the barbarians gather for the last assault on his lines might have felt, and said, much the same about the Church.

Late in 1933 a Cabinet Committee was appointed to consider the situation. It excluded the contingency of war with America, France or Italy. But it acknowledged that in the Far East we were very weak, and it frankly avowed that pacts and conferences were no defence against a nation rearming as Hitler's Germany was. We had time, but not too much time, to make our defences sure; but whether the public could be brought to see that the defence of the Low Countries was still a British interest, the Committee doubted. And the Treasury did not doubt, it knew, that the contemplated expenditure was beyond our financial resources. The Committee asked for £78,000,000. The Chancellor could

---

* One example, *instar mille*. At a by-election in 1934 a fly-sheet was circulated, "The Unionist party want war. Your husbands and sons will be cannon fodder. More poison-gas will mean dearer food. Register your disgust of the war-mongers by voting Labour."
   Baldwin said: "A more nauseating and lying document I have never read—not even in the days of Chinese slavery."

not find more than £50,000,000. Nor would he pledge himself to a continuing programme. Baldwin signed the Report, and it fell to him as Lord President to announce the programme on which the Cabinet was agreed.

Meanwhile, and all through the sittings of the Committee, he had spoken, at not very frequent intervals, but always on the same theme. On February 8th, for example, replying to Churchill: either the Disarmament Conference succeeds in producing a convention or it fails. If it fails, we must look to our own interests; if it succeeds, we must arm up to the limits agreed on with the other powers. Some weeks later, on March 8th, the occasion being the Estimates for the Air Ministry, Churchill invited him to declare, with the authority of the Cabinet, what the Government policy was. His answer was still the same. If no general convention could be achieved, they would endeavour to bring about an air convention in Europe. If that failed, then the old formula must be made good: "No inferiority to any country within striking distance." He repeated it on May 18th. But in the public reception of these speeches, there is heard a note, not yet of distrust, but of doubt moving towards distrust. What needed to be said had been said. But what was being done? Once more—Baldwin always hits the nail on the head, but it never seems to go any further.

True, there were signs that public opinion was beginning to respond. The real nature of Nazism in Germany was becoming more manifest. The extremer pacifism was abating in the Trade Unions. At Twickenham, on June 22nd—a return match for East Fulham—the Conservative increased his party's majority. The atmosphere was changing, and the method of well-spaced instruction seemed to be bearing fruit. So we reach July 19th—the five-year programme of forty-one new squadrons, making seventy-five for Home Defence, and the sentence which in a few moments had flashed round the world. On the 30th Baldwin spoke first. The proposals of the Government, he said, might be criticized on one of three grounds: that they were excessive or inadequate or untimely. With each of these he dealt in his quiet, patient manner, just not wearying the House but at no point exciting it. He was of necessity compelled to go back to his not very happy phrase "the bomber will always get through" and to point out that because an enemy submarine might sink a food ship, it did not follow that we need build no cruisers. On the large issue—the relation of armed strength to moral influence—he quoted Haldane in 1923:

> We wish to reduce armaments and expenditure, but we cannot get anything accomplished with a diplomacy that is impotent for want of power behind it.

He spoke of Walpole,

> who wanted a lasting peace, but he did not believe it could be got by an insular peace, but by a European peace, and that is . . . what we all hope to achieve.

He cited Oliver's "great book on Walpole"*—one of the very few books that influenced Baldwin's lonely mind:

> If we allow our prestige to be impaired, if we shirk responsibility and let things of moment go by default . . . if we cease to care whether our strength is recognized or not, whether our voice is audible or not in the councils of Europe, we lose the chief security for our independence. . . . Confusion and disaster will follow as certainly as if one of the planets in the solar system should cease to pull its weight. If aloofness is inconsistent with our own safety, it is equally inconsistent with public morality. To be a good European is no mean patriotism.

"Those are great words," he said. And then:

> Since the day of the air, the old frontiers are gone. When you think of the defence of England you no longer think of the chalk cliffs of Dover; you think of the Rhine.

A thunder of applause on the right did not excite him to a peroration. He quoted Asquith in 1924 and asked the approval of the House for what was not only necessary but the least that the Government ought to ask.

Anyone familiar with the customs of debate would anticipate the Opposition reply: that Baldwin had averred that no defence against the bomber could be found, and now he was pretending that it could; that by mentioning Walpole he meant to return to the bad days of the Balance of Power; that when he said that not all the nations were animated

---

* *The Endless Adventure* by F. S. Oliver (1930–35).

by our ideals, he was canting, or talking the language of the Kaiser: all the mean sophistry, the dreary distortions with which, session after session, the Labour Party obstructed the defence of their country. If, setting all this aside, we try to reduce the debate to a rational exchange of views, the issue is very simple. The Government wanted to begin re-arming at once. The Opposition saw, in their urgency, distrust of the League in general and of Disarmament Conferences in particular. And such distrust was not an error: it was a sin.

Behind the League of Nations Union, sanctifying its sometimes unscrupulous operations, was a body of faith: and the light which streamed from the Sacred City blinded the worshippers to certain practical considerations which an earthly Government could not ignore. It was undoubtedly to be desired that Germany and Russia should be brought into the League, and indeed America. Not less to be desired that the aerial forces of mankind should be in the hands of one body, international, owing allegiance only to the League, swift, irresistible. The fallacy—and one must believe that it was sincerely held for truth—lay in the conclusion that until these things were achieved England might safely go unarmed while Germany armed to her heart's content: armed secretly and mysteriously, it was rumoured, in caves and forests, for the day when she might launch a thousand planes—or it might be ten thousand—and London would be no more than a smouldering heap. Faith, fear, and ignorance were masters of the moment.*

On November 23rd, speaking at Glasgow, Baldwin disclosed his mind with something more than his usual plainness. Japan and Germany being absent, no collective system was practicable. He would never sanction the use of the Navy for a blockade unless he knew what the United States would do. And then

> I remember once talking to a keeper in the Zoo. We were looking at a very large python, and I said, "That would be a nasty fellow to handle if he escaped." The keeper said, "It would take a dozen men to handle him and you have got

---

* An eminent man of letters wrote an article to show that we had purchased *Codex Sinaiticus* as a fetish to protect London from air-raids.

to trust them all." Well, when I have to help put a python
back in his cage, I mean to be sure who the other eleven are
and what they are going to do.

But, parables apart—and the parable of the python was
to come very exactly true when fifty nations gave judgment against Mussolini and left the execution of it to
one—where in that autumn of 1934 did England really
stand? The answer was given by Baldwin on November
28th.

> [Germany's] real strength is not fifty per cent of our strength
> in Europe to-day. As for the position this time next year, if
> she continues to execute her air programme without accelera-
> tion and if we continue to carry out at the present approved
> rate the expansion announced in Parliament in July . . . so
> far from the German military air force being at least as strong
> and probably stronger than our own, we estimate that we
> shall have in Europe a margin—in Europe alone—of nearly
> fifty per cent.

How did he know? And one reservation went far to nullify
the assurance. Three to two in Europe alone, provided there
was no acceleration in Germany. But what was the rate of
production in Germany and from what level did it start? On
the morning of the debate two statements were before the
Cabinet. The Air Ministry reckoned the number of German
aircraft at 1,000 of which 300 were available for front line
units. The Embassy made the figure 600. The French said
1,100. The *Daily Telegraph* had its own figures. So had
Churchill. But who knew?

The Secretary of State for Air at this juncture, Lord
Londonderry, was not on easy terms with Baldwin. The
Under Secretary, Sassoon, was an excellent departmental
spokesman, but hardly of the calibre to represent the Air
Force in the Commons. As a consequence Baldwin had to
speak for the Ministry. He ought therefore to have maintained a close relation with his colleague in the Lords, and
this he could never bring himself to do. Both in composition
and in direction the Air Ministry was notoriously weak: it
needed constant supervision from above. Baldwin lacked the
industry required for checking reports, collating tables,
cross-questioning witnesses. Nor could he have brought to

bear on a weak department the energy which Lloyd George or Curzon, Churchill or Beaverbrook would have shown, making every official feel that his life depended on it if his facts were loose, his figures hazy or his contracts extravagant. One might almost say that in these critical months the office of Prime Minister was neither filled nor vacant. MacDonald could not; Baldwin would not; and the Government of which they were joint heads was hardly better equipped to deal with defence than the Labour Government in 1931 to deal with finance.

One incident tells its own story. On November 29th 1933 a peer raised the question of defence, and Londonderry replied in a carefully drafted statement. Many of the Commons were listening, and one of them mentioned it in debate. He was ruled out of order. But surely it was a Government statement? "To be quite frank," Baldwin said, "I have not the slightest idea what has been said in another place."

And a second, disclosed by Churchill to the House of Commons, repeats the tale. In September 1934 he, with his scientific adviser, Professor Lindemann, travelled to Aix to lay before the Lord President a plan of research into the whole subject of defence against air attack. "He appeared to be interested." Austen Chamberlain was brought in and in February 1935 the group were received by MacDonald. He was sympathetic. On March 19th he announced that a special sub-committee of the Committee of Imperial Defence had been appointed. By the middle of June it had met twice.

After the reconstruction of the Government in 1935, Londonderry, loyally, but bitterly, made way for Cunliffe Lister, and was solaced with the Leadership of the Lords. Before very long, Cunliffe Lister was raised to the peerage and Halifax became Leader. I can only recount these facts: I cannot explain them. But, years later, Londonderry wrote:

I think, looking back, that you, Neville, and Ramsay lost confidence in me because you were frightened by the propaganda of Winston and Rothermere which asserted that the Germans were overwhelmingly strong. You had refused to listen to our advice on rearmament and I am sure you became anxious lest the propaganda might be correct, and that then you would be confronted with the charge of having failed in your duty of establishing the security of this country. I think that is why you threw me to the wolves.

It was one reason perhaps. Another was that Londonderry had involved himself in relations with German leaders out of which a German party would grow. There was undoubtedly much sympathy with Hitler, and to many Englishmen the restoration of Germany as a barrier against Communism was not unwelcome. In 1936 Londonderry visited Germany. He came back convinced that the German rulers desired friendship with England and that their preparations in the air were not nearly so far advanced as was commonly believed. Baldwin did not answer his letters: he did not even see him. And it may be doubted whether on either question, the extent of German rearmament or the trend of German sentiment, Baldwin had thought enough even to ask the right questions. The seer was baffled: the cloud would not take shape. To the realists—Vansittart and our ambassador Eric Phipps—Germany was the instrument of a group of gangsters bent on the utmost mischief that wickedness could devise or power effect. Others—like Arnold Wilson, who gave his life to atone for his error—thought there was something heroic in Germany's resurgence from the awful humiliation of 1918. Churchill felt that too. The sentimentalists, Lothian at their head, could not believe that Hitler really harboured any evil intent against England. And in these surging, crossing currents there were no marks by which Baldwin could steer.

CHAPTER XVIII

INDIA AGAIN

Since *we* became masters of the country: *our* native subjects: and other phrases of similar import constantly occur in books and familiar conversation. In the lower orders these ideas rise to the height of despotism, and are liable to all the excesses of despotism.

Warren Hastings

The fulness of time means *now* to India and *never* to certain die-hards.

S.B.

LATER events were to give an importance to Rearmament so overwhelming that we may be led to forget the other cares and concerns of 1935. An election was not far off, and the quidnuncs of the party and the press were particularly inquisitive to know where Lloyd George would be found. Some time before, Baldwin was advised by a friend, speaking from the most intimate authority, that Lloyd George's unbounded activity was making him a nuisance to himself and his surroundings. He wanted action, not office, a Commission on agriculture, perhaps, under Baldwin, not MacDonald. But as time went on, his ideas—"he goes from strength to strength, he is the Brougham of our age"—grew more capacious. He had a programme: he would make a party: he could put three hundred candidates in the field. They would no doubt help the return of many Socialists, and his own party added thereto would reduce the Conservatives in the House to a very narrow margin. A lively prospect for the Government, and encouraging rather than otherwise to certain foreign powers. But, he thought, he might lend a hand there. Hitler had often invited him to Berlin and, in office, he also might be of some use in placating the Führer. All which was duly reported to Baldwin, who had been taking soundings for some months past. The results were not favourable to Lloyd George. And no one, gossip said, was more unfavourable than Mrs. Baldwin.

At the same time there was evidence that, as in 1927 and 1928, the people were getting tired of the Conservatives, while the Conservatives were certainly getting tired of MacDonald and of Simon.

I regard the Government as at present constituted [so a colleague wrote in February] as surely doomed. The rot has set in strongly in the House and the country. Only early and drastic reconstruction can save (1) any National Government, (2) the Conservative party. I can't disguise from you that I don't think we can carry on with Ramsay as Prime Minister or Simon at the Foreign Office. Unless you become P.M., we are lost.

The inclusion of Lloyd George, he thought, would split the party. A large group of Tories would go into definite opposition.

Even if a new combination with L.G., *ergo* Winston, with Rothermere's support, won the next election, the Conservative party would be morally discredited for ever. It will be difficult enough to reunite the existing breaches, improbable with Ramsay, impossible with Lloyd George.

And then the real, innermost grievance.

I hope you would include in your Cabinet Anthony Eden, Duff Cooper, Malcolm MacDonald, and Brown or Burgin. If you can get a good *honest* businessman, not in Parliament, so much the better, if he is not too old. Young and new men are wanted, and the maximum number of departmental changes among the old hands. The country is bored by every single one of us in our present jobs.

Baldwin was not above taking advice, and the burden of sustaining his Prime Minister was growing very heavy. It had to be very delicately hinted to MacDonald that by clinging to office he was inviting a revolt which might fatally harm his son's career, and the reconstruction of the Government which accompanied the exchange of offices between Baldwin and MacDonald in June did make room for some of the younger men—Brown, Malcolm MacDonald and Eden. But not for Lloyd George. And not for Churchill.

I once said to Baldwin: "It must have been clear to you,

and MacDonald and Neville Chamberlain, that Churchill at all events was *safer* inside the Cabinet than outside. What kept him out?" "One war at a time," he answered, "India. He had gone about threatening to smash the Tory party on India, and I did not mean to be smashed." I have already spoken of the immense significance in Baldwin's eyes of an Indian settlement, detached from, and uninfluenced by, any party discords at home. And the time seemed to be ripe. In June 1933 he had promised "to take counsel" with his party when anything concrete emerged from the year-long enquiries and investigations into India. Very briefly—and Baldwin gave little heed to the details of this, or any other, measure—the first Plan had provided for local, provincial autonomy, with safeguards at the centre for the maintenance of order and stability. The situation was altered when it appeared that the Princes would join in a Federal scheme. The way was now clear to a true and permanent settlement —the White Paper of 1933—and the promise to "take counsel" with the party was discharged at a great meeting of the Central Council of the Party on December 4th 1934, held to determine the Conservative attitude to the report, arising out of the White Paper, of the Joint Select Committee. Baldwin, having briefly given the history of those years and the part taken in the evolution of India by the Conservative Viceroys Minto and Curzon, came to his favourite analogy, his favourite warning—Ireland, which,

> by an inscrutable decree of Providence, was pitchforked into the party warfare of England. The lines were drawn up in battle, and so hard-bitten were the two policies that accommodation became impossible. You had an alternative policy according to the Government which ruled in this country, with the inevitable result that the end was chaos, and the settlement one that neither party would have looked on, ten or fifteen years before, as even possible or desirable.
>
> That is what we want to avoid in India. You remember that in May last year I declared openly in favour of the principles underlying the White Paper. From that day I have done what some of my friends have found a difficulty in doing —I have muzzled myself.

He was thinking of the strangely named India Defence

League, founded in 1933 "to combat and expose the dangers of the White Paper."

But the Report is issued and I can no longer with decency or dignity maintain that position. I say, as Leader of the Conservative Party, with a full sense of responsibility, that I accept the Report as a basis of legislation and I recommend this Council to accept it too.

Remember: what have we taught India for a century? We have preached English institutions and democracy and all the rest of it. We have taught her the lesson and she wants us to pay the bill. There is a wind of nationalism and freedom blowing round the world and blowing as strongly in Asia as anywhere in the world. And are we less true Conservatives because we say: "the time has now come"? Are those who say "the time may come—some day", are they the truer Conservatives?

It is my considered judgment in all the changes and chances of this wide world today, you have a good chance of keeping India in the Empire for ever. If you refuse it, you will infallibly lose India before two generations are passed. That to my mind is the choice. Believing that, I can do no other than give you the advice I do. I ask you to support me. It will be a good thing for the world to know that the Tory party dares to take risks for the greater end and the greater good. If I stood alone, I would put these views before you. But I am not alone. I know I have the support of all my colleagues in the Government. I believe it will be seen I have the support of a large Conservative majority in the House. I am convinced I have the support of a large majority of all parties in the country— and the support of the Empire.

The voting was 1,102 to 390.

On February 5th he broadcast on the same theme and took the occasion to capture his audience with another of his delightful phrases:

I sometimes think, if I were not leader of the Conservative party, I should like to be the leader of the people who do not belong to any party. At any rate I should like to feel I had got them behind me as I have already got the great bulk of the Conservative party.

And so, very simply, to the business in hand.

We have learnt from experience that we shall preserve our Empire if we succeed in giving the units of it the right amount

of liberty in the right way at the right time. We are pledged
to the development of self-government in India since 1919.
We should have failed in one of our main Imperial undertakings if we were not able to extend the field of self-government in India. And we who invented this system of government, and pride ourselves on understanding it, will be there
to watch over, and preside over, its further development. The
British Raj is not cravenly withdrawing from India. It will
remain there until its work is complete and its presence no
longer necessary.

The debate on the second reading of the Government of
India Bill was for February 11th. That morning—a morning
of wild rumours in the City, of dissolution and a general
election—Baldwin received a warning letter from Salisbury.

> The left wing are restless: the right profoundly estranged.
> Your strength lies in the Conservative party. If they will not
> help you, even if you accept the tender mercies of Lloyd
> George, you will only estrange them still more. It is essential
> to consolidate the party. If tomorrow you close the door
> absolutely this cannot be done.

But it was done. The Bill passed by an overwhelming
majority. The Opposition were promised thirty days in
Committee instead of the fifty they demanded. The rumours
died down. The general election was postponed. As a lobby
correspondent wrote: "Mr. Baldwin spoke: and the crisis
was over. He is the most powerful man in the House of
Commons." The idealist of Empire was never out of touch
with the party chief. And the Middle Multitude, the "people
who belonged to no party," enjoyed his skill—so often on
the edge of disaster and always avoiding the fall—while
they profoundly respected his high integrity, the simplicity
of his moral code. One of his Dominion colleagues, Menzies,
wrote about this time:

> Your capacity to excite enthusiasm among the English people
> for something above their average level of thinking strikes
> me as without equal in our time.

Baldwin knew that not even Churchill could excite
enthusiasm among the people for the maintenance of the
British Raj. But—our pledges must be kept—that they could

understand, to that they would respond. Good faith, and good faith only, would save India for the Empire. But "What do you suppose educated Indians think about Kipling?" I once asked him. "It never occurred to me," he answered. "See if you can find out." He once met Gandhi, in November 1931. "What did you talk about?" "I really can't remember," he said. Will India remember Baldwin? I wondered.

CHAPTER XIX

IS IT PEACE?

FROM a distance it might seem that the England of those early months of 1935—the England which would soon be called upon to make choice of rulers—had three main problems to face, and if possible to solve. One was Unemployment, sometimes better, sometimes worse, but not, it seemed, to be dealt with by any measures within the financial order, the financial habit one might say, of the times. Or conceivably, its political habit. It is evident, from his speeches, that Baldwin at this time was anxious about the growth of a Fascist, totalitarian way of thought and action. I find him, most unexpectedly, calling for a return of Shirts, their colour and what they symbolised. And he knew, the General Strike having demonstrated its own futility, that the revolutionaries were full of a new device—to use Parliament for the destruction of Parliament by Enabling Acts and Orders in Council. All this needed to be watched. The second problem, India, was at least in a way to solution. The third, most intricate of all, was Defence, and here anxiety was growing keener as the months went by, the strength of Germany reawakened, and the strength of France seemed paralysed by internal discord.

In the winter of 1934–35 a group of high officials proposed to the Prime Minister and the Lord President that the time had come for a White Paper on defence in all its bearings to be prepared and laid before Parliament, and they suggested the broad outlines which such a Paper should take.

The principal aim of our Foreign Policy, they said, was the establishment of peace on a permanent footing: first by support of the League of Nations, and the promotion of international instruments making for a sense of security among the nations: the Quadruple Pacific Treaty; the Nine-Power Treaty; the Briand-Kellogg pact for the Renunciation of

War, and the Locarno Treaties. In the second place, we had done our best to bring the ex-enemy countries back into the comity of nations: reparations had been virtually disposed of; the Rhineland had been evacuated five years in advance of the Treaty date; all the ex-enemies had entered the League, and Germany was a permanent member of the Council. Finally, with a view to the reduction of armaments throughout the world, we had negotiated the Washington Treaty of 1922 and the London Treaty of 1930; and we had taken the leading part in the Disarmament Conference which opened at Geneva in February 1932.

An admirable record, but one, the signatories thought, which had led public opinion to assume that no more was needed and that we could gradually dispense with those other methods on which we had hitherto relied for our security. The assumption was premature. Nations were still prepared to use or threaten force, and "when once action has been taken, the existing international machinery for the maintenance of peace cannot be counted on to provide an adequate protection."

It would perhaps have been simpler to say that no machinery of any kind existed which could protect the most innocent of powers from attack by an aggressive neighbour. But, even so cautiously and moderately expressed, the dictum of the officials would undoubtedly have given offence, emotional offence, to a very considerable multitude. The phrase "collective security," embracing all the hopes and banning all the fears of mankind, had acquired a sanctity which was not to be violated by any anxious enquiry into its exact significance.

The draft was carefully studied, and, naturally, in places amended. It has often been said that the relations between Whitehall and Westminster conform to Oliver Cromwell's dictum: "What people want, or what is good for them—that is the question." Whitehall must keep its official eye fixed on public welfare and public security, and on nothing else: it must be candid, logical, convincing. And it is, for the most part, addressing an audience of picked men, men with experience in administration, policy and finance. But, in Westminster, to be logical—as Baldwin was for ever remind-

ing his public—may be mischievous: to be persuasive is at
the moment more effectual than to be convincing: and to be
candid at the wrong time may be suicidal. There lies the
weakness, and, in time of stress, the danger, of government
by debate. "With words we govern men." Shall we say that
our security is at stake, or, more outspokenly, our survival?
To some hearers one word may seem too mild: to some, the
other word will seem extravagant. Will it brace our people
to be told that if our sea power fails to guard our communications we shall starve, or will it seem no more than the
common change of debate—the clamour of service-men
"garrisoning the moon to defend themselves from Mars"—
of warmongers, in a word, a charge as damaging as Papist in
another age, and often as meaningless?

One of the officials wrote personally to Baldwin on February 26th 1935.

> Some of the amendments proposed at Monday's Cabinet
> in the wording of the draft White Paper on Imperial Defence
> seem to me to ignore the purpose for which that document
> was intended.
>
> The consideration which principally influenced those of us
> who were responsible for suggesting to the Cabinet the idea
> of a White Paper was that our own British public should be
> educated as to the vital necessity of putting our defences in
> order. Our draft, therefore, was addressed to our own people,
> and if it were taken in any foreign country as a cause of annoy-
> ance, that surely would be a very important element in its
> justification. We are so convinced (a) of the reality of the
> danger of war, (b) of the profound ignorance of our own
> people, (c) of the degree to which they have been misled by
> so called pacifist propaganda, that we feel that if any docu-
> ment is to serve a useful purpose it must be downright in
> its expression, and avoid all half-hearted or unconvincing
> phraseology.
>
> Any document whatsoever, however mealy-mouthed, if it
> contains one scintilla of truth cannot fail to tickle up the
> Germans, who, as we know perfectly well, are set on making
> themselves the most powerfully armed European state, and
> are in this mood not for mere display but for action when they
> think the time has arrived. The choice then seems to be
> between having no document at all if we are to be primarily

concerned with foreign and in particular German reactions, and having one which warns our own people in simple, unvarnished language.

The chief trend of the Cabinet variations is to weaken the warning which I have always imagined it is common ground that our public badly needs. And it seems to me that the one thing of supreme importance is that our public should be warned in no uncertain language.

I do therefore trust that the Cabinet may reconsider its attitude towards the purpose and form of the document, and address its mind not to gilding the pill for German consumption, but to ensuring that the pill provides the effective stimulation so much required by our sluggish-minded people.

The White Paper, as amended, was laid before the House on March 4th. The immediate consequence was unexpected. Hitler, who had invited Simon to Berlin for a friendly talk, contracted a bad cold and could not see him. At the same time, the White Paper, as the writer of the letter had foreseen, fanned the subsiding pacifism into fresh fury. A motion of censure was put down for March 11th.

Attlee's speech could for the most part have been written by any lobby correspondent of a Socialist habit of mind.

The nationalist and imperialist delusions that run all through this document are far more wild than any idealist dreams of the future that we hold. But we say that if there is this menace, it is not going to be met by any policy of alliances. It is not going to be met by attack. . . . We in the Labour Party . . . believe that the policy as outlined here is disastrous, and it is rattling back to war. The Lord President . . . said that the air menace must be dealt with by the young men. . . . Will he go to the country and ask what the young men think? I believe that the young people will reject it all over the world.

That the young men of Germany, Italy, Russia and Japan would have voted against the rearmament of England may well be true. But that is hardly what Attlee meant.

Baldwin spoke for less than an hour.

I think [he said] that this document will be one of historic interest. It is one in which a democratic Government tells what it believes to be the truth to democracy, and I hope to

show . . . that one of the greatest perils that have met de-
mocracies in the past, and meet them to-day, is when their
leaders have not the courage to tell them the truth.

Then, after some dutiful remarks on the League of
Nations:

> I want now to turn to questions of armament. . . . But before I
> do that I should like to make an observation to right honour-
> able and honourable gentlemen opposite. . . . I do not think
> they will help to produce that atmosphere in Europe which
> is so desirable by issuing papers headed "Hit Hitler". Let
> me ask them if they think it would make our feelings better
> towards any foreign country if they issued a document
> headed "Lam Lansbury"?

Then to the facts—the departmental facts. First, the Fleet.
We accepted limitations at Washington and London; and
we have not built up to our limits: much of our tonnage is
over-age. Japan is building—so is America, so are Italy and
France. Russia—the army raised from 600,000 to 940,000;
more than 2,000 front line aeroplanes. And we—from 1925,
the year of Locarno, to 1933, our defences dropped every
year. It was a risk. But it was a risk all parties took, and with
their eyes open. Then some quotations. From MacDonald
in 1930 broadcasting to America:

> If we cannot get an agreement we may be forced to expand.

From Alexander, First Lord of the Admiralty in the second
Labour Government:

> You can go too quickly . . . unless you can get other countries
> in Europe to go as quickly as you. You find a steady decline
> in our naval expenditure and a steady rise in almost every
> other country, and you begin to ask whether it is a sane
> policy.

From Tom Shaw, in the same year, but this time on the
Army:

> Example does not produce the results that I had hoped. . . .
> The example was shown, but the result did not come; and
> I cannot shut my eyes to the facts of life because I hold a
> beautiful theory that ought to work out but does not.

"I wish Mr. Shaw were here to-day," Baldwin added, and the reader of these debates has always to remember that one thing. There was very little likelihood of any Labour minister being called upon to form a Government within any time that could be foreseen. The Opposition therefore was not hampered, or sobered, by the reflection that it might have to defend what it was now assailing, and to reject much that it was now defending. The one thing that might bring them back to office was a pacifist surge like that which had engulfed East Fulham. So—to keep the country in good humour, to damp down the pacifist fires, to lift the constituencies over the election, to secure another term of office and so ensure continuance of the new policy of moderate rearmament, that, so far as Baldwin's instinctive movements can ever be set down in consecutive sentences, was the aim he had set himself.

A fortnight later he spoke to the Junior Imperial League at the Albert Hall.

> I would urge you, as thoughtful young politicians, to learn to see the wood in spite of the trees. Do not mistake acceleration for civilization. Each may be good in itself, but they have nothing in common.
>
> You are bombarded by a series of utterly disconnected impressions; unless you can put yourselves outside the events of the day, you will lose your perspective, and find yourselves unable to maintain that careful, steady and balanced judgment which is essential in politics. The spirit of enquiry is good. But do not forget that the faith which unites us is based on very old principles—the principles laid down by Disraeli: the maintenance of the Constitution, of Religion, of the Empire, and the welfare of the people.

Then he passed to the question of questions: peace and rearmament. The friends of the League had pitched their hopes too high, and reaction had followed.

> An Englishman was talking to a most distinguished Chinese, and the great advantage of the Chinese mind is that it does not hurry. The Englishman said, "Do you not think the French Revolution has had a profound effect on the future of humanity?" The Chinese scholar replied, "Do you not think it is rather too soon to say?"

Baldwin could not have drawn more truthfully the picture
of his own mind. Never to hurry; to stand quiet under
the bombardment of impressions; to cultivate perspective,
balance, the long, and sometimes misty, view. "What is
killing me," he said to me, in the time of distress between the
ending of the Hoare affair and the opening of the Abdication crisis, "is that I never have more than ten minutes for
anything." And indeed to combine an almost mystical
quietism with the occupation of an administrative chief in
time of peril is hardly within the power of man.

Two days later he spoke in Liverpool:

> For good or evil the days of non-interference by Governments
> are gone. We are passing into a new era. The full-fledged
> gospel of *laissez faire* ruled for about a century, and, whatever
> the ideals of the men who preached it, in practice it meant
> "every man for himself and the devil take the hindmost."
> Since the war of 1914 you may take it that that gospel has
> gone—as the slave trade went. Many things that were done,
> and innocently done, in the nineteenth century, cannot be
> done in the twentieth century. I am quite sure that the change
> which is coming calls for the greatest measure of statesmanship,
> on the part not only of those who are called statesmen but of
> those who are responsible for the conduct of business and of
> the Trade Unions.

It was observed, and is perhaps characteristic, that, speaking
in Liverpool, he said nothing about shipping. But—*con-
cordia ordinum, pax totius Italiae*: year after year he had reiterated and adorned this one theme, the one theme, we
might say, of which he was really master; and his oratory
was never more happy or abundant than in that spring of
1935, when he was sixty-seven and beginning, though not
yet very decidedly, to look forward to retirement. By now
the public had come to realize that the Lord President was
a great orator—it would have disturbed him to be called a
great rhetorician—an impeccable master of pathos and
humour, noble declamation and conversational grace;
a man so reasonably, so simply and firmly planted on
a few sound principles, that he had no need to raise his
voice in attack. The Opposition was a group of sincere and
honest men who had not yet seen the light: that was all. So

long as they showed themselves good Parliament men, he
was ready—a great deal too ready, some supporters thought
—to meet them half way. And in defence of Parliament he
would accept allies wherever he found them.

> It would be putting it too high [he said to the Press Gallery]
> to say that our Parliamentary system is endangered. But
> it is difficult for us in England to realize that so far from foreign
> countries admiring and desiring to emulate our system, in
> most countries that system, so far as it has been tried, has
> failed completely. But in these days ideas fly about with extra-
> ordinary rapidity and infection may pass from country to
> country. Now, no one cares less for criticism than I do: it
> is not complacency and it is not conceit. But I do resent criti-
> cism of a kind you see in a small section of the press, criticism
> of Parliament. There was never a time when it was more
> necessary for our stability that Parliament should be respected.
> Any organ that belittles the work of Parliament, that treats
> statesmen as fools or incapable or dishonest, can work an
> infinity of harm. If Parliament were killed it could never be
> replaced. I think it will live: and in its life I am convinced
> that the ultimate security and welfare of mankind, certainly
> in Europe, is involved. We have often had to stand alone in
> Europe. To-day we stand almost alone in Europe, in defence
> of that ordered liberty which has evolved itself through the
> centuries among our people. If that liberty is to live in Europe,
> it can only live by this people being faithful to its trust. If it is
> to be faithful, it must not only hold that banner aloft, it must
> be ready to defend it at every cost.

And from this height he sailed gracefully down to talk
about his age and the Herefordshire farmer who said to a
friend, "'We are both suffering from the same thing. We
been about a bit too long.' It was under the shadow of that
observation I felt it was time I gave notice that I could not
go on for ever doing the work I am doing now."

On April 8th he addressed the National Council of the
Evangelical Free Churches at Llandridnod Wells. The words
of the presiding minister are worth recording because they
do express, with no more exaggeration than the courtesy of
such occasions requires, the feeling for Baldwin, and about
Baldwin, which any mixed assembly, in England, Wales or
Scotland, at that time entertained:

No man in public life has made greater sacrifices for the common weal. He has held to his exalted conception of public life in face of multiplex and embittered opposition that would have overwhelmed a feebler man, steadfastly refusing to disappoint the legitimate hopes of India or to repudiate the plighted word of Britain. No one who has held such high office has more worthily embodied the best elements of the English character: simplicity, downrightness, candour, sympathy, a firm grasp of principle, linked with hospitality to new ideas. More than once I have heard Germans discussing British leaders. One after another has been named with adverse comment, and then has followed the phrase in a very different tone—*Aber der Baldwin.*

Roses, roses, all the way.

At the end of his speech Baldwin made an appeal for understanding in the vital matter of defence.

It is an easy thing to say, "We will have no armaments: we shall be all right." If you knew what was going on: if you were in London: if you saw the millions there, the women and children: if you knew that yours was the responsibility to decide whether any steps should be taken, or how, to protect them, you might perhaps judge more kindly than you do the decisions of a statesman on whom the responsibility does lie.

I may hate the prospect of an increased air force as much as any of you do. But I have to ask myself—may this or may it not make the difference? May it or may it not save the lives of those people who put me in power to do my duty? If I decide it is my duty to see that a greater deterrent is set up, and the way of the aggressor made harder, then I appeal to you to remember that dilemma and respect the decision of the statesman even if you do not agree.

But, somewhat later, I happened to remark to Baldwin, "The Secretary of the Treasury seems to be much concerned about our defences." "Better be minding his own business," Baldwin snapped. Public men learn how to deal with untimely, perhaps impertinent, curiosity. But in the tone of his voice I thought I heard the accent of a conscience not quite at ease. "We want a quiet man at the top," a Dorset farmer said, "and then there will be no wars." But the letter of February 26th, I felt, had stirred a doubt whether at that juncture a quiet man was the leader whom England

needed. Baldwin could indeed frame to himself unanswerable
reasons for remaining in office. The old King was nearing
his end, and Baldwin was convinced that he—and he only—
could guide the monarchy into safe waters. The storm of
pacifism was abating, but the wind was still blowing strong,
and if some mischance reawakened the tempest, what would
be the fate even of those limited and tentative efforts at rearmament to which the country on the whole seemed to be
reconciling itself? On every ground he must make sure of
the next election.

But had he done, was he doing, all that he might to prepare
the people for the necessity that was coming on them, the
necessity to which the Memorable Speech, as Churchill called
it, of November 1932 so directly pointed? I always felt that
the nerve, injured in October 1933, the East Fulham nerve,
never quite healed: he was afraid of the pacifists: he could
not bring himself quite to say, perhaps not quite to think,
"Germany is arming and we must arm too." And he was
not sure of himself. He could never master the logistics, as
we afterwards learnt to call them, of defence. All his shortcomings combined to keep him off that ground—his indolence, his lack of scientific interest, his indifference to administrative concerns. "I always make mistakes," he dole-
fully acknowledged, and in May of that fateful year 1935 he
had to acknowledge a mistake of the first magnitude. On
March 19th, in answer to Churchill, he repeated the old
formula "no inferiority to any power within striking distance." On May 2nd Hitler told Simon that parity had been
achieved. The reaction to this avowal—whether it was true
or false makes no difference: we were bound to assume its
truth—was immediate and almost violent. The Air Council
proposed that the existing programme—3,800 machines by
1939—should be pushed forward to 1937. Weir, who had
been Director of Aircraft Production in the first war, was
called into council. He was, very naturally, taken aback.
The new programme meant turning industry upside down.
And what, he asked, was the concurrent programme of air
defence? And the Army: what artillery, what tanks, what
machine guns, what ammunition? Baldwin had been warned
that a hurried, a panic, expansion in the air would react

dangerously on the other arms. But, politically, emotionally one might say, aircraft held the field. "They may," Weir said, "but if I am to visit industrial leaders and assess the capacity of their works, I must know, more exactly than I do, what the emergency is, and with what earnestness and sincerity the essential measures will be taken. We do not want to introduce war-practice or the war spirit into our factories in peace time. Quietly and rapidly we must find a way of our own not a copy of Hitler's." And then, in a letter to Baldwin, the wisest words spoken in this long debate. "What I always feared has happened. The technical structure behind our production is too weak to carry such a load as is now to be thrust on it." The programme was scaled down to 1,500 by 1937, all first-line craft with reserves. On May 22nd Baldwin acknowledged his error.

The occasion was indeed remarkable, and the House was crowded as it had not been since Grey spoke on that memorable August day of 1914. Again and again our statesmen had publicly pleaded with Germany to return to the League, to say something, to do something which might remove the shadow over Europe. And at last it seemed that Hitler had listened. He had spoken plainly: it seemed that he had spoken candidly, and in that spirit, Baldwin said, his declarations would be received and studied. But,

> I should like . . . to contrast the position of a democracy such as ours and the authoritarian State in regard to their security. If the authoritarian State . . . wishes . . . to increase its national defences, it can do so in absolute secrecy. It can draw a curtain round all that is happening in the country; nothing appears in the Press . . . nothing is said in Parliament, and the world is presented with a *fait accompli*. But . . . a year or two ago I said that one of the gravest causes of fear was ignorance as to what was going on behind some of these screens. Ignorance begets rumour. The veil has been partially lifted in Germany. I hope it will be fully lifted soon, so that we may be perfectly frank with each other.

Then the confession:

> First of all with regard to the figure I gave [in November] of German aeroplanes, nothing has come to my knowledge since that makes me think that that figure was wrong. I believed it

was right. Where I was wrong was in my estimate of the future. There I was completely wrong. . . .* Neither I nor any advisers from whom we could get accurate information had any idea of the exact rate at which production was being, could be, and actually was being speeded up in Germany. . . . We could get no facts and the only facts at this moment that I could put before the House are those which I have from Herr Hitler himself, and until I have reason to doubt them, which I have not at present, I put those figures before the House.

Hitler in fact had told Simon that he had achieved parity with England and was approaching parity with France. And taking that as our guide, our programme would provide for 1,500 first-line aircraft. First parity—or equality: then limitation, with a maximum for all. That is what Hitler seemed to be offering, and indeed what common sense would approve. There is no occasion for panic, but

> I will say this deliberately, with all the knowledge I have . . . that I would not remain for one moment in any Government which took less determined steps than we are taking to-day. . . .
> I had a peroration—I am not an orator, but I think that it was not a bad one—but it has been torn up because it was impossible to deliver it after the speech which was delivered in Berlin last night. I propose to end on a different note.

He set himself to woo the Opposition:

> I know how many Members of this House must be feeling. . . . It gives me an opportunity, moreover, of saying something that I hope they will forgive me for saying, but which I have wanted to say for some time. . . . Whatever may be said of this Parliament in years to come . . . and whatever may be said of the right honourable gentleman's party, I believe that full tribute will be given to him and his friends. . . . They have helped to keep the flag of Parliamentary government flying in the world. . . . They have equipped themselves for debate after debate, and held their own. . . . I know that they, as I do, stand for our Constitution and our free Parliament, and that has been preserved against all dangers.

* One of the officials engaged on these estimates thought it right to offer his resignation as having misled the Prime Minister. "I misled myself," Baldwin said.

A theme that Baldwin never wearied of was the valiant leadership with which Lansbury brought his broken legions into the field and kept them fighting. "They might have sulked, they might have seceded, and they never thought of it. When the history of that Parliament is written, see that Lansbury gets his due."

And then, the almost terrifying close, delivered with a passion rare in Baldwin's speeches:

> I tell the House that I have been made almost physically sick to think that I and my friends, and the statesmen in every country in Europe, two thousand years after Our Lord was crucified, should be spending our time thinking how we can get the mangled bodies of children to the hospitals and how we can keep the poison gas from going down the throats of the people. . . . I look for light wherever I can find it. I believe there is some light in the speech that was made last night. . . . I believe an opportunity may be open even now, at the eleventh hour . . . when in time measurable in our lives we may see banished from the world the most fearful terror and prostitution of man's knowledge that ever was known in the world.

The debate took the usual course. The question was carried by the usual majority. But in a thin House at dinner time, one Labour member dropped an observation—it is not even indexed in Hansard—of truly prophetic import.

> I would mention a case which . . . is before us even now. If the Government display the same pusillanimity in this case as they did in the case of Japan and Shanghai, we shall be presented with I know not how many more armament Votes. I refer to the Italian dispute with Abyssinia. . . . If we fail there we shall alienate the support of every minor Power in the world. They will say: "What is the good of the League of Nations?" and they will be justified in asking. Our attitude in that matter will have a very intimate relation to the policy of this country in preventing another world war.

A few days before, Abyssinia had demanded at Geneva the application of Article 15 of the Covenant of the League. That Article carried with it Article 12, and Article 12 led up to Article 16—the severance of relations with the Covenant breaker; the prohibition of all intercourse; and the use of armed force to protect the Covenant. If the clouds were thinning over the Rhine, they were growing darker over the Mediterranean. On June 27th MacDonald and Baldwin changed offices; the Government was reconstructed, and Baldwin became Prime Minister for the third time. Two months later—the interim included the Jubilee—Churchill gracefully yielded to necessity and declared that his opposition to the Indian legislation of the Government ceased with the Royal assent. In other words, if a Minister of Defence were needed, such a minister was at hand. "You have gathered," he wrote to Baldwin, "a fund of personal good-will and public confidence indispensable to our safety. But there lies before us a period of strain and peril which was not equalled—no, not in the Great War, certainly not in the years before it. Naturally, this will never fail to guide my actions."

And Churchill's warnings were beginning to tell in an unexpected quarter. On September 5th the Trades Union Congress, led by Ernest Bevin, resolved, by an immense majority, to support any action taken by the League in defence of peace, knowing full well, as the debate showed, that in defence of peace we must prepare for war. Here, at last, was the thing which Baldwin had always said was vital to any policy of armament and defence—the cooperation of the Unions.

He invited one of his most trusted friends in the Labour movement to come to Chequers. He spoke to him of his own duty to the public, the need for prompt rearmament, the unpopularity that must be faced and incurred. His visitor suggested a private conference with representatives of the Congress, to whom Baldwin could safely disclose what was in his mind: in particular the rate of rearmament in Germany. The chairman of the Congress was confidentially advised of what was in the air, so that he might be ready if sent for. And nothing happened. As in 1926 languor prevailed: the springs of action would not flow: the hand was put out to grasp the clue, but the fingers did not close.

I have sometimes asked myself—What should Baldwin have done? And when I think of the place he held in the public eye, his ascendancy and what it was grounded on, the trust and affection of a whole people: his mysterious significance in Europe,

> discreet, impalpable, invisible, efficient:

it seems to me that a wise counsellor, knowing Baldwin's strength, and also his weakness, could have said one thing only—"Make the sacrifice, resign. Tell the world that the task to which you set your hand is accomplished: that you are a man of peace, and that we are entering on a Passage Perilous where other gifts are needed. You will startle the world: you will dismay the country. But that dismay is the shock they need. The most frantic pacifist never called you a war-monger, and if you, released from office, discharged from party, say Arm, even pacifists will listen."

We have come to the turn, the reversal, in Baldwin's fame and fortune, and some day that reversal might well be taken as the theme of a tragedy after the classic pattern, the tragedy of the good man who lacked the one virtue which the occasion required. So one of his Greeks might have seen it, and among Englishmen, I once said, only one could write this life—Robert Browning:

> I go in the rain, and, more than needs,
>   A rope cuts both my wrists behind,
> And I think, from the feel, my forehead bleeds,
>   For they fling, whoever has a mind,
> Stones at me for my year's misdeeds.

CHAPTER XX

THE FAITH OF A ROMANTIC

ANY man born in 1867 grew up in a world of fierce controversy over the foundations of the Christian faith. For all
which Baldwin cared little or nothing. Once I found him
looking for Browning's *Death in the Desert*: "I told my
daughter," he said, "that that was my religion." In his last
sad days he drew some comfort from the offices of the
Church. But at all times he was a religious man—penetrated
with the mystery of the world and the Power behind the
world and the slow coming of the Kingdom of God. To the
Bible Society he said:

> To the man or woman that reads the Bible . . . what is Jewish
> or Greek or Oriental falls away, and there emerges, and must
> emerge, the universal appeal to mankind of the personality
> of our Lord . . . if I did not believe that our work was done
> in the faith and the hope that at some day, it may be a million
> years hence, the Kingdom of God would spread over the whole
> world, I could have no hope, I could do no work, and I would
> give my office over this morning to anyone who would take it.

To the Wesleyans:

> Wesley's supreme legacy to this country was his conception
> of a practical religion for the ordinary man and woman. He
> aimed at finding—and here I come back to that calm mind of
> his century—a reasoned balance between individual con-
> version and collective worship. . . . He knew England . . . and
> he knew Englishmen. Historians now realise that they
> cannot explain the nineteenth-century England until they can
> explain Wesley. And I believe it is true to say that you cannot
> understand twentieth-century America unless you understand
> Wesley.

To the Baptists:

> You have stood from the earliest days for the completest inde-
> pendence of the soul . . . you proclaim the responsibility and

the right of every man to pray and to worship as he chooses. . . .
In that belief you throw a most tremendous responsibility
on the individual. And in that you are doing in the sphere
of religion exactly what the spirit of the age is doing in the
sphere of politics. Democracy means nothing if it does not
mean the realisation by the individual of his responsibility. . . .
He is the salt; he is the leaven; he is the grain of mustard seed.
And it is only in so far as the individual, whether it be in
religion, or in politics, can live the life that is demanded of
him for the health of the whole, that that whole can live at all.

Always the Individual: not in isolation, though, but freely
uniting for the service of the whole; respecting the law because he had helped to make it; and taking from the old
radical Bentham that motto of a good citizen, "to censure
freely and to obey punctually." That is democracy: and
democracy is a most difficult form of government, being at
once a political arrangement and a social ideal; regarded
from one side, a fact; from another, still an aspiration.

It was characteristic of Baldwin that the widest, most comprehensive statement of his political philosophy—shading off
into his religious creed—should have been delivered, in
Coventry, at a Conference of the Brotherhood movement,
and in memory of John Clifford, a man whom admiring
followers sometimes called the greatest Protestant since Cromwell. Baldwin had been out of office for a year, and the discontent within his own ranks made it doubtful whether he
would ever be in office again. So he came not as a party
leader but as "a spectator who stands back for an hour to
gaze on the arena where the battle is being fought." There
were, he said, two main sources from which our political
ideas were derived. One was Greece—the practice of the
city states, their moral decline, the speculations thereon of
their historians and philosophers. The other was the self-
governing congregations of the seventeenth century, whose
ideals were summed up in one famous phrase of the Puritan
Colonel, Rainborough, "I think that the poorest he that is
in England hath a life to live as the richest he." Here, in
those tiny congregations, we had democracy on the infini-
tesimal scale. In Greece, we saw it on the municipal scale.
Our colossal task was to take over these principles of

personal participation in government, co-operative discussion and active consent, and apply them to the immense populations, all free and all enfranchised, of a modern state. And this too at a time when the main current of political thought in Europe was splitting into two channels where it ran all the more violently—Caesarism and Communism. From what did they draw their power? From disappointment; from impatience; from the failure of faith.

Here, at home, all parties were deeply committed to intervention in the lives of the people. But there was no constitutional machinery to record the results of these assaults on human personality, and yet it was the quality of that personality which would determine the fate of the country. Character is built by innumerable acts of choice. But if the crucial choices are made by the state, what becomes of Colonel Rainborough and the democratic ideal? When, by redistribution of the national wealth, we have completed the fabric of public services—some protective, some constructive —will John Smith be a better man: will his life be fuller; will he feel more keenly his own responsibility for the government which ultimately he and his like control?

Commonplaces. Yes, but the common places, the *loci communes*, of European speculation from Aristotle and beyond. Thucydides would have understood our problems and our troubles, and there is no variety of man in public life, Baldwin was fond of saying, that you will not meet in Aristophanes. It is the tradition in which so many of our statesmen had been reared, but in Baldwin's mind it ran into that other tradition, all our own, of individualism, non-conformity, toleration: mirth, mystery and romance. And as Newman had said in words which Baldwin had read at Harrow and never forgotten:

> What is Christian highmindedness, generous self-denial, contempt of wealth, endurance of suffering, and earnest striving after perfection, but an improvement and transformation under the influence of the Holy Spirit of that natural character of mind which we call romantic?

Romantic—but the word bears more senses than one. "Where he himself is the subject, Baldwin's memory is not to be trusted." Such was the warning once given me by the wisest and kindliest head in Fleet Street. It was not untruthfulness so much as an overriding play of fancy which one learnt to discount: a very harmless play, because in all matters of deep concern Baldwin was direct, exact, downright, sincere. But he liked to romanticize his burdens, and they were heavy: his sacrifices, and they were keen. "For twenty years I have never seen the pageant of blossom in the Vale of Evesham from the first damson to the last apple." And, I used to think, though he was not indifferent to the emoluments of office, the rewards he cherished most, and which were hardest to forgo, were those which England had always reserved for favoured statesmen, like fairy tales for good children: the splendours of the Temple or the Mansion House: the sumptuous ritual of an installation: the hounds meeting at Chequers: visits to the great houses of England: intimacy with the Royal Family: dainty missives to the young princesses: the Garter, the Earldom, the Coat of Arms with the sprig of broom indicating his wife's Plantagenet descent. A certain vein of sentiment verging on the sentimental was there too, but it was salted with a ready, half-rustic humour, pungent and broad at once,* and never trespassing beyond the limits set by provincial propriety.

Many statesmen have left rules for the guidance of their successors: Baldwin never assumed the part of tutor. But all he had to say to those who would serve the democratic state was said in one broadcast:

> Use your commonsense: avoid logic: love your fellow men: have faith in your own people, and grow the hide of a rhinoceros.

Or, as Wellington had said before him:

> There is only one line to be adopted in opposition to all tricks: that is the steady straight line of duty, tempered by forbearance, levity and good nature.

And of these, levity was not the least: "the English laugh— the healthiest sound in the world."

---

* His masterpiece in this mode must remain in a translation furnished by the Board of Education :

> Aulam hospitalem Maximus subit noster :
> Intrat : sedet : circumspicit : notat nemo :
> Cogantur ut notare, quid facit ? Pedit.

CHAPTER XXI

ITALY

The Peace Ballot of 1935 had disclosed an extraordinary re-shaping of opinion; of nearly 12,000,000 balloteers only one in five had rejected military action against a declared aggressor: and in the circumstances of the moment the decision might be read as a vote for collective security or as a vote against Mussolini, whose designs on Abyssinia were now patent. Conversations having failed to produce any form of compromise, the dispute was due to be considered by the Council of the League on September 4th. On August 23rd Baldwin was brought back from Aix, and on the following day the Cabinet decided "to uphold the obligations of Great Britain under the Covenant." In this sense Eden spoke at Geneva, followed a few days later by Hoare.*

"To make the will of England prevail among the nations": so, many years before, Baldwin had declared his resolution. And now it seemed the moment had come. Ten million voters had bound themselves to fight for the League. Those were not the words, but that was the meaning, and with that determination charging his sentences, Hoare spoke on September 11th. Whatever doubts the Assembly may have felt when he rose, there was no question, when he sat down, that the will of England had prevailed. Never did our name stand higher in Europe than at the close of that day. It seemed as if England had learnt to speak once more with the voice of Palmerston, or Pitt, or Cromwell.

There were indeed certain material questions remaining to be answered—whether the League would fight for itself, or leave England to fight for it; whether Mussolini would accept its judgment with becoming meekness, whether economic sanctions would lead to military sanctions, and if so

* Hoare was Foreign Secretary; Eden was specially charged with League of Nations affairs.

what the end might be. Italy had no friends; Germany
would do nothing to embarrass the League; the United
States might even help. Our fleet in the Mediterranean had
been reinforced and Mussolini told plainly why—because
of the threats that were daily noised by the Italian press.
So far, we were strong. But there remained the uncertainty
as to the attitude of the other powers, even of France. Could
we count on being allowed to use the French ports for
docking and refitting? If we acted, should we find ourselves alone? If we did not act, should we not be accused
on every platform of deserting or betraying the League?
And what would be the result of an election fought on
that issue? Defeat for the Conservative Party—and the
sequel? War with Italy, for which we were not prepared? We
must follow the path marked out at Geneva : above all, we
must keep step with France. But would an attack on Malta
or Egypt engage either France or the League on our side?
Single-handed we could doubtless make war on Italy,
though our losses might be heavy. In capital ships we had,
it is true, the preponderance. But Italy was far stronger in
submarines. Our defences against air attack were still weak,
and a raid in the Narrow Seas, between Italy and Africa,
might cripple our Fleet. Above all, and again, what ports
could we use if France stood neutral? France meant Laval.
He was believed to be half-hearted even as to sanctions. It
was certain he would take no military measures against
Italy; he would never consent to join in a blockade. We
could only hope that moderate sanctions would incline
Italy to a settlement, and then—we must not be intransi-
gent, we must give Italy some satisfaction in Ethiopia. The
Pact which was nearly to overthrow the Administration,
which did bring about Hoare's retirement in December,
was in contemplation already, eight weeks before the
election.

On October 9th, five days after the Italian declaration of
war against Abyssinia, the estimate was, if anything, less
favourable. For the first time the members of the Government had before them a complete view of our defences,
until now considered only in committees : and Neville Chamberlain drew the only possible conclusion. "Hitherto," he

said, "the position had been governed by financial considerations. They must be reviewed—and in a very different light."

Rarely can our history have known a Government in such
a case. An election impending: with every hope of a victory
for the party in office. The national finances in order; the
national temper cheerful. A popular Prime Minister, a
feeble Opposition. But the brighter the prospects in the
country, the gloomier were the debates in Cabinet. On
October 16th a Committee was appointed to draw up the
Election Programme of the Conservative Party. That same
day the Cabinet learned that Laval had discovered an excuse
for not pledging France to our support. Our reinforcement
of the Fleet in the Mediterranean, he said, was action outside the League: it amounted to a provocative act. France
thereby was absolved from common action. It was known
that Laval was in communication with Mussolini: the French
Admiralty would not allow its officers to discuss plans of co-
operation with our Naval staff. The Sea Lords were profoundly anxious. They had supposed, in case of hostilities,
that France would act in the air over North Italy: that we
should hold the Straits and the Eastern Mediterranean,
France the centre. Now it was doubtful—worse than
doubtful—whether we should have the use of the French
ports. "Don't let us quarrel with France as well as Italy,"
Baldwin exclaimed. But the conclusion was not to be evaded.
Keeping step with France meant moderate sanctions for
Italy—sanctions in principle, so to speak, and a simultaneous
search for ground of accommodation. If that failed, then we
must gird ourselves to fight, without France on our side.
True, by October 23rd, Laval, in answer to enquiries, had
given assurances that might be taken as satisfactory by those
who trusted Laval. So far we were in step: we need not, and
would not, reduce the Fleet in the Mediterranean. But, that
understood, we must work toward an accommodation with
Italy and be gentle with our sanctions.

It is to be remarked that in all these discussions Germany
was barely mentioned. Yet there could not be much doubt
that fear of Germany had led the French Government to
settle its differences with Italy early in 1935, or that, as
Churchill said, the free hand in Abyssinia had been thrown

in. In return, France got the equivalent of ten divisions
moved from the Italian to the German frontier. The most
high-minded of French statesmen might very well have
paused before he committed his country to war against
45,000,000 Italians, with 60,000,000 Germans biding their
time, waiting the moment to march into the Rhineland.
Hoare's words were brave; the spectacle of fifty sovereign
states concerting economic action against an erring sister
was heartening: the grey lines of the *Hood* and *Rodney* steam-
ing eastward through the Straits, a magnificent demonstration of power in defence of law. So long as it was certain that
Mussolini would not fight. If he did—then monstrous and
incredible as it might sound, England might be forced to
capitulate to the upstart autocracy of the Quirinal; the
League would be in ruins; Germany might strike by land,
Japan in the Eastern seas.

Parliament was dissolved on October 25th, the Election
was fixed for November 14th. The programme of the Party
was on familiar lines: support for the League but no isolated
action: forces adequate to our obligations and the security
of our food supplies: the gaps in our armaments to be closed:
the general limitation of all armaments to be pursued: and,
in the air, no inferiority to any power within striking distance.
The Prime Minister's own broadcast lacked nothing in firmness or clarity. "I will not be responsible for any Government
at this time, unless I am given power to remedy the defi-
ciencies which have occurred in our defences since the War."

But Baldwin had a previous engagement to address the
Peace Society on October 31st.

> I must speak to you [he said] in some sense as Head of the
> Government, but I do not wish my remarks to be taken as a
> contribution to the election torrent. There is no need for that;
> I am talking of Peace, and I see no issue between the parties
> in their love of peace. Perhaps, also, you will think of me as
> speaking personally, as one citizen of this country facing a
> question which no honest citizen, man or woman, can evade.
>
> Now that question will in the end be answered not by
> Governments, but by peoples. There may be Governments
> deliberately planning the future, leading reluctant or un-
> suspecting people into the shambles. It sometimes looks as if
> it were so. I confess that in my own political experience I have

not encountered Governments possessed of all these malevolent
qualities. Most Governments seem not much better or worse
than the people they govern. Nor am I on the whole disposed
to conclude that the people are such a helpless, ineffective
flock of sheep as those who claim to speak in their name often
imply. They have in fact a way of making their opinions known
and heard when they feel deeply.

I have a second reason for treating the subject as a personal
reality.

And now the enchanter was weaving all his spells in a passage
of such eloquence as neither that audience, nor any other,
had ever heard from him before.

Most of us, when we consider the subject, do not see great
movements, deep moral or legal issues, groupings of Powers,
or any of those "huge cloudy symbols." We catch our breath
and think of something far more intimate, much more dear,
the lives of our children and grandchildren, of the familiar
sights and institutions of our own land, all the boundary
stones of our spiritual estate. We live under the shadow of
the last war and its memories still sicken us. We remember
what war is, with no glory in it but the heroism of man. Have
you thought what it has meant to the world to have had that
swathe of death cut through the loveliest and the best of our
contemporaries, how public life has suffered because those
who would have been ready to take over from our tired and
disillusioned generation are not there?

Perhaps we avert our thoughts from these terrors and
send them roaming over this "dear dear land." We think
perhaps of the level evening sun over an English meadow with
the rooks trundling noisily home into the elms; of the plough-
man "with his team on the world's rim creeping like the
hands of a clock," one of those garnered memories of the long
peace of the countryside that a wise man takes about with him
as a viaticum. To what risks do we expose our treasures, irre-
placeable treasures, for you cannot build up beauty like that
in a few years of mass production? Make no mistake: every
piece of all the life that we and our fathers have made in this
land, every thing we have and hold and cherish, is in jeopardy
in this great issue.

But what was the issue? In one word, Abyssinia. Would the
League of Nations, could the League of Nations, restrain
the ambitions of Mussolini? By representations—by a vote

of censure—by economic sanctions—in the last resort by
sending the fleet to look at him and closing the Suez Canal?
But:

> Judgement may lead to action, cautionary action, restraining
> action, at the extreme to coercive action. We mean nothing
> by the League if we are not prepared, after trial, to take action
> to enforce its judgement. Look at the alternative. When I
> spoke, so inadequately, of the horrors of war, was it not clear
> that we must be prepared to take risks to prevent that evil
> thing stalking again across the world?
>
> The judgement of the world, given, as it must be, unani-
> mously in open Assembly, after long discussion, is no light
> and hasty thing. The last few weeks have taught us what it
> means. *Securus judicat orbis terrarum.* That is the power of the
> League of Nations.
>
> I am not asking you to search the skies, to look for clouds
> on the horizon, much less to give way to imaginings of possible
> grounds or signs of trouble: nor to talk of such things. I think
> that all such talk of trouble is evil: and it forecasts a feeling of
> nervous excitement which is itself an unhealthy condition.
> Do not fear or misunderstand when the Government say that
> they are looking to our defences . . . do not fear that it is a
> step in the wrong direction. You need not remind me of the
> solemn task of the League—to reduce armaments by agree-
> ment. But we have gone too far alone and must try to bring
> others along with us. I give you my word that there will be no
> great armaments. We are "bound over to keep the peace,"
> and it may not be an easy task. But we accept it.

This address might rank as Baldwin's masterpiece in the
vein of high, impersonal persuasion. He asked for no votes:
he announced no policy. Rather, one may say, and it is perhaps the essential achievement of the orator, he created a
mood. One listener wrote: "It was like the first hearing of
a great symphony." And Neville Chamberlain:

> I will frankly confess that at times I have felt some transient
> impatience when it has seemed difficult to bring your thoughts
> down to the earthy decision I wanted. But when I read a
> speech like that I can only think of our good fortune in having
> a leader who can raise us so far above ourselves, and can ex-
> press what we should like to believe we had thought ourselves,
> in such moving words.

But when the last wave of music or of emotion had died away, what did it all come to? That war was a dreadful thing: that we must not think about it too much: that somehow the League of Nations might avert it or end it: and that meanwhile we must arm, but also not too much. But gnawing at the speaker's mind all the time was the innermost conviction that the League could not stop the career of Mussolini; that France would slip out; and that without France we could not hold our own in the Mediterranean and the Eastern Seas. We did not, could not, arm to the level of our needs in 1934. Therefore we depended on France in 1935, and France was faithless. But—the election had to be won. And it was won. It was the quietest election on record and the Conservative majority, though naturally lessened, was still 428 to 184.

When Baldwin spoke to the Peace Society, sanctions had been applied to Italy by Order in Council to take effect on November 18th. In the Debate on the Address Hoare was able to report that they were going well. As regards oil, there had been delays—at the request of Laval—which gave opportunity for further efforts. But Hoare was worn out. Four years at the India office, then the Foreign Office "weekdays and Sundays, day and night, the spate of telegrams and dispatches, problems and crises, had never ceased." The doctors ordered him to take an immediate rest. He planned to go to Switzerland with his wife on December 7th, knowing that within a few days the Cabinet would have to decide whether it would agree to complete the economic blockade of Italy by an embargo on oil and face the danger of an Italian attack on Malta or Egypt. At the same time no agreement had been reached with France upon any proposals for peace that might be laid before the League or the belligerents.

At this point, just as he was starting, an urgent message, backed by our Ambassador, reached him from Laval. The French Prime Minister begged him to travel by way of Paris, and meet him there. The conversations lasted over the first day well into the second. Then Hoare escaped to Switzerland, fell on the ice and broke his nose in two places. Meanwhile, on the day after the Paris meeting, certain

French newspapers published sensational and inaccurate accounts of what the two Ministers had agreed upon. The London press took the alarm, and before the unfortunate negotiator had time to explain what he had done or not done, the tide of feeling was sweeping him out of office. "I don't profess," Tweedsmuir wrote from Ottawa, "to understand exactly what happened. . . . but what seems plain is that public opinion suddenly took a hand in directing the game, which is a most interesting phenomenon and proves that after all we are a genuine democracy."

What had Hoare done? He had preserved, in form at least, the unity of the Stresa Front, the good understanding between the old allies, France, Italy and England. He had assented to proposals which might be a ground of peace between Italy and Abyssinia. He had saved the League of Nations from collapsing under a burden which it was manifestly too weak to carry. He had in fact treated the Italo-Abyssinian conflict as a war like any other war to be settled by mediation and hard bargaining on either side. And public opinion in England regarded it as a monstrous defiance of the League which England was committed to support. Very rarely in our history has there been an outburst of popular indignation so vehement and so spontaneous.

Baldwin's insight had failed him. When therefore he found the whole press ablaze, and his postbag bursting with wrathful letters, he was utterly at a loss. Always loyal to his colleagues, his first impulse had been to accept the arrangement proposed by Hoare and give it the approval of the Cabinet. But the debate on December 10th disclosed that, in condemning the agreement, a great body of opinion, perhaps a majority of the party, was at one with the public. Eden could not stem the tide. Neither could the Prime Minister, feeble, toneless and unhappy. Hour by hour it was plainer that the Government was discredited, that defeat was possible—defeat in the House first, and then, after dissolution, defeat in the country. Hoare made his leader's way easy. "Convinced," he wrote "that a Foreign Secretary must broadly represent his countrymen's views, and that owing to a series of mishaps and misunderstandings I had lost the confidence that had previously been shown

me from so many quarters, I at once resigned my office."
On the following day, December 19th, he made his defence
before a House sympathetic but resolute.

Indeed, if Attlee had not overplayed his hand he might
have had Austen Chamberlain on his side and between them
they might have brought the Government down. But he
used words,

> There is the question of the honour of this country, and there
> is the question of the honour of the Prime Minister. If, as is
> suggested in some quarters, the Prime Minister won an
> election on one policy and immediately after victory was
> prepared to carry out another, it has an extremely ugly look,

which touched the loyalty and chivalry of the old statesman.
Baldwin could only repeat that his judgment had been at
fault, that he recognized when the conscience of the people
was aroused, and that the League of Nations was still the
keynote of our policy. But Chamberlain declined the place
in the Cabinet which the Prime Minister offered him.

Baldwin in those days wore the air of a man crushed by
some appalling disaster. For his own well-being the shock
could not have been more unhappily timed. The King's life
was drawing to its close. On the night of January 20th he
passed peacefully away, and Baldwin knew, as no one else
did, the trouble that might follow. But at the time of the
King's dangerous illness in 1928 he had gone down to meet
the Prince at Folkestone. They talked all the way to London,
and as they parted the Prince said, "Now you do understand, don't you, that you can always talk to me about
everything?" That assurance Baldwin kept in mind. But
for the moment there was no apprehension of mischief to
come, only sorrow and hope, themes exquisitely blended in
Baldwin's broadcast speech, from its opening text,

> After he had served his own generation by the will of God, he
> fell on sleep and was laid unto his fathers.

to its close (only the first few lines were written, scribbled in
pencil):

> All eyes are upon him [the Prince], as he advances to his
> father's place, and, while he is no stranger to public duty, he is
> now summoned to face responsibilities more onerous, more

exacting, more continuous, than any he has hitherto been asked to discharge. . . . He inherits an example of kingly conduct, of virtue, of wisdom, of endurance. King George's reign was marked by far-reaching constitutional and Parliamentary changes without precedent in our long history. He earned the loyalty and respect of all parties in the State, new and old. He hands down in turn to his son the throne he himself received from his father, and he hands it down with its foundations strengthened, its moral authority, its honour and its dignity enhanced. It is an incomparable and awe-inspiring inheritance.

The young King knows the confidence we all repose in him. He knows that he commands not only the allegiance, he knows that the understanding, the affection and the prayers of the countless multitudes of his subjects are with him at this hour. May God guide him aright and God save the King.

When Austen Chamberlain died, Baldwin repaid his loyalty most nobly.

He has left us. In . . . that country-side where I was born and where old English phrases linger . . . even now I hear among those old people this phrase about those who die: "He has gone home." It was a universal phrase among the old agricultural labourers, whose life was one toil from their earliest days to the last, and I think it must have arisen from the sense that one day the toil would be over and the rest would come, and that rest would be home. So they say "He has gone home."

When our long days of work are over here there is nothing in our oldest customs which so stirs the imagination of the young Member as the cry which goes down the Lobbies: "Who goes home?" Sometimes when I hear it, I think of the language of my country-side, feeling that for those who have borne the almost insupportable burden of public life there may well be a day when they will be glad to go home. So Austen Chamberlain has gone home . . . the best thing we can do to honour his memory is to cling more closely to the two things to which he clung throughout his life. He always maintained that public service was the highest career a man could take. . . . He had an infinite faith in the Parliamentary system of this country. Let us resolve once more that we can best keep his memory bright by confirming our own resolution that government of the people by the people shall never perish on the earth.

CHAPTER XXII

SANCTIONS AND THE RHINELAND

OUR export of coal to Italy had ceased and 30,000 miners were out of work. The Mediterranean Fleet was at war strength: already the strain on men and ships was making itself apparent: and a concentration in those waters meant weakness in those more distant seas where Japan was already formidably strong. Commercial relations between England and Italy were suspended, and business houses were lodging claims for compensation and unrecovered debts.

These warnings, from the Admiralty and Board of Trade, could not be ignored. And behind them was the most formidable truth of all, that Italy, whatever the League might say or do, would continue to receive oil from the United States and Venezuela. There was no question of declaring the Italian ports blockaded, and that being so, the oil would come through. Crude oil; whether the Italian refineries could handle all that Italy needed, might be doubtful. But at the most, the embargo could only add to her difficulties, it could not bring her activities to a stop. Yet—even this might be enough. And the coal trade was dead already for want of sterling exchange. The good name of the League was at stake, and perhaps American sentiment might be stirred by the spectacle of the nations doing justice on the strong and on behalf of the weak. In England that sentiment was working strongly, not least among the Trade Unions, whose good will was essential if our own defences were to be restored. And not England alone was concerned. The Dominions were watching, with some distrust, what might be interpreted as the play of rival Imperialisms in European waters: and the confidence of the Dominions was a vital element in Imperial strategy.

So the debate rolled, backward and forward, till the whole ground had been covered. Then Baldwin spoke. His own position, he said, was at stake, and though that might not mean much to him, the prestige of the Prime Minister was a matter of concern to the Government as a whole. The electors had decided to give the League a fair trial: the world was entitled to know, experimentally, whether the League could be made to work. To hold back now meant political disaster—party disaster—at home: and if the Dominions were to co-operate they must first be satisfied of our sincerity and right intentions. So must the Trade Unions.

It was agreed that sanctions should be continued.

On March 2nd the Cabinet decided that the White Paper on Defence should be published on the following day. The Opposition resolution, moved by Attlee, in effect sums up the policy of the Labour Party, in foreign affairs and, by implication, in defence; the policy which that party would doubtless have pursued if the Abyssinian incident had placed it in power.

As the safety of this country and the peace of the world cannot be secured by reliance on armaments but only by the resolute pursuit of a policy of international understanding, adherence to the Covenant of the League of Nations, general disarmament, the progressive improvement of international labour standards, and economic co-operation so as to remove the causes of war, this House cannot agree to a policy which in fact seeks security in national armaments alone and intensifies the ruinous arms race between the nations, inevitably leading to war; views with alarm proposals for the reorganisation of industry on a war basis which will enormously extend the vested interests in arms manufacture and create a serious menace to organised labour and to trade union standards; and has no confidence in His Majesty's Ministers whose unworthy and ambiguous foreign policy has largely contributed to the present state of world unrest.

Here was a gap, a chasm rather, between the parties, and what could fill it? Nothing, it might seem, but the ruins of the League. "We must try the League," one Minister declared, "and if it fails—break it." It had broken itself. And who, besides ourselves, had moved a ship or a man in its defence?

Eden returned from Paris on March 5th with an impression of deep anxiety in France. There it was believed that if sanctions were intensified, Italy would withdraw from the League and denounce the Locarno Treaty. The result would be a coming-together of Mussolini and Hitler and a German occupation of the Rhineland. It was clear that the Cabinet and the country had to decide whether, if the Germans did march and the French took counter action, we were bound by Treaty to move with France. Would public opinion, in the last resort, countenance war with Germany to expel Germans from their own territory? The French, unsure of themselves, were asking where we stood, and till they knew they would not risk a breach with Italy. Where did we stand? Once more the debate moved over that only-too-well-trodden ground, our obligations were clear, as clear as our incapacity to make them good. In five years we need fear no one—but we might not have five years. Only one course was possible—to postpone and postpone again: to negotiate with Hitler, to secure, if only for the moment, some agreement in the air.

This was the decision of Thursday March 5th. On Saturday, Hitler proclaimed the reoccupation of the Rhineland and the German army marched. Meanwhile, on the Friday, Eden had seen the German Ambassador and repeated his suggestion (it had been made twice before, on December 13th and February 27th) that the Locarno Powers should proceed with a pact for mutual security in the Air. On the following day the German Ambassador informed him that, in the view of his Government, the Franco-Russian agreement had cancelled Locarno, and Germany was now free. On the 10th Eden and Halifax saw the French Ministers in Paris. There they found that our policy—to acknowledge our obligations by formally condemning Germany's action and then proceeding to negotiate on the basis of an accomplished fact—was acceptable neither to the French nor to the Belgians. Italy explained that while exposed to sanctions she was clearly not in a position to act in defence of Locarno. But if Locarno broke, then what course could the French Government take except the old course of alliances to pin Germany down? A few months before Hoare had felt him-

self driven to sacrifice Abyssinia to keep the Stresa Front
intact. He sacrificed a principle in order to save a system.
Must we now accept the remilitarisation of the Rhineland in
order to save, and extend, Locarno? There was indeed this
difference. Public opinion was against Italy in Abyssinia.
But the popular wisdom in which Baldwin so profoundly
believed had pronounced in favour of Hitler, "Why shouldn't
a man walk into his own backyard?" It was reported too
that among soldiers of the last war feeling against France
was very bitter. In short, England would not fight over the
Rhineland—that was clear. Equally clear to those within
the Cabinet circle was that England could not fight for the
Rhineland—or for anything else. Nothing remained but
diplomacy, the kind of diplomacy with which the Venetian
Republic had concealed from the world the fact that Venice
was no longer a great power.

Postpone—and postpone. But should we be any better
off if ever the war we were postponing did come? French
Ministers, who knew their people and the precarious balance
of French parties, said no: "either now, or in 1939." And
those who had explored the underworld of French politics
had good reason to doubt whether by 1939 the French
Government or the French forces would be in any better
state to answer a German challenge. Should we? "Locarno,"
Baldwin said, "was grounded on two assumptions—that
France would always be strong, and Germany always disarmed. Now—disarmament had failed and Germany was
armed. We had begun, but we had been caught at a dis-
advantage because it takes time to educate opinion in a
democracy. It was no friendly act of France to force us into
a decision for which we were not ready. They must be made
to realise our condition: and surely they could be brought
to see that a Germany crushed by France and Russia
would be a Communist Germany?"

Late in the evening of March 11th Eden made his proposal to the German Ambassador, condemning the action
of the German Government and urging them to reduce
their troops in the Rhineland to a token force in order to
make negotiations possible. Outside the Cabinet only the
High Commissioners of the Dominions knew what had

been decided and they were warned not even to telegraph to their Governments. There is no reason to suppose that any of them failed to observe the secrecy enjoined on them. Anyone endowed with moderate forethought might have seen that, to the German Embassy, the chance of showing the two Powers, England and France, at odds, and England negotiating behind the back of her ally, was too rich to be let slip. The next morning, the whole story was in the papers, and we were in the unhappy position of having to tell the French that, in effect, we had decided on a course which we ourselves knew would be unacceptable to France. And the reason? That military action against Germany was excessive in view of what Germany had done—the backyard argument rendered into the language of diplomacy. If Germany was not content with the Rhineland, if Germany moved against Belgium or France, then England would fight. It might be said that this was 1914 again. It was 1914. Only, the insular security from which we had always struck out in defence of the Low Countries, that had gone. Instead —the gas attack on London in a low-lying fog.

The League had failed. But the Western Alliance must be preserved. And here that unexpected, inflexible resolution which Baldwin could show in a crisis, comes into play. From the dissolution of 1922 to the Abdication, the pattern is always the same: "the cloud takes shape and then I know what to say." It took some courage to say, in that climate, in the teeth of Lloyd George and a public half-convinced that secret conversations were the cause of the First War, that mutual defence meant staff talks with France and Belgium, and negotiations with Germany from a common strength. But the courage was not wanting, in the Cabinet or its chief, and the Western Alliance was saved.

CHAPTER XXIII

CONFESSION

THE White Paper of March 3rd, 1936, reaffirmed the principles of March 1934, and both of them the inherent dualism of the Covenant.

> The members of the League recognize that the maintenance of peace requires the reduction of armaments to the lowest point consistent with national safety, and the enforcement by common action of international obligations.

The steps taken to enforce those obligations in the case of Italy and Abyssinia had weakened us, dangerously weakened us, in the Eastern Seas. So it might always be. In other words, collective security might in practice prove to be individual insecurity, especially if the aggressor was prepared and the League was not. But one thing was self-evident. The White Paper of March if duly executed—and all three arms were to be strengthened—would make us a formidable power. It would also involve us in great expenditure. The coordination of our defences and the mobilization of our industry would therefore be a task requiring great energy, great authority, intense devotion to the subject matter. To whom would the task be assigned? The outer public nominated Churchill. There were voices for Hoare. Baldwin thought of Neville Chamberlain. The party did not want Hoare. Hitler certainly did not want Churchill, and Hitler's feelings had to be considered. So the Prime Minister selected a distinguished lawyer, the Attorney General, Sir Thomas Inskip. And from that day to this no one has ever known why. Had he powers unrevealed which Baldwin had detected? He never disclosed them.

The truth, I think, is that, as in 1927, but with nearly ten years more to carry, Baldwin was broken in mind. That imperturbability which he cultivated never went very deep, and this last shock had taken him in his most sensitive, his proudest spot, his understanding of the English people. From the highest place in public esteem and confidence he had sunk to very nearly the lowest, and the torment of those months was a forecast of what awaited him when war came in 1939. Austen Chamberlain asked, very reasonably, where the thinking of the Government was done. Certainly not in Downing Street. On March 31st Lord Eustace Percy resigned because he could find nothing to do in his office. The following day the Government were defeated by a little revolt on equal pay for women. And on April 6th, six months after the election, the Prime Minister was forced to ask for a vote of confidence. He got it, of course. But the honours of the day were with Churchill and Austen Chamberlain. We had not saved Abyssinia. We had alienated Italy. We might go on or we might stop. Only, which was it to be? Had anybody, had the Prime Minister, thought? Baldwin replied, at Worcester, a fortnight later, in a speech which might have been headed "I told you so." If one man prefers fighting to arbitrating, there is no way to stop him. Sanctions mean nothing without a blockade. But blockade, Baldwin had always maintained, was contingent to war. And anyone following the debates of that unhappy spring must at times have asked himself, if the Peace Balloteers had been reassembled and asked "Are you for war with Italy?" how would they have voted? And behind that is the question which no one can answer now, or could answer then, Would Mussolini have fought? "I wish he would die," Baldwin once exclaimed with passion. Doubtless that would have been the best solution, but one not easy to contrive.

 It was noticed, and it is significant, that Baldwin seemed in these days to be losing his Parliamentary skill. On May 6th the Government introduced a bill for the compulsory amalgamation of collieries. Violent opposition was threatened by the owners. Changes were agreed which Runciman promised to introduce as amendments. But it was generally, and rightly, thought that the Bill should be re-drafted. Baldwin consented to postpone the Second Reading and issue an explanatory leaflet. Then he changed his mind, agreed to re-draft the bill and leave it over till the autumn. The old man's grasp was relaxing. And he felt, very keenly, the trouble and mischief that arose out of a budget disclosure by his colleague and old Labour friend Thomas: to the end of his life he never believed that Thomas had had fair treatment. On the greater issue, it was plain that sanctions had failed, Neville Chamberlain describing them as "midsummer madness." "It was," said the Prime Minister, "his personal reflection, delivered to an exclusive audience of politically educated people."

But by June it was clear that, everything short of war having been tried, the wretched episode must be wound up, and there were not a few—not adversaries this time but old supporters—who were coming, if reluctantly, to the conclusion that the end of it all must be the retirement of the Prime Minister. And by June his nearest friends must have wondered whether his term had not been reached. "I watched him," one lobby correspondent wrote, "huddled up on the Treasury bench, the picture of forlorn misery, while Lloyd George delivered the most tremendous Philippic directed against an Administration since the war." But even in that fierce weather the courtesies were observed. Attlee had spoken severely of the Prime Minister's absence from a debate. Learning the truth, that Baldwin was suffering from sleepless nights, he hastened to express his regrets and his sympathy.

It was never safe to think that Baldwin was beaten. He retired to Chequers, leaving London all agog with rumours of resignation. He reappeared on July 2nd, greeted in the House like a long-lost friend, in his gayest and most buoyant mood. At a dinner that night he made genial fun of all the stories that had been circulated, repeated what he had so often said, that he meant to keep the country out of war even if he was called a coward for his pains, and told his anxious friends that he would retire at his own time and no one else's. But this year he did not feel strong enough for the journey to France, and possible recalls to emergency Cabinets, so he spent his holiday, or his convalescence, in Wales and Norfolk, at the houses of friends. And then Mrs. Baldwin's diary records: "Nov. 16. Very grave news." News to make Italy and Abyssinia forgotten, and, for the moment, Baldwin's own speech in the House, only four days before.

The occasion was an amendment to the Address on the private manufacture of arms. The new minister Inskip defended the programme of March and its execution. Churchill was not satisfied, but as so often happened he lessened the effect of his attack by the excess of his rhetoric. "The Government," he said, "cannot make up their minds: or they cannot get the Prime Minister to make up his mind. So they go on, in strange paradox, decided only to be undecided, resolved to be irresolute, adamant for drift, solid for fluidity, all-powerful to be impotent. So we go on preparing more months and years, precious—perhaps vital— to the greatness of Britain—for the locusts to eat." So it was, so it always had been, with Churchill: he had never won that reputation for good judgment in civil affairs which makes eloquence of his kind effectual: "adamant for drift, solid for fluidity"; the phrase-making was obtrusive, even crude. And, after all, everybody knew that he was exceedingly angry. He had expected to be Minister of Defence. He thought he understood why he had been passed over. His appointment would have been a declaration against Germany, an acknowledgment that Germany was arming and that we were arming against her. In that sense it would have been a declaration of war. At home, it would have shocked the pacifist elements, still unconverted, still active in Parliament and the country. After all, if there was one man on this side the North Sea to whom the word war-lord could without extravagance be applied it was Winston Churchill. Well for us that there was that one! But whatever the theme, Socialism or India or Germany, he thought in terms of combat, as naturally as Baldwin though in terms of reason and conciliation. So it was on November 12th. Never was the Prime Minister more conciliatory, more reasonable, more candid.

Not once but on many occasions . . . when I have been . . . advocating . . . the democratic principle, I have stated that a democracy is always two years behind the dictator. I believe that to be true. It has been true in this case. I put before the whole House my own views with an appalling frankness. . . . You will remember . . . that . . . the Disarmament Conference was sitting in Geneva. You will remember at that time there was probably a stronger pacifist feeling running through the country than at any time since the War.

All of which was true even to platitude.

You will remember the election at Fulham in the autumn of 1933, when a seat which the National Government held was lost by about 7,000 votes on no issue but the pacifist.

True, no less. Then followed the confession.

My position as the leader of a great party was not altogether a comfortable one. I asked myself what chance was there—when that feeling that was given expression to in Fulham was common throughout the country—what chance was there within the next year or two of that feeling being so changed that the country would give a mandate for rearmament?

That all depended, one might reply, on how those years were spent. But,

Supposing I had gone to the country and said that Germany was rearming and we must rearm, does anybody think that this pacific democracy would have rallied to that cry at that moment? I cannot think of anything that would have made the loss of the election from my point of view more certain.

Never I suppose in our history has a statesman used a phrase so fatal to his own good name, and at the same time so wholly unnecessary, so incomprehensible. One can think of half a dozen ways of ending that passage, all convincing and all true.

I set myself, without using language that might have created panic at home or resentment abroad, to prepare our people for the necessity that might come upon them. There was the White Paper of March 1935: the White Paper of March 1936. And so to-day we have a Government fully empowered to do all that our national security demands.

That is what he might have said, because that is what he might fairly claim to have achieved. But East Fulham—always East Fulham. He clung to it as the justification of all he had done, or failed to do. Of the election of 1935 he never spoke to me. But once, in the last summer of his life, our conversation happened to drift that way. He rose

with difficulty from his chair, walked painfully to the
window, and looked at the sky over the hills. "I have never
seen clouds quite like that before," he said. And of 1935 no
more.

Baldwin, it was well known, had a habit of thinking aloud,
with little or no regard to what the hearer might suppose
him to mean; trying out an idea, as it were, by putting it
into words. "We may have to reduce our exports." "Imports?" queried a back bencher. "I said exports." Once he
said to me: "I doubt if we can go on like this: we shall have
to limit the franchise." But the disclosure of November
12th was of a different order, and, without going beyond
the limits of fair debate, an opponent—even a friend—might
say that Baldwin had confessed to concealing the truth in
order to win an election. What it did mean, in Baldwin's
mind, this narrative must have made clear.

Birdwood, now Master of Peterhouse, offered the true
interpretation:

> You gave the House your very excellent reasons for not press-
> ing at that time for huge expenditure on armaments, realising
> that, if you did, you might at that time be unable to carry
> the country with you, in which case we might have headed
> for a Socialist Government and disaster.

(Unless it can be supposed that, returned to office, the Socialists, burning what they had adored and adoring what they
had burned, would themselves come forward for rearmament. Which seemed unlikely.)

> But when you felt you were in a position to carry the country,
> you then came out with what you felt to be essential.
>
> But what annoys me mostly is this. No credit apparently
> is given you for the fact that by sitting tight, as you did,
> you were able to build up the resources of the country and
> bring it to its present high state of prosperity: you enormously
> increased the number of men in employment and gave
> industry the very great fillip it has had. Having done this, and
> with the country in its now prosperous state, you can attack
> the main object in view as you are now doing.

Baldwin's own apologia, a week or so later, was as frank
as his avowal. He had, he said, nothing to withdraw, nothing
to retract, but something to explain. The question was—

should the Government have gone to the country on re-armament in 1934? That year we decided to increase our air force. In March 1935 we published our White Paper. Then came conscription in Germany. Then came Italy and Abyssinia. And the electors gave their verdict in 1935.

True. But—the words had been spoken, and *nescit vox missa reverti.*

CHAPTER XXIV

THE ABDICATION

If in any cataclysm the Crown vanished, the Empire would vanish with it. It is a link which once broken can never be repaired, and so long as the tradition to which we have been accustomed, the tradition which guides those who sit on our august throne, so long as that tradition lasts, it will be blest to our country and no power on earth can break it.

S.B. May 3rd, 1935

KING GEORGE V, exemplary in other relations of life, was not a sympathetic parent, and in Edward, Prince of Wales, there was not the strength of purpose to get the better of his upbringing. He was neither made nor disciplined for kingship. Indeed, it was widely, and by a few confidently, believed that, realizing his unfitness, he had wished to decline the succession, but had never brought himself to say so; and that the unhappy face which was seen, with pity and some apprehension, by thousands on the day of the old King's funeral, was the face of a man who knew that he had made an irreparable mistake; or, if not irreparable, only to be redressed by marriage with the woman with whom he was deeply and passionately in love. He could never have been a good king; but single, he could not be a king at all. That the woman of his choice had been twice married and once divorced; that the circle in which she moved, and he moved with her, repelled those who should have been his friends: these were things that went for nothing. But he was honourable—"I always knew," Baldwin often said, "that his word once given, he would never go back"; with sympathies easily touched, a liker of his fellow-creatures; at forty still much of a boy, but a boy overstrained by the effort to master his timidity, his shyness, his fear of authority, and so running over into a boyish egoism,

232

which none the less left him kindly, straightforward and responsive. In a word, he showed himself of the same stock as George IV, without his brutality but also without his culture; with something also, perhaps, of the Young Pretender.

Early in the new reign, anxious and unhappy messages came to Downing Street from the Palace, disturbed about the King's habits—his indiscretion, his extravagance, his relations with the Household. His Private Secretary was resigning, but before he went he begged the Prime Minister to do all he could to impress on the King the danger he was running. But at the same time he made it clear that against a passion so overmastering it was very doubtful whether words of reason would be of any avail. Baldwin, shaken by the storm still raging over Italy and Abyssinia, was in no state to take on himself a fresh anxiety, and in his early conversations with the King he said nothing of what he and all those in his confidence were thinking. Twice the Court Circular announced that Mr. and Mrs. Simpson had dined at St. James's Palace. On one of these occasions the Baldwins were among the guests. It was the only time that Baldwin ever met the lady, and the encounter intrigued him. Mrs. Baldwin's comments, then and after, were less bland. For her, and for women like her throughout the Empire, Mrs. Simpson had stolen the Fairy Prince.

Throughout that spring and early summer the pressure of Cabinet business was intense. By July it was plain that Baldwin was breaking down, and the doctors were emphatic that he must take at least a three months' rest. In August he retired to Wales. The King went with a yachting party to Greece. Among his guests was Mrs. Simpson, who had already instituted divorce proceedings against her husband. The usual request (dating from Queen Victoria's time) was sent from the Palace to the press, asking that the King's privacy on holiday should be respected, and, with one or two exceptions of no great consequence, the English papers complied. But the Continental and American papers were free to say what they liked, and at Downing Street cuttings and comments and questions were arriving in a daily increasing stream. The voluntary discretion of the English papers concealed from the public a situation which the people of the United States were watching with excitement, France with amusement, and Canada with some anger and some alarm. In Scotland feeling was already beginning to find voice; and early in October, Sir James Barrie, the dramatist, and a friend of Baldwin, remarked to the Editor of *The Times* that at any moment some Scottish minister might feel called to take up the part of John Knox and denounce the sins of the Court.

From Wales Baldwin had gone to Blickling in Norfolk. He came back on October 12th, to all seeming as fresh and cheerful as if he had not a care in the world, and spent some hours studying the letters that had been coming in during his absence. The next day he was summoned to the Palace. Nothing of consequence passed, and in the evening he went to Chequers. On October 15th it became known in London that Mrs. Simpson's divorce petition would be heard at Ipswich, probably in the following week. Then the silence of the press would be broken, and Baldwin decided that he must speak to the King as soon as possible. It was settled that they should meet on Tuesday 20th at Fort Belvedere, the King's house near Windsor. The Baldwins spent the week-end with Lord Fitzalan. Hardinge, the King's new Private Secretary, was there; Lord Kemsley; Lord Salisbury; the Duke of Norfolk, who, as Earl Marshal, would have the ordering of the Coronation. After luncheon on Sunday, Baldwin said, pointing at Lord Kemsley, "I want a word with my friend there." They retired to the library and Baldwin told his tale, ending "And so, what do you think?" Lord Kemsley answered, "Prime Minister, the Nonconformist conscience is not dead." "I believe," said Baldwin laughing, "you ought to be in charge of this, not I."

On Tuesday the King and Prime Minister met. Baldwin began: "You remember, Sir, when we came up from Folkestone together, you said I might speak freely to you about everything. Does that hold good when there is a woman in the case?" "Yes," said the King. Then, speaking not as Minister offering formal advice but as an old friend, Baldwin put into the King's mind certain considerations which he would do well to take into account—opinion at home,

opinion abroad, opinion in the Empire; and what the world
expected of the English throne. But he was speaking to a
man who did not see things in the same perspective, and they
parted under a certain misunderstanding. The King mis-
conceived the nature of Baldwin's sympathy, and Baldwin
thought the King had taken his counsels more earnestly
than, in fact, he had. One positive suggestion tendered by
Baldwin the King refused to accept—that Mrs. Simpson
should not proceed with her petition. That, he said, was a
matter in which it was not for him to interfere; and he could
not be brought to understand that, silence once broken,
public anxiety was sure to find voice in the press. It so
happened that Mr. Mackenzie King, Prime Minister of
Canada, was at that time in England. He spent the night of
October 23rd at Chequers, and on the 27th he had an
audience. He spoke of the feeling for the Crown in Canada,
but as he dwelt rather on the affection of the Canadian people
in general than on their judgment of this issue in particular,
he also seems to have left the King under the impression that
his relations with Mrs. Simpson were a personal, not a public
concern. Mr. Bruce, High Commissioner for Australia, left
no doubt in the minds of Ministers that the Commonwealth
was as deeply affected as the Dominion.

Baldwin still hoped, though with no great confidence,
that the thoughts he had lodged in the King's mind would
take root and bear. He decided therefore not to press for
another audience. But meanwhile he was testing opinion in
private conversations, and, after the Armistice service on
November 11th, he opened the matter to a few colleagues,
MacDonald and Chamberlain, Halifax, Simon and Runciman—on whom he relied throughout for advice on the
attitude of the Free Churches. At a second meeting on
November 13th, ministers had before them a letter from the
Editor of the *Morning Post*, Mr. H. A. Gwynne, the doyen
of the London press, asking in effect for guidance. The
papers, he said, were finding it difficult to maintain their
self-imposed censorship on the King's Affair, but they might
continue in silence if only they were assured that the Government had the matter in mind. The Prime Minister saw Mr.
Gwynne and gave him leave to say that it was not yet a

Cabinet matter, but that he and certain of his colleagues were keeping close watch on the situation as it developed.

In these discussions Chamberlain, as might be expected, always took the more rigorous view, and he drafted a submission of which it is no more than truth to say that if it had been made, and published at that time, the country would have been swept with a wave of sympathy for the King. Edward was popular as no sovereign before him had ever been, and his popularity rested on qualities which his Prime Minister could understand and rate the strength of: his personal charm, his readiness to be friends with all, his sincere desire for the welfare of the people. On that Armistice Day he was given a thunderous reception by the British Legion at the Albert Hall; again by the Fleet at Portland; again by the miners in South Wales. Baldwin knew that there were those standing by to use this popularity for their own ends. But what durable strength was there in it? Sir Frederick Maurice, who knew the British Legion through and through, reported that the vast majority of its members never troubled their heads about the King's private life. But the King's marriage was not a private concern; and not even his popularity could stand the shock of marriage with Mrs. Simpson.

Baldwin's intention, at this time, was to await the King's return from South Wales and then ask him plainly whether, in pursuit of his private happiness, he was prepared to sacrifice all this affection, all this loyalty, and accept the consequences. But on October 26th Geoffrey Dawson, Editor of *The Times*, showed the King's Private Secretary, Hardinge, a letter summing up the state of opinion in America, and with Baldwin's knowledge, though not at his instance, Hardinge wrote to the King on November 13th, reminding him that if the Cabinet tendered advice and he rejected it, Ministers must resign; and urging him to send Mrs. Simpson quickly abroad. Edward's relations with Hardinge were not always happy. But at least he decided that he would send for the Prime Minister. They met on November 16th, Baldwin having, for the first time, spoken to Attlee, the Leader of the Opposition. It was clear that any hopes he might have entertained were groundless. He told the

King plainly that marriage with Mrs. Simpson would not be approved. The King replied, "I mean to marry her and I am prepared to go." "Sir," the Prime Minister replied, "this is grievous news." On the following day he saw Queen Mary. She told him what her son had already told her and his brothers—that he was determined to marry and to abdicate. Three days later, on November 21st, Lord Beaverbrook, who had sailed for America, hoping to find relief from his asthma in Arizona, and had turned in his tracks on reaching New York, visited the King at Fort Belvedere.

So far the issue had been clear cut. But in the course of the next few days, a compromise was suggested—the product, it was widely believed, of Churchill's warm heart and active brain. On Monday 23rd, the Prime Minister was to see Esmond Harmsworth, Chairman of the Newspaper Proprietors' Association, and find out from him how much longer the press could be expected to keep silence. But he found him full of the new idea—that the King should marry Mrs. Simpson as a private man, so that she should not become Queen. On the following Wednesday, November 25th, Baldwin saw the King, who at once asked him to consider what came to be known, incorrectly, as the Morganatic Plan. Baldwin replied that if the King so desired he would consult the Cabinet; but, speaking for himself, he was confident that Parliament would never pass the necessary legislation. Then, in graver tones than he had so far used, he warned him that his popularity could not protect Mrs. Simpson if the fury of the people was once aroused. This, he said to a friend, was the only time that something like anger showed itself in their talks.

On Friday 27th, the Cabinet, specially summoned, decided that the Dominions must be informed, and that day the first messages went out, asking each Prime Minister to give his own views, and his estimate of public opinion in his Dominion, on the three possibilities—marriage with Mrs. Simpson as Queen, marriage by special legislation (the Morganatic Plan), and abdication. Thereafter there were constant communications with the Dominions until the end of the episode.

It is to be borne in mind that, so far, even the inner public

in Westminster and Fleet Street had little knowledge of
what was proceeding, the outer public no knowledge at all.
Miss Irene Ward, whom Baldwin had taken into his confidence, reported that in the North of England the story was
becoming known to the middle-classes, but had hardly
reached the working classes. But almost while she was writing
the Bishop of Bradford, in an address about the Coronation Service, used words which were universally, though
wrongly, taken as alluding to the King's relations with Mrs.
Simpson. The silence was broken; concealment no longer
possible. The provincial papers, headed by the *Yorkshire Post*,
spoke first, and on Thursday, December 3rd, the whole press
broke loose.

Meanwhile, on Wednesday 2nd, the Prime Minister had
seen the King again and reported the result of his promised
enquiries into the morganatic proposal. The Whips were
sure that the Conservatives would be almost unanimous
against it; almost: a significant reservation which meant
that some elements might hope to form a King's Party in
the House. Attlee was satisfied that the Labour Party
would be wholly unanimous. The replies that had come
from the Dominions showed an identical response. But if the
King would not give up Mrs. Simpson, if the Empire would
not accept her as Queen, if the Morganatic Plan was ruled
out, only one possibility remained, abdication. "I have
known that all along," the King replied, and never spoke of
the Morganatic Plan again. But one thing troubled him.
Royal persons are not commonly subject to criticism in the
press, and the King was startled by the outspoken language
of the provincial newspapers—"They don't want me," he
said, picking up the *Birmingham Post*. He had heard that
The Times intended an attack on Mrs. Simpson and he
asked the Prime Minister to forbid it. In vain Baldwin
pointed out that the press was free, and that he had no more
authority over *The Times* than over any other paper. Late
that night, with many apologies, he told the Editor that the
King would be satisfied if he himself read over the intended
article. At midnight a proof was sent to Downing Street.
Baldwin had gone to bed, as he had gone on the night of the
General Strike.

On Thursday 3rd, Attlee by private notice asked the Prime Minister whether any constitutional difficulties had arisen and whether he had any statement to make. In a carefully drafted sentence Baldwin replied that while there did not then exist any constitutional difficulty, the situation was of such a nature as to make it inexpedient that he should be questioned about it at that stage. But, Attlee went on, in view of the prevailing anxiety, could he assure the House that he would make a statement at the earliest possible time it could be made? "I have all that very much in mind." Churchill rose. Could the Prime Minister give an assurance that no irrevocable step would be taken before a general statement had been made to Parliament? Baldwin answered coldly, "I have nothing to add to the statement I have made, at this present moment. I will consider and examine the question my right honourable friend has asked." The House proceeded to discuss Railway Freights, Trunk Roads, Armament Contracts and International Trade. That evening the Prime Minister was summoned again to the Palace at nine in the evening. Though he was taken in by a back entrance, his visit did not escape the vigilance of the press. The King read him the draft of a broadcast he proposed to deliver to the Empire on Friday night. Baldwin replied that he must consult his colleagues, but, speaking for himself, he had no doubt of their answer—that the proposal was thoroughly unconstitutional. "You want me to go, don't you?" the King interjected. "And before I go, I think it is right, for her sake and mine, that I should speak." "What I want, Sir, is what you told me you wanted: to go with dignity, not dividing the country, and making things as smooth as possible for your successor. To broadcast would be to go over the heads of your Ministers and speak to the people. You will be telling millions throughout the world—among them a vast number of women—that you are determined to marry one who has a husband living. They will want to know all about her, and the press will ring with gossip, the very thing you want to avoid. You may, by speaking, divide opinion; but you will certainly harden it. The Churches are straining at the leash; only three papers would be on your side, the *News Chronicle*, the *Daily Mail* and the *Daily Express.*" Besides all which, there was a point of great delicacy which Baldwin felt bound to mention. Mrs. Simpson's decree would not be confirmed till May: and it was not at all unlikely that some muddle-headed busybody would seek to delay the proceedings by an unjustified intervention.

On Friday 4th the Cabinet met early to consider the King's proposal. Very soon, a message came from Attlee that he could not avoid putting a question, and the Cabinet agreed that the Prime Minister must be in the House to answer it. Returning, he had to report a strange and disquieting scene in the Commons. Once more Attlee asked whether the Prime Minister was now able to make a statement. Once more Baldwin replied that he was not. Once more Churchill repeated his demand for an assurance that no irrevocable step would be taken before a statement had been made to the House. But this time he was cheered—an ominous sound which might mean that a King's Party was forming. The House swarmed out, and an insignificant group wrote assuring the King that they would support him in any action he might take to defend his constitutional rights. What they meant, they might have found it difficult to say. But the Chief Whip reported that Churchill and Beaverbrook were in consultation with one another and with the papers which supported the Morganatic Plan.

The situation, that Friday, was both complicated and unhappy. Baldwin had hoped that the King's resolution— to abdicate and marry—would issue in a communication to Ministers which they would lay before Parliament without any previous publicity or popular excitement.* This was no longer possible. But it was for every reason to be desired that his decision should be taken and announced as soon as possible, while at the same time anything that might be interpreted as pressure on the King, was to be avoided. Left to himself, the King would probably have taken his decision when he realized that the Morganatic Plan was inadmissible —it was, in fact, still strongly urged in certain papers—

---

* The nearest constitutional parallel was furnished by Queen Victoria. She first acquainted her Prime Minister with her intention to marry Prince Albert, and the Cabinet brought it to the knowledge of Parliament.

The Abdication
Baldwin leaving 10 Downing Street, 8 December 1936,
followed by Walter Monckton

and now the contemplated broadcast had come in to com-
plicate everything. The conclusion at which the Cabinet
arrived was to keep the two things apart—to make known
to Parliament that neither here nor in the Dominions would
the Morganatic Plan be accepted; and to tell the King that
so long as he remained King he could only broadcast in
words approved by his Ministers. As always, he accepted
their decision, and of the broadcast no more was heard. The
Morganatic Plan was disposed of that afternoon in an answer
to Attlee, drafted, with exquisite skill, by the Home
Secretary, Simon.

> The lady whom [the King] marries . . . necessarily becomes
> Queen. She herself, therefore, enjoys all the status, rights and
> privileges which, both by positive law and by custom, attach to
> that position, and with which we are familiar in the cases of her
> late Majesty Queen Alexandra and of Her Majesty Queen
> Mary, and her children would be in the direct line of suc-
> cession to the Throne. The only possible way in which this
> result could be avoided would be by legislation dealing with
> a particular case. His Majesty's Government are not prepared
> to introduce such legislation. Moreover, the matters to be
> dealt with are of common concern to the Commonwealth
> as a whole, and such a change could not be effected without
> the assent of all the Dominions. I am satisfied from inquiries
> I have made that this assent would not be forthcoming.

There, by rights, the story should have ended: a Cabinet
Committee was drafting the Act of Abdication; the Duke of
York was advised of the destiny awaiting him; all that remained was the word from the King. There were, indeed,
some who did not mean it to end with Baldwin still in office:
but what alternative was left? That the King should ignore
the Dominions, reject the advice of his Ministers, compel
the Cabinet to resign, send for Churchill and so provoke
a general election on the most unhappy issue that had divided
the country since the days of Queen Caroline? Those who
nursed these fancies understood the King as little as
they understood the people. "Whoever writes about the
Abdication," Baldwin said to me, "must give the King his
due. He could not have behaved better than he did." But that
was looking back. Looking forward from that Friday, the

Cabinet could not feel quite so sure. London, feverish and bewildered, light-hearted and light-headed, cynical and sentimental by turns, was a rich breeding-ground for mischief. The word was "Give the King time." But the King, who after all was a man of forty, had had by now the best part of six weeks in which to make up his mind, and the tension could not be prolonged much further without grave danger at home, possibly from abroad. A paralysing pre-occupation had settled upon industry, on business, on private life, which could only be ended in one way, and by one man.

I once said to Baldwin, "I believe you were the only man on Friday who knew what the House of Commons would be thinking on Monday." He replied, with a smile half shy and half triumphant, "I have always believed in the week-end. But how they do it I don't know. I suppose they talk to the stationmaster." On Monday December 7th, the tide of provincial opinion came pouring into the Capital and the Chamber. Churchill, gesticulating and protesting, was almost shouted down, and it was plain to all serious observers that the story had reached its end.

None the less, those days were a time of tense anxiety for the Prime Minister. On December 3rd the King had asked him whether he might see Churchill, as an old friend with whom he could talk freely. Taken by surprise, Baldwin said yes. When the Cabinet met on December 4th he began, "I have made my first blunder." His colleagues comforted him by assurances that he had done rightly. But he confided to one of his staff, "It was the only way I could carry it off—owning up to a mistake."

That same day, the King made a new proposal. He was, very naturally, disturbed by the Prime Minister's warning, and asked whether some special action could be taken to expedite the dissolution of Mrs. Simpson's marriage. Baldwin instructed two members of his staff to discuss the question with the King's solicitor and Mr. Walter Monckton, Attorney General to the Duchy of Cornwall, in whom King and Prime Minister throughout placed entire and well-deserved confidence. They agreed that, an approach to the Courts being out of the question, the best way out of the difficulty might be by legislation. As it turned out, these long discussions proved to be no more than a tiresome parenthesis in the narrative, of no significance in the outcome. What troubled Baldwin was a more serious matter, the danger that the crisis might be prolonged.

After his meeting with the King, Churchill wrote to Baldwin that the King was in no fit state to give a decision and it would be "cruel and wrong" to extort one, while a rumour, wholly false, ran through Fleet Street and Whitehall that the King's physicians had been summoned to certify that he was not equal to the discharge of business. But Baldwin could not be sure how far the King had been influenced by the Simpson press, as it had come to be called, which was never more vehement than on that Sunday. He decided therefore to go to the Fort on Tuesday for a quiet talk, which might well be their last. The King must decide. "He must wrestle with himself in a way he has never done before, and if he will let me, I will help him. We may even have to see the night through together." Something of the old Wesleyan strain is audible perhaps in this utterance. But the red earth showed through also. Speaking later to another friend he said, "Only time I was frightened. I thought he might change his mind. But I need not have been. He had given his word and that was enough."

That the record might be complete and clear, the Cabinet addressed the King:

> Ministers are reluctant to believe that Your Majesty's resolve is irrevocable, and still venture to hope that before Your Majesty pronounces any formal decision Your Majesty may be pleased to reconsider an intention which must so deeply distress and so vitally affect all Your Majesty's subjects.

The King replied:

> His Majesty has given the matter his further consideration but regrets he is unable to alter his decision.

When the two men met, a few sentences were enough to satisfy Baldwin that the King had made up his mind. Indeed, earlier that day he had said to one of his brothers, "I made it up long ago. Why should I change now?" That evening, alone of all the party, he was at his ease. The crisis was past, and on December 10th Baldwin spoke to a House, a People and an Empire, united in pity, in admiration and in pride.

From every corner of the land, from every part of the Empire, from foreign countries, letters of thanks and admiration poured in. The most malignant scrutiny could find no one point on which to fasten blame, and the Prime Minister's career as a public man ended in a cloudless glow of praise and gratitude. If his life had ended also, he would have been remembered as the best beloved of all English statesmen. Another myth might well have grown up around his memory: "Baldwin would have thought of something, and there would have been no war."

But after the battle came the collapse. From the opening skirmish in October till the moment when the Clerk's voice faltered as he uttered the final words, "Le Roy le veult," Baldwin was swift, resolute, almost gay in the confidence of his own mastery. But, "you will pay for this," Lord Dawson said; and when it was all over he knew that whatever he had left undone other hands must finish. After Coronation Day, when he almost divided the cheering with the royal pair themselves, he wrote:

> The last few days have been a strange time: a time that comes only once and cannot recur. All hearts seem open for the moment: most will close again: some perhaps be kept ajar; but it is very wonderful. I feel tired, happy and at peace, and mighty humble. I wish my dear Dickens hadn't destroyed what is really a very beautiful word: but you will know what I mean by it.
>
> I still have that sense of wonder that the Blessed Damozel shewed in her face as she leaned over the gold bar of heaven. It wore off: so will mine. But it leaves something good, I hope, behind.

A Liberal, not unfriendly, said:

> Britain's consciousness of her strength is one legacy he leaves to his successor. The other is a set of unresolved, neglected problems on which the issues of peace and war depend.

CHAPTER XXV

LAST WORDS

BALDWIN's last speech in the Commons, on May 5th, 1937, went back to the unforgotten utterance of March, 1925, and was the summing up of a hundred others. An ugly, vicious little dispute had broken out in the mines again. Men were dismissed, families were evicted from their homes. Baldwin rose:

> The whole world [he said] has its eyes to-day on London. . . . I appeal to that handful of men with whom rests peace or war . . . to rend and dissipate this dark cloud which has gathered over us, and show the world that this democracy can still at least practise the arts of peace in a world of strife.

Members silently tore up their speeches, and the debate died away. Ten days later he delivered the last of his great public addresses, to the Empire Youth at the Albert Hall.

> I have had my hour. I pass soon into the shade . . . a responsibility rests upon each one of you whether you like it or not. . . . When I talk of your country I mean all its activities—everything it comprehends—the well-being and contentment of its people, their education, their religion, their professions, its businesses, public affairs, the government of village or town or county, of the province, of the country, and their Parliament. All that is inevitably committed to you. . . . The brotherhood of man to-day is often denied and derided and called foolishness, but it is, in fact, one of the foolish things of the world which God has chosen to confound the wise. . . . We may evade it, we may deny it; but we shall find no rest for our souls, nor will the world, until we acknowledge it as the ultimate wisdom.

His last Cabinet was on May 26th: his last appearance in the House on May 27th. For a brief interval he was Sir Stanley Baldwin, Knight of the Garter, before he passed to the Upper House, carrying with him the fixed resolve never to make a political speech, "never to spit on the deck and never to speak to the helmsman." And if ever he was tempted, the example of Lloyd George was there to restrain him. Keynes wrote:

> It is rather sad that after all these years he is quite unable to be philosophical and look back on the past with a little regret, a little wonder and a little large-mindedness, in the light of all that has happened since. All he can do is to work over his hoards of paper, snipping out anything capable of being made to do duty in an unrelieved tirade of self-justification, without mitigation or relief of voice.

Six months after his resignation, Baldwin was entertained at a dinner by members of the Athenæum. Lord Macmillan was in the chair and in proposing the health of the guest quoted first the words that had already been written of him as one,

> who can raise debate to the level of philosophy, who can illuminate controversy with nobility, and who dares to seek the truth that begins where argument ends.

He spoke also of the passage, already famous, in which Baldwin had recalled the evening in Italy when he had heard the sound of an English bell: passed with some words of admiration over the three great crises of Baldwin's political life, the General Strike, the averted catastrophe of 1931, and the Abdication: and ended with a few graceful sentences on the felicity of his humanism. The Archbishop of Canterbury spoke of the magnanimity of the man, who belonged to all parties because in his own person he was the spirit of England behind all parties: the Happy Warrior that every statesman should seek to be.

The speech which Baldwin delivered in reply was in effect his political testament. When he first took office, he said, universal suffrage had introduced an unknown element into politics. There were dangerous feelings abroad among the people, and the shadow of class war was projected on us from the Continent. The country needed peace, and it seemed that the parties could not give it peace. In these circumstances there was a likelihood of Labour becoming

Keystone

With Lady Baldwin, 1937

embittered and extreme, unless they were taught to realize
the importance of the House of Commons. And, mishandled
in the House, they would have said, "Those people are using
against us the education which we have never had."

> Remember, [he went on] they do not speak the same
> language: words have a different meaning to them. . . . Once
> I was chatting with a Labour Member in the Smoking Room,
> and a stranger looked in. "That's a queer looking customer,"
> I said. He replied, "It's not a word I like to use but if I did
> I should say—" "Well, out with it," I said—"I should say he
> had a Sinister Appearance."

We had to reason with them, not to score or seem to
score. Those who supposed that the Englishman could not
reason were wrong. Only—he had an instinctive faculty for
converting ideas into practice, and when once he had
decided "that won't work," all argument was at an end.

Of the General Strike he said that nothing could have
averted action by disappointed men out for blood. But when
it was over, the word was—never again: and from that
moment relations began to improve. In 1931 seat after seat
was won for the Conservatives by the unemployed men
voting for reductions in their own benefit. He praised, as he
always did, the fine conduct of Lansbury and his opposition of
ninety: and as his last word, he spoke of the misery he had felt
watching Ireland aflame while parties fought in Parliament,
and his resolve that India should not become a second
Ireland. Of defence—nothing.

Baldwin was worn out. For a year he could neither read
nor think. Then he went to the poets: *The Excursion*, *The
Prelude*, Hardy's *Dynasts*, and found his way back to history
and prose, by way of Froude's *Letters of Erasmus*. There he
saw the break-up of a civilization, no one knowing whither
the world was tending. "And so I recovered my poise."

In 1939 he twice crossed the Atlantic. In April he delivered
three addresses at Toronto, summing up all the old themes,
warning his audience not to change the basis of their constitution from party to ideology, because party is founded
on mutual tolerance, while rival ideologies aim each at the
extirpation of the other. That is why we could have no
dealings with Fascism or Communism. Either would

destroy the soul of our people. By trial and error we had
discovered the method of co-operation, in domestic needs
no less than in those of wider import, and in the Crown we
had a guarantee of stability for democracy. But the danger
of our time, the "terrible danger," was the mass-mind, of
"democratic totalitarianism," extinguishing spiritual freedom. And no form of government was more difficult to
work than the true democracy.

In his third lecture Baldwin surveyed the history of
Europe since the close of the first war.

> It has taken Mr. Lloyd George fifteen hundred pages to tell
> the truth about the Peace Treaties, so I cannot expect to do it
> in fifteen sentences. There are statesmen who have never made
> a mistake. I am not one of them. I leave judgment to those
> who come after. None of us is free from blame.

What, really, had happened? The abstention of America
and the collapse of President Wilson took half the power out of
the League. True, the Treaty vindicated international right,
liberated the oppressed, broke up huge armaments, and provided for the revision of its own enactments. But it had to be
enforced in an atmosphere of mingled victory and defeat, and
the despotisms of generations were soon to return more terrible
and cruel than ever. Reparations ruined Germany and
dislocated the economics of Europe. England and America,
with the best intentions, forced a hothouse expansion of
German industry. Then came collapse, and the catastrophe
in world trade—thirty million workers idle—out of that
morass of misery, sown with dragon's teeth, came Hitler.
And now we saw, not Bolshevism but Nazism sweeping over
Germany—a greater menace to justice and liberty because
it was backed by the genius for organization of a nation which
for generations has been taught to regard the career of arms
as most glorious.

> The theory of the Covenant was admirable. I am glad
> the experiment was tried. I am not dismayed by the first
> failure. But it proved that justice is not the first fruit yielded
> by the tree of knowledge, but the last. If you advance too
> far for the conscience of men, you have to retrace your steps.
> National states are no better than their citizens. They are
> rarely magnanimous; they can be cruel; none is completely

rational. I am speaking of course only of Europe [he added with a smile]. There has never been a logical Government in England. All I have ever had to deal with were shot through with inconsistency and compromise. But the trouble with the Covenant and its dominant signatories was that they were logical. They sought to give the clauses a show of moral sanctity, alien to the nature of political things, to the potential might of Germany. Neither our policy of conciliation, nor the French policy of coercion was ever tried out. [Did the speaker still wince at the recollection of Poincaré in 1922?] The result was a policy which neither crushed Germany nor placated her. And so we arrived at April 1939—Nazism triumphant, and not in its own land only. Therefore England is arming. We are looking to the defences of body and soul.

To my mind war is the greatest folly that can afflict mankind. Whoever starts it knows that he is condemning to death, mutilation, and famine as many civilians as may be killed in the fighting services. Of the great works of man, works which distinguish him from the beasts, more may be destroyed in four years of bombing than Goths and Huns and Vandals could accomplish in a century.

But—we were there when the Spanish galleons made for Plymouth. We were on those bloody fields of the Netherlands when Louis XIV aimed at the domination of Europe. We were on duty when Napoleon bestrode the world like a demigod. We answered the roll-call, as you did, in August 1914. And if the challenge comes again we shall be there. We can do no other. So help us God.

On the way home the Baldwins had a sight of the ship that was to take the King and Queen to Canada. Their next crossing was nearer to the hour of disaster. He went to speak at Columbia on education for citizenship. With him, on the same errand, was Ernest Bevin. Baldwin spoke of the dignity of man, his individuality as a child of God: Bevin of the social services which had saved England from revolution. They were not very far apart. Returning, the ship was diverted from Havre to Cork. War had come.

CHAPTER XXVI

LAST YEARS

With millions of others, I had prayed hard at the time of Dunkirk and never did prayer seem to be more speedily answered to the full. And we prayed for France, and the next day she surrendered. I thought much and when I went to bed I lay for a long time vividly awake. And I went over in my mind what had happened, concentrating on the thought you had dwelt on, that prayer to be effective must be in accordance with God's Will, and that by far the hardest thing to say from the heart, and indeed the last lesson we learn (if we ever do) is to say, "Thy Will be done." And I thought what mites we all are, and how we can never see God's plan, a plan on such a scale that it *must* be incomprehensible. And suddenly for what must have been a couple of minutes I seemed to see with extraordinary and vivid clarity, and to hear someone speaking to me. The words at the time were clear but the recollection of them had passed when I seemed to come to, as it were: but the sense remained, and the sense was this: "You cannot see the plan," then "have you not thought that there is a purpose in stripping you one by one of all the human props on which you depend, that you are being left alone in the world? You have now Me upon whom to lean and I have chosen you as my instrument to work my will. Why then are you afraid?"

S.B. July 23rd, 1940.

After the fall of France, Baldwin was advised, or warned, not to come to London. "They hate me so." When, in June 1940, he unveiled the memorial to Thomas Hardy in Dorchester, the authorities showed some anxiety: "he seemed to have death in his face—leaning on a stick, trembling." The same feeling made itself heard in the House too. The gates at Astley were of local ironwork, the gift of the constituency, and were not removed in the general drive for iron. One member asked, "Does not Lord Baldwin need

them to protect him from the rage of the people?" After
a while he resumed his visits to London and he often spoke
of the kindness with which Churchill received him at Downing Street, the time he could find to entertain him, his fascina-
ting talk. But journeys tired him, he was always in pain.
He could hardly walk the length of the garden, and deaf-
ness was growing on him too.

One last brief, happy holiday he had. In the summer of
1941 he took a "typically English drive" by way of Stratford
and over Edgehill, through Aylesbury and Tring to Berk-
hamsted, and his loyal and beloved Davidsons. There some
old friends, Dawson of Penn his doctor, Walter Monckton of
the Abdication, Horace Wilson, "wise, calm and serene,"
on whom he had leant so heavily in the dark years of the
armament debates, and the Welsh fairy, Megan Lloyd
George, came over to see him. Thence to Hatfield, a sand-
bagged hospital with much traffic of ambulances and lorries,
and thence to Panshanger and another friend, Lord Des-
borough.

> On pulling up at the front door, there was a large placard
> with a printed inscription. Closer inspection revealed a strange
> device

POST NATAL CLINIC

> I got beyond all surprise at anything years ago, so, bearing in
> mind that I had qualified for admission seventy years ago, I
> marched in and the old butler led me past a milk-bar (dreams
> aren't in it with reality!) and ultimately into Willie's old den.

At home every day seemed the exact copy of every other.
I used to contrive my uprising and downcoming so that I
entered the breakfast room as nine was striking. I always
found him either helping himself at the sideboard or just
spreading his napkin—never by a quarter of a minute behind or in front. Then to the library: his chair back to the
light, by the table that carried his pipes—I once counted
forty-seven—and a score of books, gifts for the most part of
friends. The *Birmingham Post* was read with care, *The Times*
languidly: the morning's mail was opened and answered at
once. Then he was ready to talk—not for long at a time: to

extract odds and ends from his boxes, each with some anec-
dote attached, of cousins and old colleagues. It was a rule
that every new name in Parliament should be looked up in
Dod's Companion first, and then traced through *Who's Who*,
if need be, up to *Debrett*. So the morning would drift past to
luncheon, the afternoon to tea and the never-omitted crossword, the evening to dinner, and bed betimes.

Early in the war Baldwin offered the spare rooms at Astley
as a place of rest for exhausted civil servants. But they were
wanted for evacuated school-children, and close on the children came a thief and with the thief went much of Lady
Baldwin's jewellery. One by one the rooms were dismantled
or closed: the garden was neglected; and though his daily
life was carefully arranged and guarded, first by his wife and
then after her death by his daughter, and though he could
still be unforcedly cheerful, good at a story, ready with a
humorous retort, still the fretfulness and timidity of old age
made themselves felt: he could not suffer a cushion out of
place, and journeys filled him with fear. He had ceased to
read, but to the end his memory, whether for books or incidents, was astonishingly tenacious and exact. I noticed that
his account of some Parliamentary affair, twenty years
earlier, would agree to the last detail with the record; and
I was often followed home with some triumphant note: "It
is in *Martin Chuzzlewit*—the Todgers chapter: I knew it
was."

More than once, in his last years, the fancy would come
over me that there was a third party to our talks in the
library at Astley—Walter Scott. It seemed to me that just
as Scott by pure force of imagination kept in being a social
order which, in truth, had passed away, so Baldwin was
living in a landscape no longer to be seen from any window.
It was not, I used to think, old age, with its rounding of
forms and mellowing of tints, but a certain intensity of
imagination, commoner perhaps in youth, always at work,
and always on one theme—England. Often, as he drew upon
his memory of old times—a country saying, a curious
name in a churchyard, an election joke, that long walk
down the Windrush and so round to Cirencester, the
carven angels in a Norfolk Church, the state still kept at

Woburn, why Lord Coventry refused the Garter (because he could no longer kneel to do his homage) and Lord Willingdon (because he could not share it with his wife)—I used to ask myself: of all our statesmen, who knew better, or half so well, the homely things of England? Once a fourth figure joined our talks: I told him of the Lord Protector's saying: "I have been in all the counties of England and I think the husbandry of Devonshire is the best." "It must have been pretty good in the Vale of Evesham," he replied, "but I expect when he was here he was too busy to notice it."

But for the most part, week after week, month by month, when there was no guest, no visitor; all through the years of war, of trial and victory; the break-up of one administration, the fall of another, the proclamation of social revolution by a third—he sat silent, looking at the fire, meditating on his fingertips, doing his crossword: and what was passing in his mind beyond a languorous drift of memories, no one could ever guess. To have succeeded, so unexpectedly and so greatly; to have seen the amusement, the tolerance, the contempt even, of his early associates giving way to the admiration and affection of a whole people; and in its turn this affection, this admiration converted to the bitterest hatred: to have staked everything on that one virtue, integrity, and to know that far and wide throughout his own England men and women under the rain of death were cursing him as the politician who, to gain a few months or years of office, had lied to the people and left them defenceless against their enemies. There was not much to comfort him in those years. But one thing there was. Through and through he was convinced that he had done what no other man could have done—by courtesy, by tolerance, by the simple assertion of his own simple ideals, he had restored and maintained the unity of the nation in the face of all perils within and without. Once they had felt that: now they had forgotten it. Some day they might recognize it for truth. And then, not excusing his errors, and not overlooking his shortcomings, might they not number him among those Ministers who have most faithfully served England in time of peace?

When Lady Baldwin died, shortly after the Labour victory of 1945, a friend in condoling wrote:

> The supreme test of your statesmanship between 1924 and 1937 is now at hand. If this Government shows itself ready to govern constitutionally it will be because you taught them to be a Parliamentary and not a Revolutionary party. It has always been my conviction that whatever else you achieved this transcends all others. It was, as I know from talks we had in those days, your constant and conscious aim, and I believe that history will credit you, more than any man of our generation, with having saved Parliamentary Government.

Not knowing of this letter, I wrote to Baldwin that Christmastide in almost the same words. I believe them to be the truth.

Baldwin died in his sleep, in the early hours of December 14th, 1947. His ashes were laid with his wife's in the Cathedral church of Worcester.

THE END

INDEX

France, Gerald
congratulates S.B. on speech on the Address, 47–48.
Free Trade
see Protection.
French Academy of Moral and Political Science
S.B. honoured at, 153.
French Revolution
Chinese scholar on effect of, 196.
Fulham, East
pacifism defeats Tory candidate, 177; S.B. afraid of losing General Election, 229.

Gandhi, Mahatma
understanding with, 157; S.B. meets once, 190
General Strike
possibility of alliance of Unions, 34; threatened, 98; interpretations of, 110; troops moved in readiness for, 112; threatened, strike at Daily Mail, 115; begins, 116; cannot succeed, declared illegal, ends, 117; King congratulates S.B. on handling of, 118; S.B.'s indolence after, 120–122; S.B. likes to recall, 122; possibility of legislation against, 122–123; Trades Disputes Bill, 123–124.
Geneva
S.B.'s only visit to, 29; Naval Disarmament Conference at, 129.
George III
S.B. compared to, 56, 113.
George V
startled to read S.B.'s remarks to press about U.S.A., 46; "doesn't read the Daily Mail," 116; S.B.'s reply to his congratulations on handling of General Strike, 118–119; nearing his end, 200; dies, 218; S.B.'s broadcast, 218–219.
Germany
Anglo-French discord about, 37–38, 60–61; France marches into the Ruhr, 61; reparations concluded, rearmament called for, 173; defences insufficient against, 178; arming secretly, 181; air strength, 182; conflicting views, 183–184; reaches air parity with Britain, 200–201; deters France from fighting Italy, 211–213; French fear of, 222, occupies Rhineland, 222–224.
Gheluvelt
S.B. describes visit to, 132–133.

17*

Government of India Bill
passed, despite rumours of dissolution, 189.
Gratitude
not a political category, 142.
Gwynne, H. A.
asks for guidance on King's Affair, 235; sees Baldwin, 235–236.

Haldane, Lord
supports Lord Thomson, 76; grateful for S.B.'s MacQuisten speech, 94; S.B.'s tribute to, 137; on need for arms, 180.
Halifax, Edward Wood, Earl of
letter to S.B. (going to country over Protection), 66; letter from S.B. (cost of teaching democracy), 103; pledges Dominion Status for India, 145; myth of meeting with S.B., 146; S.B. on reasons for his appointment, 147; repeats Dominion Status pledge, despite Conservative's warning, 153; S.B. disavows his declaration, 158; S.B. on his great work, 160.
Halifax, George Savile, Lord
S.B. likened to, 54, 55.
Halsbury, Lord
his interpretation of Trade Union laws, 31.
Hardinge of Penshurst, Lord
at Chequers meeting, 234; letter to King, 236.
Hardy, Thomas
S.B. unveils memorial to, 250.
Harkness, Edward
makes S.B. Chairman of Pilgrim Trust, 162.
Harrow
S.B. at school at, 20.
Hawtrey's
S.B. at school at, 19.
Health
S.B. youthfully active at fifty-five, 29; bad fall, 136; sick in mind, 226; sleepless nights, convalescence, 227; "death in his face," 250.
Hearst, W. R.
attacks S.B., 152.
Highland seer
S.B. compared to, 55, 144.
Hitler, Adolf
becomes master of Germany, walks out of Disarmament Conference, 176; conflicting views on, 184; tells Simon that Germany has air parity with Britain, 200; reoccupies Rhineland, 222.